ADVENTURES IN AVIATION

An Autobiography of Captain Kimball J. Scribner

Edited by Kim Scribner, Bourdon Scribner, P.A.A. Captain (Ret.) Eugene Banning, Mary Richey, Marla Rawnsley, Jim Jackson, and Jim Barry

Composed by Jim Barry (The Focus Group), Daytona Beach, FL and Susan Scribner (Mansfield Publishing), Long Beach, CA

Caricatures by Richard C. McNeil and John Downer

Special photography by Jim Barry and Baron John G. von Feilitzch

Printed by Wimmer Brothers, Memphis, TE

ACKNOWLEDGMENTS

I owe a great deal to my very good friend, Jim Jackson, as editor and adviser for this book and my daughter, Susan M. Scribner, for her dedication and computer work in the initial drafting of my handwritten text. Her friend and partner, Mary Richey, provided many hours of editing for which I am very grateful.

Pan American Captain Eugene Banning (Ret.) made numerous corrections to help in the many specifics about Pan American.

My brother, Bourdon F. Scribner, conducted numerous reviews of the book's preparations. His scientific background and experience as an author made his comments invaluable.

I have been very fortunate to establish an ongoing friendship with Jim Barry, Director and Partner in The Focus Group, who has adapted his professional background and computer expertise to the restoration and finish of the many photographs and cartoons used in the book. His fantastic computer know-how of imagery development and graphic design contributed significantly to the style of this book. His charming wife, Marla, an attorney, provided her many skills in the review of my efforts to write this book.

I am very proud of my friends and family for their help and considerations - it has been a lot of fun.

CONTENTS

Chapter One

LET THE FUN BEGIN

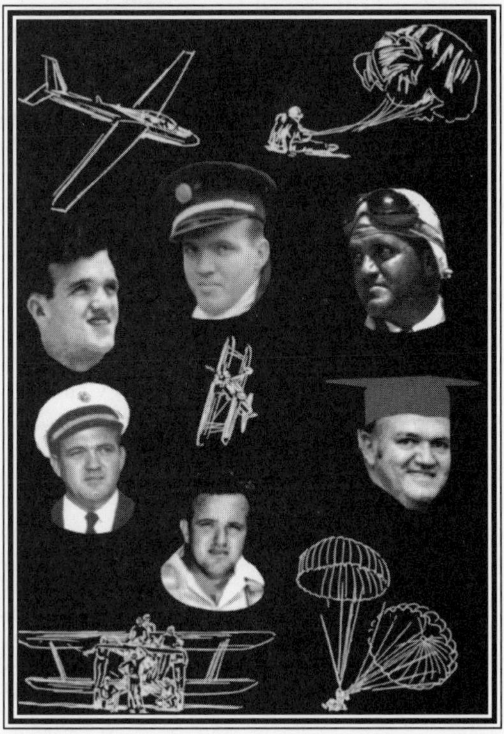

TOP LEFT: My sister Jane and brother Bourdon standing behind me at my grandparent's home
RIGHT: My grandparents, Captain and Mrs. William F. Mansfield, on their 50th wedding anniversary
BOTTOM LEFT: Their home in Westernport, Maryland

Bourdon and I standing on grandfather's farm. We inherited the farm along with our sister and 13 cousins. We later sold the farm at an auction to Amish neighbors.

Chapter One

I was not the first member of my family to be called captain. My maternal grandfather was Captain William F. Mansfield, a tall, distinguished looking gentleman whom I assumed had earned his captaincy serving in the Spanish American War or other military action. I was somewhat surprised later when I learned that he was a retired Cumberland and Pennsylvania Railroad conductor. It seems the practice of calling a railroad conductor captain was initiated during the Civil War when conductors were given the unofficial status of captain during the war period, because they assumed the responsibility of caring for military troops on their trains. This custom of referring to a rail conductor as captain continues to this day.

And now, much later, I am a retired captain of Pan American World Airways, even though there were times I did not feel in control of my airplane's movements. Control was always shared with the elements, instruments, air traffic controllers, and, more recently, with computers. No one calls me captain much any more, except an occasional pilot or flight attendant who flew with me, or shared with me some of

1924

Raymond Morders (right) and I (left) in the 1st grade

1925

1926

Charles Lindbergh flies Atlantic alone

1927

Earhart first woman to fly over Atlantic

Me at Age 12

1928

1929

My first position as "Captain" at age 14

1930

Doolittle crosses country in 11 hours

1931

the discoveries, adventures, misadventures, and fun that this book is all about.

My first adventure took place in Piedmont, West Virginia, on the side of a mountain where I was born and lived with my parents and older siblings Bourdon and Jane. When I was two years old, I would often travel with my mother to visit her parents who lived only a mile away in Westernport, Maryland. I would ride my kiddie car with her down the steep hill into the town of Piedmont, across four railroad tracks, over the Potomac River bridge into Westernport. From there a right turn, down a block, and we were at Grandfather Mansfield's house.

On the morning of my earliest adventure, my mother carried my kiddie car down several flights of stairs. After she had placed me onto the car, she told me she had forgotten something, and she asked me to wait for her while she made a trip back into the house. Now I had made this trip many times. I knew the way. She knew the way. So why wait? The hill was steep, so all I did was raise my feet up and off I went. Down the hill, over curbs and cross streets, no way for mother to catch up with me. Full speed ahead into town. People moved aside, and many waved to me as I went by. They had often seen me go by in tandem with my mother.

My Mother,
Nellie V. Mansfield

I had to push myself along when I reached the downtown area. When the flagman at the tracks saw me coming, he gave me a hand across the railroad tracks. I went up and over the bridge, and down Church Street to Grandfather Mansfield's house. With great satisfaction, I am told, I opened the front gate, and wheeled into the front yard. My first solo.

I don't remember any more such trips during that time, not because I was a menace to traffic, but because we moved to Washington, D.C. when my father was selected as chief of the paper section of the National Bureau of Standards. Bourdon Walter Scribner, my father, had been chief chemist for the West Virginia Pulp and Paper Company in Luke, Maryland after graduating from Pennsylvania State College, and he and my mother had set up their home on the steep hill near the paper mill.

The mill is another poignant memory of my boyhood. Those who have lived in a paper mill town, I know, share similar thoughts to mine about the smell which drifts for miles, the smokeless residue which kills trees leaves the area barren. The chemical effluents released into rivers turn water and rocks yellow far downstream. The environment of Washington was wonderful at that time; for, in 1923, the city was uncrowded, almost pastoral country located far enough down the Potomac to escape the paper mill's yellow stain.

There is a good chance that you have been in touch with my father's work. At the Bureau of Standards he developed the specifications for paper used in the United States currency, introduced in smaller dollar bills in the 1920's. The paper utilized silk and preservative ingredients which foiled counterfeiters. For this achievement and other work, he received the highest award from the Technical Association of the Pulp and Paper Industry.

We lived in Tenleytown, a suburb in the northwest section of Washington, D. C., where I began the first grade in a private Catholic school. My brother and sister had primed me with terrorizing descriptions of school through stories of the horrors of the discipline of the teacher nuns. Bewildered and intimidated by the nuns, I had no success in getting a good start in my first shot at school. As a matter of fact, I failed first grade in the Catholic school, and my father decided to send me to public school. In my second year of first grade I fared a little better, though my teacher complained to my parents that my body was in the classroom, but my mind was always on the clouds and sky outside.

Most persons who speak of their aviation careers usually indicate that their search for adventure leading them toward flying began on the ground. My own interest in

Bourdon W. Scribner, Authority on Paper Technology, Dies

Bourdon W. Scribner, 67, nationally known authority on paper technology, who is credited with saving the Government millions of dollars by developing a better grade of paper for currency, died March 5, 1952 of a heart ailment at Emergency Hospital. He had been ill for 10 days.

Since 1923, Mr. Scribner had been chief of the Bureau of Standards' paper section in the Division of Organic and Fibrous Materials. He lived at 3901 Connecticut Avenue N.W.

In the late 1920s he directed the project which changed United States currency paper. The important changes were in the fiber content and manufacturing techniques.

Develops Glass Fiber Paper.

Last December he was responsible for developing a paper made of glass fiber which heretofore has been thought an impossibility. Its primary importance is as a filter paper. Such a filter is valuable for gas masks and respirators used by fire fighters, industrial and medical workers and military personnel.

In gas mask tests in a smoke-filled room it was proven that only one smoke particle in one hundred thousand passes through the glass paper.

In World War II he was instrumental in developing a map paper used by the military which was highly resistant to wear and a good water repellant.

Mr. Scribner and his associates did pioneer work in developing basic methods used in testing the strength, durability and quality of paper. In 1945 he received a gold medal from the Technical Association of the Pulp and Paper Industry given yearly to the person who makes outstanding contributions to the industry.

Graduate of Penn State

Mr. Scribner was born in Ridgeway, Pa., and graduated from Pennsylvania State College. Before coming to the Bureau he worked for the West Virginia Pulp and Paper Co., in Luke, Md.

He was a member of the Friendship Citizens' Association, Phi Delta Theta Fraternity, American Chemical Society and Technical Association of the Pulp and Paper Industry.

The Washington Daily News

19th Year - No. 281 Three Cents Entered as Second Class Matter at D.C. Post Office

WASHINGTON, D.C., SATURDAY, APRIL 19, 1930

Hero Rescues Five Chums Trapped in Sewer

Five boys involved in the near sewer tragedy (left to right): Carroll Bilbrey,11; Ned Denton, 12; Kimball Scribner, 12; Louis Snyder, 13; and Billy Johnson, 13.

exploration began underground as a result of being an avid reader of the Tom Swift series of books. One of his adventures involved the search for the city of gold. That search stimulated four of my friends and me to explore caverns and caves. There are no caverns and caves in Washington, D.C., however, there are storm drains below the streets which collect water from the street gutters. In our neighborhood, near the Bureau of Standards, there was a wooded area where a storm drain pipe about four feet in diameter emptied into a small stream which took the street water into the Potomac River.

After school my friends and I would bring our flashlights down to the "pipe", as we called it, and enter single file into the storm drain to explore the intercepting pipes under the streets. After considerable time spent walking bent over, with only the lead boy using his flashlight, we would eventually become tired, and ready to enter the world above. To make our exit, we would climb up the metal rungs of the manhole ladder which protruded from the side of the four foot diameter tower like a cement tunnel, rising about 35 feet to the street level. Two of us would stand together on one ladder rung below the cover. Listening carefully for automobiles, we waited for quiet. When all was quiet, we would cautiously lift the manhole cover, push it off, crawl out, and replace the manhole cover.

On Friday, April 19, 1930, our explorations took five of us into an older area where, unknown to us, gas had seeped into the pipe. One by one we became overwhelmed by lack of oxygen in the gas filled tube. On Saturday, April 20, 1930, many articles in the Washington papers revealed the story. The *Washington Star* wrote:

FIVE BOYS ESCAPE DEATH
EXPLORING GAS-FILLED SEWER

Gameness of Leader in Seeking Help Credited with Saving Band. Cries for Aid Heard by 9-Year Old Student. Rescue Squad Members Brave Fumes to Bring Adventurers Out of Trap

Search for adventure within the inky blackness of a storm water sewer near their homes in Cleveland Park lured five youngsters to the threshold of death late yesterday afternoon.

Only the feeble cries of one of their band and the alertness of Johnny Cragoe, 9-year old Janney School student saved them from death by asphyxiation in the gas filled tube, where they were playing follow the leader.

The boys, Ned Denton, 12, Louis Snyder, 13, Carroll Bilbrey, 11, Kimball Scribner, 12, and William Johnson, 13, were all well on the road to recovery at Georgetown

Hospital today.

STARTED ON EXPLORING TRIP

The youngsters, equipped with flashlights, told companions they were going to "explore" the sewer and entered the outlet at Reno Road, near the Bureau of Standards, and began their perilous journey through the long, black conduit.

Accumulated sewer gasses began to affect them after they had crawled nearly half-mile through the mud and slime of the sewer, and the four collapsed as they neared a manhole in front of the Cragoe residence.

The Schneider boy, himself a sufferer of asthma,

FIVE BOYS ESCAPE DEATH EXPLORING GAS-FILLED SEWER

Nine-year-old Johnny Cragoe and his father, Carl Cragoe, at the manhole through which five youngsters were brought to safety late yesterday when the Cragoe boy heard the cries of Louis Snyder.

kept on, however, and fought against the deadly effects of the gasses until he came upon a ladder leading up 35 feet to the manhole opening. Groping his way up the rungs he tried to push up the cover, but failed and cried out for help.

Johnny Cragoe, playing on the front lawn of his home, heard the shouts and ran into the house and brought out his father who seized a poker and opened the manhole cover with the help of two of his neighbors. They found the Schneider boy clinging to the ladder and pulled him to safety. "Are there any others down there?" Cragoe asked."Yes sir," the boy mumbled and lapsed into unconsciousness.

SEES BOY IN WATER

Peering into the gloomy interior of the sewer, Cragoe made out the form of a boy in the water. He raced into his house and called the Fire Department for the rescue squad. The lad later turned out to be Bilbrey.

One member of No. 12 Truck Company climbed into the manhole without a mask and brought out two boys he found unconscious in the shallow water. He was sickened by the gas fumes after the second rescue and was given first-aid treatment. Two members of a second engine company rescued the remaining boys.

Members of two rescue squads went to work over the youths with respirator apparatus. They were later rushed to Georgetown Hospital. It was expected that the boys would be discharged from the hospital late today.

After having survived my exploration beneath the city streets I turned my interests and adventures to explorations above the ground. In 1932, my best friend, Ray Morders, and I were 15 years old, and enchanted by the exploits of his older brother, Howard, who was a licensed pilot and owned his own open OX Travelair Biplane. Ray regaled me with his exciting

stories of having been up in this biplane several times with his brother. I both enjoyed and envied these adventures. I had never been off the ground. Every Sunday we hitchhiked twenty miles to Congressional Airport, then a large grass field on the outskirts of Rockville, Maryland, where Ray's brother kept his biplane. There we would mingle with the "flying aces", and watch the flying and parachute jumping.

Ray's brother introduced us to the professional parachute jumper, Eddie Butler, who gave us our first flying jobs. Ours was the task of attracting the attention of people driving by in cars, inducing them to drive into the airport to watch the parachute jumps. We leapt at the opportunity. To accomplish our jobs we had to stand out on the road in white flying suits, provided by Eddie, and yell at the passing cars: "parachute jump today." Those drawn into the park would then be caught by Eddie Butler and his fantastic spiel aimed to talk them out of their money. Eddie's modus operandi was to pass his helmet in front of them to accept the money they were expected to drop freely for the pleasure of his making a parachute jump. Of course, we collected the "donations" from those who arrived after Eddie was aloft for the jump. The final task was a joyous one. We got to drive his old Essex on the airport to pick him up after he landed from his parachute jumps.

Eddie cut quite a figure. He was in his early thirties, a deep sea diver, a former high diver for a carnival, a parachutist, and an excellent parachute rigger. We were devoted to him. Getting him out of trees, extracting him from the Tidal Basin in Washington, near the Lincoln Memorial, helping him pack his parachute, learning a great deal about parachutes, and jumping was very high pay for the services we rendered. Eddie promised that when we were 16, with our parents written permission, he would check us out to make parachute jumps. Of course, he would make the money on the jumps and we would have the experience.

In February, 1933, when we were both 16 years old, we

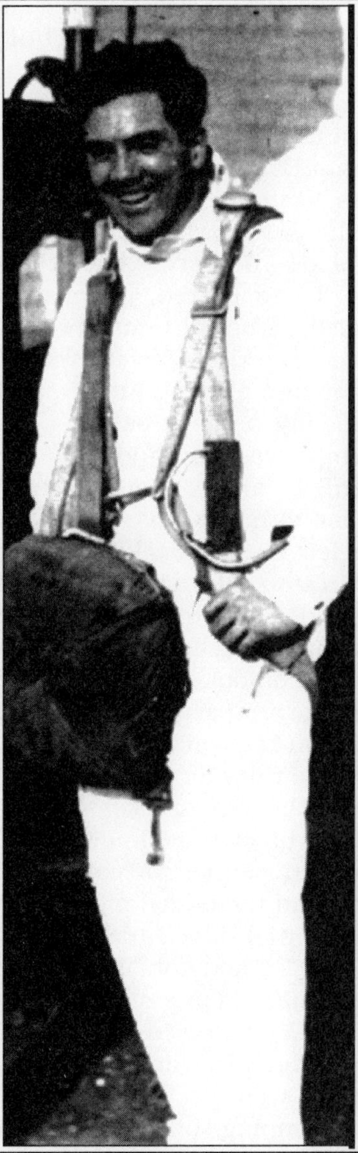

LEFT: Eddie Butler - professional parachute jumper

TOP RIGHT: Baron John G. von Feilitzsch - professional photographer from Ormond Beach, Florida. Standing in front of his "Travelaire" (same plane in which I had my first ride)

BOTTOM RIGHT : Both 16 years old, Ray (right) and I take our first parachute jumps in June, 1933.

delivered to Eddie a forged letter purportedly from each set of parents giving him permission for us to make parachute jumps under his guidance. I told Eddie: "My dad agrees it would be a real experience for me to jump out of airplanes." Ray, of course, said the same thing, and in May of 1933, we made our first parachute jumps at Beacon Field, Virginia, a grass airport south of Alexandria, Virginia. Having watched many of Eddie's jumps from the seat next to him in the airplane, I was certain I could do the very same thing. However, when the time came, I was scared. Suppose I fainted. Suppose the chute failed. Would I remember the proper technique of pulling the ripcord on the emergency parachute while holding the contents of the chute in both hands, throwing it away from me like a basketball?

On our first parachute jumps we both landed off the airport. Ray landed in a cornfield and I came down in telephone wires between the poles with legs crossed and my arms over my face. I made a few swings back and forth beneath the wires until I came to a stop. Still a few feet off the ground, all I had to do was step down to the ground after releasing the straps on my parachute harness. I was hooked.Later that spring, Eddie Butler took Ray and me with him to Winchester, Virginia to make jumps at the air shows of the famous Annual Apple Blossom Festival where we made three jumps each day, sold airplane rides for the pilots, and then passed the hat for our pay for the jumps. Occasionally, we were allowed to fly the airplane a bit on our climb to 2,000 feet to make our jumps. We slept in the hangar on cots which we had brought from home, and had the added pleasure of eating at the local boarding house with Eddie Butler and two special barnstorming pilots, Woody Edmonston and Squeak Burnette. At night Ray and I would make a small detour before laying out our cots to sleep. We observed our ritual of sitting in every plane pretending to fly it. In Washington, Ray attended Tech High School and I went to Western High, allowing us to compete in our jumping, one high school

against another. During this time we first met the famous local radio announcer and avid pilot, Arthur Godfrey, who had us visit with him on his delightful radio show. He gave us a big introduction at the First Annual Junior Birdmen's Field Day, introducing us as the youngest parachute jumpers in the United States, declaring us the first of the new group of Junior Birdmen. **Arthur Godfrey**, an aviation minded man, avid flyer, and great supporter of all us adventurers, became a lifelong friend.

Chapter Two

UP HILL, DOWN WIND?

VARIETY

Hughes plane hits 350 miles per hour

The Atlanta Journal.

Pan Am Launches Orient Air Service

San Francisco Chronicle

The City's Only Home-Owned Newspaper

Turner flies across country in 10 hours

Sept 1. Colonel Roscoe Turner flew from New York to Los Angeles today in ten hours, two minutes and 51 seconds, beating the old record (his own) by two minutes and 39 seconds. His Wedell-Williams Racer averaged 250 mph. He made the trip in only four stops.

Turner and pet after the flight.

Thousands gather to see Scribner, Edmondson, Morders stunt at rodeo

The Washington Daily News

DC-3, carrying 21, makes initial flight

American Airlines hopes the DC-3's 21 seats will turn them a profit

Young chute jumpers to stage show today

He Won His Leap For Life

IN TIDAL BASIN - Eddie Butler, Washington parachute jumper, took his life in his hands last night to make a 2000 ft. parachute leap into the Tidal Basin and avoid hitting the crowd at the Monument grounds.

Fourth Annual

AERIAL RODEO

LYNCHBURG'S 150th BIRTHDAY

AUSPICES

LYNCHBURG LIFE SAVING AND FIRST AID CREW

PRESTON GLENN AIRPORT

LYNCHBURG, VIRGINIA
OCTOBER 16th - 17th

1936

JUNIOR BIRDMEN OF AMERICA

Raymond Morders andKimball Scribner, charter members of the Washington wing Junior Birdmen, will launch out as full-fledged professional parachute jumpers Sunday afternoon at Hybla Valley, near Alexandria, Va.

Morders and Scribner made their first jumps from Eddie Butler's tutelage at the first outdoor field day held June a year ago when they catapulted from Johnny Euans plane at Hoover Airport.

Chapter Two

In 1933, my first solo airplane flight came in an unorthodox manner. At the Hybla Valley Airport in Virginia, about thirty miles south of Washington, D.C., I met a man who had recently purchased a second hand little 39 horsepower Taylor Cub, one of the first ones built. He quickly agreed to rent me his cub for $6.00 per hour, gas included, in order to get a return on his investment on his plane. I think his flying time totalled six hours, and he assumed that I had soloed because I told him I had never flown a plane as small as his Taylor Cub. I neglected to add that I had never soloed in any plane of any size.

He agreed to check me out in the Cub, provided that I meet him every day at 6:30 a.m. to take off at 7:00 a.m.for thirty minutes of flying. His scheduling me was built around his need to drive into Washington for work. In the three hours total flying time, his only guidance was telling me not to over control the Cub. All we did was to make takeoffs and landings, all left turns, no air time, no stalls, and no right turns. At the end of our sixth session he got out of the plane to go to work leaving me with his airplane, telling me to go

RIGHT: Cub in which I took my first solo flight in June, 1933. Performed after only six half hour periods of take-offs and landings.
BOTTOM: My first passenger was 14 year old Johnny Keeler (now Dr. Keeler). We had a very eventful flight out of Congressional Airport, Rockville, Maryland.

Congressional Airport
Rockville, Maryland

ahead and fly it. So, I took off on that grass field, flew around, made a few right turns and, to my surprise, I found that right turns were more difficult than left turns. No one ever told me that the turning of the propeller in its counter-clockwise direction made left turns easier. I was certain that it was due to my never having made right turns before.

Now that I had learned to fly, and even learned to make right hand turns, my next goal was to build up my flying time. In addition to my three hours of instruction, I accumulated three more hours solo, with takeoffs and landings at the Hybla Valley Airport. At that time, Arthur C. Hyde was establishing himself as a fixed base operator at Congressional Airport, where he owned a little 39 horsepower Taylor Cub, which he rented for $6.00 an hour. Art had seen me make parachute jumps, and when I told him I was building up flying time he agreed to rent me his plane. Though I had my log book with me indicating my flight time, Art never bothered to check my veracity, and allowed me to fly his plane. After I flew around the airport for half an hour, and made a few takeoffs and landings, I figured I was as prepared as I needed to be.

Shortly thereafter, I took my 14 year old friend Johnny Keeler to Congressional Airport to ride with me on my next flight. Since I had no license, I planned to sneak him on board to be my first passenger by landing at the airfield, down the hill from the office, where Johnny was to run out from hiding in the woods, get on board and lie down up front around the control stick. I would take off with no one being able to see him. Since he was quite small, about 110 pounds, I was certain we would not be discovered.

We drove to the airport. I let Johnny off before reaching the airport proper, and he went into the woods at the far end of the grass airfield. I met Art Hyde, we gassed up his Cub, then I got in and he pulled the prop through for me, starting the engine. I left him standing outside the office, taxied out to the top of the hill, and took off. As I left the ground I saw

Johnny Keeler (front), ten years old next to me (arms folded) at twelve years old; four years before our fateful flight.

Dr. John Keeler is the owner of an animal hospital in Rockville, Maryland. John still has the same grin he had as he looked up at me from the floor of the Cub.

Johnny Keeler to my left waving at me. I waved back, climbed to about 800 feet, and began a left turn around the airport.

I then began a series of errors. After my takeoff, I flew around the airport, and I landed down wind. Wrong. After coming to a stop, I loaded Johnny on board. Wrong. Instead of at least turning around to taxi back to use all of the airfield, I started from where I had stopped to takeoff. Wrong. I took off down wind. Wrong. I took off up hill, not using all of the available take off areas. Wrong. I began this takeoff up hill, down wind, not using all available areas WITH A PASSENGER, toward telephone wires that crossed the runway at its end along the Rockville Pike. All wrong.

When I saw Arthur Hyde still standing up by his office watching me as I came up the hill, I knew I did not want to stop and be caught with a passenger aboard. I finally raised the tail of the Cub, but the hill and tail wind did not allow me to obtain takeoff speed. I dared not put that Cub in the air too soon, or we would "mush" along right into the telephone wires and street. Johnny was looking up from the floor with a big smile. Arthur Hyde was watching from the office area - aghast!

As we came up the hill still on the ground, I kept the stick neutral, not lifting the plane off the ground until, at the last moment, I moved the stick forward then back. Barely off the ground, we eased up and over the wires, and mushed down on the other side, stalling, flying over an open field toward a big red barn. Still no speed. I knew we could not climb over the barn, and, if I did not have enough speed to turn, I might put a wing tip into the ground. I eased around the barn, using just enough rudder to make a slight turn, and missed flying into the red barn by a hair's width.

Trees ahead were no problem. I let the Cub climb just enough to clear them. I now looked down at Johnny who was still grinning, enjoying his first airplane ride. I motioned for him to get up and sit on the seat for a swell 15 minute ride. On return to the airport with Johnny back on the floor in

PARACHUTE WAY THROUGH COLLEGE

Chums, 20, Already Veterans of 4 Years Experience in Aerial Stunting

A tall, blue-eyed youth ambled into the city room yesterday afternoon, with a brief case under his arm, and announced:

"My name is Kim Scribner, and I am doing publicity for the 'Angels from Hell.' We are a flying troupe, and Sunday, at 3 o'clock, we are going to do our stuff at College Park Airport."

KIM SCRIBNER (left) AND RAY MORDERS
List Price: $25 for Ordinary Parachute Jump, $35 for Delayed Ones

Ten Stunt Pilots

"What sort of stuff?"

"Stunts. We have ten of the best stunt pilots you ever saw, and a permit from the Department of Commerce so we can do acrobatics out of the ordinary, like flying upside down so your head almost bounces the ground. Its all under the auspices of the American Legion. You ought to see it."

Yes, it must be interesting. Have you any parachute jumper?"

The tall boy considered a few moments, and said:

"I am half the parachute jumpers. The other half is my pal, Ray Morders."

Jumping Since 16

"Pretty young to be jumping, aren't you?"

"Well, we're both 20. We've been jumping for four years."

"Very dangerous profession for a boy of 20."

"Oh, we wouldn't do anything else. You see, we are working our way through college, parachute jumping."

Kim, who lives at 3802 Alton Place, Chevy Chase, and Ray, who lives at 4411 Wisconsin Ave. N.W., have for two years earned their tuition by leaping out of airplanes. They get $25 each for an ordinary jump, $35 for a delayed jump.

Kim is a sophomore at the University of Maryland. Ray is a sophomore at George Washington University. They're both studying engineering and both expect to be Navy fliers.

hiding, I made another down wind landing, let Johnny off to run into the woods, and taxied up the hill to be received by a rather acerbic Arthur Hyde. I did not try to explain my unorthodox flying. He knew of my own terror and counted on my fear to correct my mistakes. He even forgave me when he found out I had only six hours flying time. Later he hired me as a flight instructor and made me his chief pilot.

In 1936 Eddie Butler took Ray and me to the Cleveland Air Races where we enjoyed the celebrity of being the youngest parachute jumpers in the United States. The down side of that honor was that we had difficulty at first getting past guards at the gates of the airport. We solved that problem by using our badges and photo credentials which allowed us to enter the same way as the pilots who were racing or putting on acrobatic flights. We made two jumps a day, including contest jumps to land as closely as possible to the center of a white circle placed in front of the grandstand, and we participated in the mass jumps.

As we were learning parachute jumping, we gained assorted experiences such as landing backwards, being knocked out cold, twisting an ankle or knee and, of course, carrying body bruises from top to toe. Each injury carried more than one lesson for us. As time passed and accidents continued we received no sympathy, only severe tongue lashings from our mentor, Eddie Butler, who scolded us for not facing the ground as we struck it; for jumping sooner, later, or not at all to avoid landing in a tree.

In my first six jumps I never even landed on the airport, but eventually we both learned to check the wind directions aloft as we were climbing for altitude, by watching the clouds and their shadows on the ground. We learned to direct the pilot in his flight path as we were getting ready to climb out of the cockpit and, sitting next to him on the wing, spot ourselves, then roll off the wing to make our free fall jumps.

With standard procedures we had no problems, though on my second parachute jump I was a bit anxious, and as I

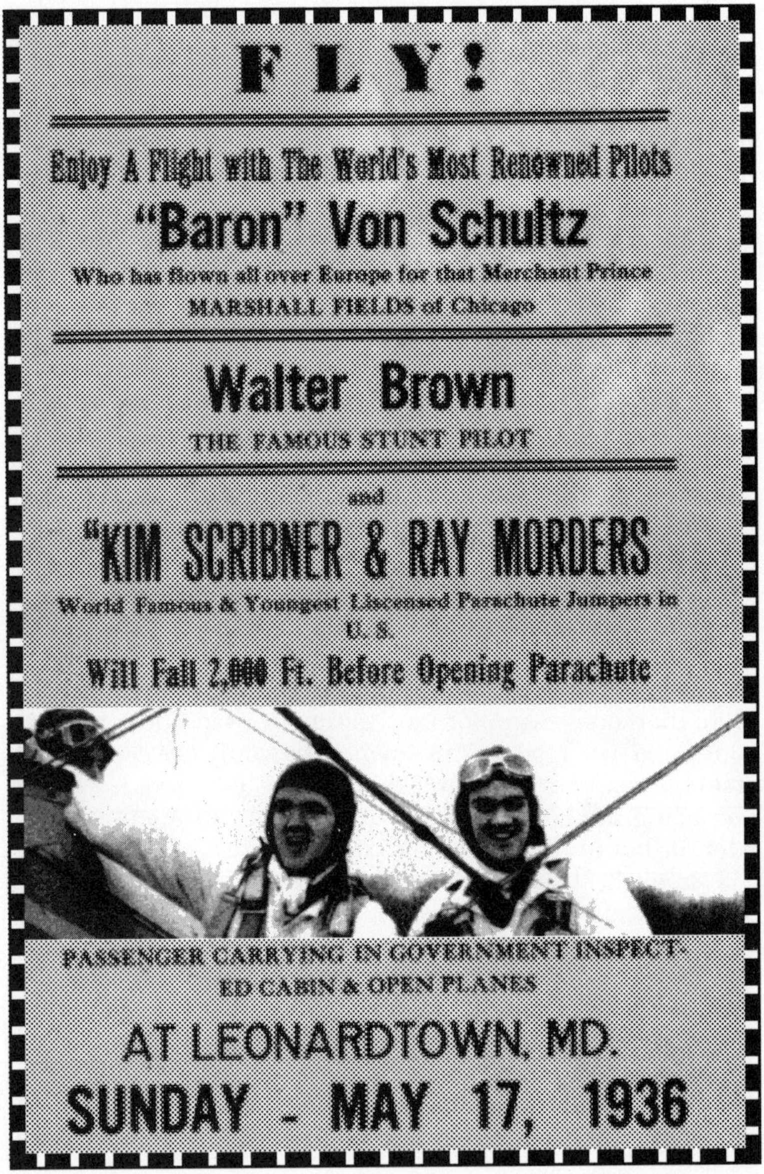
FLY!
Enjoy A Flight with The World's Most Renowned Pilots
"Baron" Von Schultz
Who has flown all over Europe for that Merchant Prince
MARSHALL FIELDS of Chicago
Walter Brown
THE FAMOUS STUNT PILOT
and
"KIM SCRIBNER & RAY MORDERS
World Famous & Youngest Liscensed Parachute Jumpers in
U. S.
Will Fall 2,000 Ft. Before Opening Parachute
PASSENGER CARRYING IN GOVERNMENT INSPECT-
ED CABIN & OPEN PLANES
AT LEONARDTOWN, MD.
SUNDAY - MAY 17, 1936

placed my hand on the ripcord, I did not notice that the sleeve on my left arm of my flying suit was caught in the ripcord housing (a flexible protective metal sleeve that encases the wire attached to the ripcord handle which the jumper pulls to open his chute). However, in this case, instead of pulling on the ripcord wire to release the parachute, I was pulling on the housing. The clasp which was intended to hold the housing to the parachute harness was, quite neatly, caught in my buttoned sleeve. I was bewildered when upon giving a positive pull on the ripcord nothing happened. I pulled again and again. Then, I remembered Eddie's advising us that we were to pull on the ripcord as though we had to break it. I followed that instruction, pulling so hard that I yanked the housing apart, unraveling the strands. Lucky me! That unraveling actually allowed the ripcord itself to function and out came my parachute to open.

On September 17, 1936, Ray rented a C-3 Aeronca, and flew down into the Shenandoah Valley outside the little town

of Teototum to visit a girlfriend and give her a plane ride. After a pleasant flight Ray landed the airplane and shut down the engine. On returning to the airplane to depart, Ray ran into difficulty. The Aeronca had brakes on its two little wheels, but no set brakes. To start the engine, one had to pull the propeller blade around. To do so properly, wheel blocks should be in place, or the brakes should be held from the inside of the plane. In this instance, Ray had no chocks for the wheels, no one to hold the brakes on from the inside, and he, by himself, had to pull the propeller by hand from behind the engine.

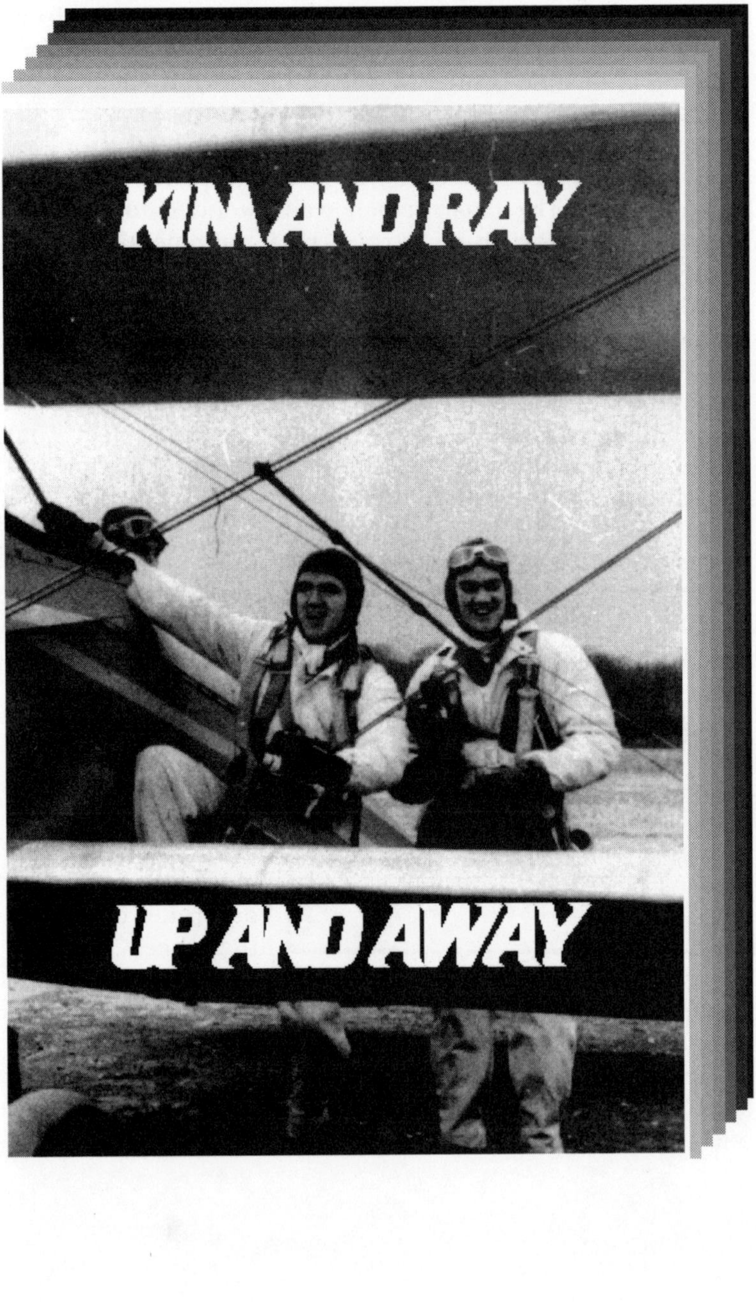
KIM AND RAY
UP AND AWAY

What to do?

Ray stood behind the propeller and pulled it through with the ignition on and the throttle slightly open. The plunger type throttle moved forward as he cranked the propeller several times. When the engine started, without chocks or brakes to keep it stationary, the plane started to move forward. Ray attempted to reach into the cockpit to close the throttle. In doing so, hc exposed himself to the propeller which, with enormous force, cut into his back. He was critically injured, weakened by extreme loss of blood, and was thirty miles from the nearest hospital. He was rescued by a driver of a long black hearse who just happened to be driving by, and saw a plane fly into the woods and crack up. Ray survived with no broken bones and became a successful TWA 747 captain. Of course, I never let him forget that TWA is known to Pan American pilots as "Teenie Weenie Airlines" or "Try Walking Across"!

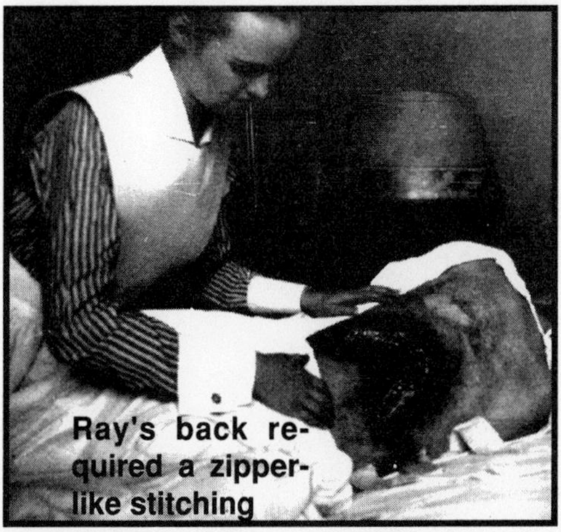

Ray's back required a zipper-like stitching

Chapter Three

DESTINATION AB-745

OHIO 1937

Yesterday
High........................92
Last Night
Low..........................69
Today
9:30 a.m..................78
10:30 a.m...............80
Noon.......................84
1 p.m.......................86
2:30 p.m.................87

The Washington Daily News

Served by Four Trunk Wires of United Press Associations

WASHINGTON, D.C., MONDAY, AUGUST 9, 1937

Partly cloudy; local showers and thunderstorms tonight and tomorrow; not much change in temperature.

Details on Page 23

Entered as Second Class Matter by D.C. Post Office

What a Gesture at 8000 Feet Altitude and Falling Fast!

Exclusive photo by Phillip McCray, Daily News Staff Photographer.

The gent making the salute to the nose is Kim Scribner, young Maryland U. sophomore. When this picture was taken, he was falling from a plane about 8000 feet above College Park Airport yesterday. "Focus 10 feet below the plane" he told the photographer, then leaped into space. The trembling cameraman hung hung grimly over the side and caught nerveless Kim waggling his fingers at him. (Note the other hand ready to pull the rip cord on the parachute.) Kim is earning his way through college jumping from planes. "It's easy," he says. "All you have to do to learn to parachute jumping is - jump."

Chapter Three

While I was enjoying these escapades, my family knew little or nothing of my aerial activities. Keeping them uninformed demanded a great deal of ingenuity on my part. I recall frequently dashing downstairs early in the morning to retrieve the newspaper before my father could read it, because the newspapers would often make mention of the fact that, at a certain airport, giving the date and time, there would be "...a death defying parachute jump race to the earth" by two high school parachute jumpers. I explained the prevalent holes in our newspapers as cut outs for articles on current events for my school work.

Angels From Hell

On a jump in August, 1937, at College Park Airport at an airshow put on by a Virginia flying group, The Angels from Hell, which Ray and I had joined, a young newspaper photographer asked to take a photo of me as I jumped out of the airplane. When I asked him if he had ever been in an airplane before, he replied that he had not. I warned him that he must wear a parachute in case I got caught in the tail of the plane.

After I had checked out the photographer fully in the use of the parachute, I brought him onto the plane with me to meet George Brinkerhoff, owner and pilot of the four-place Stinson from which I was to jump. I asked the young man his plans on taking the picture. He told me "Oh, I'm going to take it right through the windshield here." I objected, saying that the glass would cause parallax in my position. I suggested that he lie on the floor with his head and shoulders just over the edge of the door opening. I would jump out over his head and, hopefully, he'd get a good picture. He agreed and promised to give me all the photos I wanted.

I went about directing the pilot so that I might land on the airport for a change. I set the photographer on the floor with his head just over the edge of the door, holding his Leica camera against his eye and aiming it out and down to shoot the picture at about eight feet away. I tapped the pilot on his back. He closed the throttle, and I pushed myself up and out over the photographer's body. As I fell below him, I turned looking straight into his camera for the photo, and put my thumb to my nose presenting a familiar gesture for his camera.

I landed, of course, before the photographer, and forgot about the incident, because I was certain that he had not gotten a picture. The following day on the front page of the *Washington Daily News* was a photograph which won a National Photographer's Award for the year. What a shock for my father when he picked up the evening paper, and on the front page was his son "thumbing his nose" at everyone in Washington!

Later that year, Ray and I again participated in the Cleveland Air Races where I attempted a contest jump to land in a circle in front of the grandstands. I made the mistake of

AB·745
Out of 70.000 cars, I landed on a **FORD!!**

jumping too close to the stands and, in a strong wind, was heading into the audience. With the wind blowing me at about twenty miles per hour, I was being carried into the grandstands going directly into the thousands of people seated there. I opened my emergency parachute to help carry me over the top of the grandstands to avoid landing in someone's lap. I went over the top of the stands all right and found myself looking at a parking lot of 70,000 automobiles. I picked out a Ford. I hit the Ford so hard when I crashed into it that I dented the hood in and was driven through the windshield. I felt a painful crunch of my ribs on my left side as I hit the front of the car's roof. My body was stuck in the glass of the windshield and I could not move.

The rescue service for us at the Cleveland Air Races was a rather unique set up, whereby, a young chap on a motorcycle with a side car would chase and rescue jumpers who were blown off the airport. My rescuer came roaring up on his motorcycle and began to seek a way to extricate me from my predicament. As he worked, breaking more glass, I kept saying to him, "Watch out for the ribs! Watch out for the ribs!" Finally, he stuffed me and my chute into his side car, and we roared off to a hospital.

More than two decades later, as chief pilot for Pan American Airways, I flew a DC-7 from Washington D.C. to Bermuda carrying a presidential group on a special charter flight. In casual conversation with my first officer, I said, "I don't think we have ever flown together before, have we?" He replied that we hadn't. "Did you learn to fly in the service?" I asked. He answered, "No, I actually learned to fly as a civilian when I worked at the Cleveland Air Races. I started out there by picking up the parachute jumpers with my motorcycle." I said, "Oh, did you ever see anyone injured there?" He said, "Oh my God, captain, you may not believe this, but I saw this dumbbell who came across the grandstands, and hit a car so hard he dented in the hood, broke his ribs, and went right through the windshield." I asked what

Jumping over homecoming football game and landing in telephone wires.

What happened to him?
I don't know, but I'm sure that dumb bastard is dead by now.

happened to him. My copilot said, "I don't know, but I'm certain that dumb bastard is dead by now." Opening my uniform shirt, I said, "Want to see my ribs?"

Following the Cleveland Air Races, I enrolled in engineering studies at the University of Maryland. As a pledge to Sigma Nu fraternity, I was cajoled into coming into the homecoming football game by parachute. I protested to my friends that it would be against the law for me to make a jump over the town in order to land in the stadium, but they persuaded me to attempt it. I made the jump from over College Park at half time, at 2:50 p.m. Naturally, there was a strong wind. I had convinced the maintenance engineer to load the furnaces at the University so that I could see smoke rising to calculate the wind direction and velocity from the airplane.

I jumped from the plane and in a short time passed right over the top of the stadium. Everyone waved at me and I waved back. I was going fast in about a twenty mile an hour wind. I crossed over Route One and into telephone wires. When I stopped swinging, I was dangling between two cars, one foot off the ground. I had not hit anything! My reward was free entrance to the game and all the hot dogs I wanted. Good pay, and I didn't get arrested or fined.

At eighteen, Ray and I became parachute riggers, adding another dimension to our abilities to further our dreams of parachuting and flying with the best aerial artists of the day. Of course, Ray Morders achieved his moniker of "Rigger Morders" on becoming a rigger of chutes. At that time we began working on inventing and developing uncommon types of parachute jumps, because the more uncommon a jump the more money and recognition we would earn. For this show, we decided to try something that had not been attempted. We settled on having the two of us jump out in one parachute. The fact that this was a dumb thing to do did not inhibit either of us.

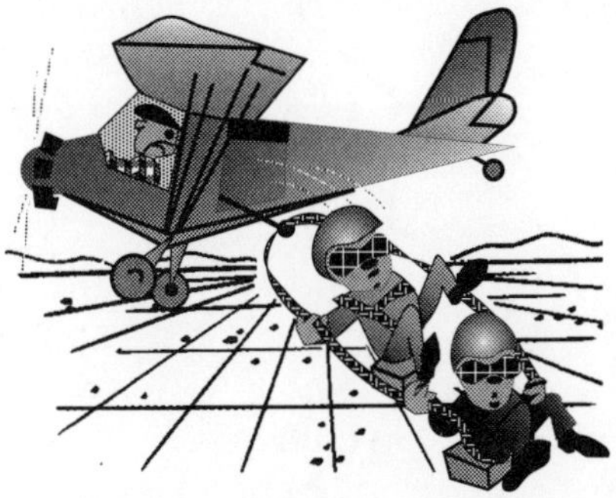

The two of us were to sit in a swinglike harness, and back out of an airplane together with one parachute packed in a bag. However, each of us would wear two parachutes independent of the one in the bag. The idea was that the line holding the bag would be attached inside the airplane. I would hold the bag with the parachute folded inside, then both of us would back out of the plane simultaneously. The bag was being held closed by light string stitching which would break when we reached the end of the rope. The parachute would then be withdrawn and open leaving two persons, for the first time, seated one above the other with one parachute. We would then each fall away from this chute and delay the opening of our individual chutes (still retaining our emergency parachutes) until we were close to the ground.

It was a hard sell to convince the people at the air show that we could make this "two in one jump" safely. In fact, they refused to allow us to try it. Undeterred, we hid our paraphernalia in the back of the seat of the airplane from which we were to jump the next day. With the governor of Virginia and thousands of others watching, we pretended to plan our usual race to earth from 10,000 feet. When we reached 5,000 feet, we dragged the rope and bag out from behind the back seat of the plane. We did not know where to tie the line holding the back, so I tied it to the pilot's seat. He

groused about that, but there was nothing he could do about it.

Just as we had planned, each of us stepped into this swinglike harness, setting it behind our knees. I leaned forward, signaling Ray to be alerted to my moving back toward him, and be prepared to back out of the plane with me. I steered the pilot beyond the airport into the wind until I thought we were in the right position. Then I backed out violently into the face of my good friend. We reached the end of the rope together. It was at this point that the stitching was to break and allow our weight to pull the parachute out of the bag. The bag, pinched between my fingers, was pulled out with us, but the rope holding the bag to the airplane broke because I held it too tightly. As a result we were out there at 5,000 feet holding the bag. There was no way to get the parachute out of the bag.

We fell from the plane so closely together we had difficulty getting untangled to get rid of the bag and open our own parachutes. We finally separated. As I looked down at the ground I saw that I was falling toward the top of a house. Still falling, I turned around facing upward for a second and saw Rigger still all tangled up in the harness above me. I knew I had to fall as closely as possible to the ground to enable him to open his parachute before I opened mine, or he would fall directly into the top of my chute. Just above the house, I opened my chute with a "WHOP". As it opened something fell past me.

I landed in the side yard of the house where a lady was standing with a rake in her hand. She was petrified, and so was I, because, lying on my back, I looked up and the sky was clear. I surmised, of course, that Ray did not get his parachute open. I asked the lady, "Did the other fellow get his parachute open?" She said, "No, he landed over here in the back yard in those bushes." I got up, and slowly ambled toward those bushes which I could see were all broken from the impact of a landing. I heard a voice I recognized saying,

"Hey boy!" As I turned I saw Ray climbing over a fence. The lady had thought there were three of us falling, but the "third fellow" had been the bag with the parachute in it which had smashed the bushes. Rigger had landed next door.

We sat down for a breather, then heard sirens from ambulances roaring to a rescue. We had fallen below the line of sight of the thousands of people at the airshow without our parachutes opening. Some people had fainted. The majority of the audience thought we had done a trick to frighten them.

As we sat on the grass we realized what had gone wrong. I had pinched the bag too tightly between my fingers, snapping the rope holding the bag, and not allowing our weight to break the stitching on the bag to allow the chute to come out and open.

Ray and I were both quite frightened by the experience. It took us another whole week to get ready to try the double jump again. At the air show at College Park, Maryland, the following Sunday, we hid our equipment again in the same type of airplane, but with a different pilot, knowing better than to request George Brinkerhoff's permission to make the double jump again from his plane. So, in our second attempt, we climbed into the wind to the position we wanted at 5,000 feet. In tandem harness we were all set to back out together with the rope again tied to a protesting pilot's seat. Ray tapped me on the shoulder and reminded me, "Don't pinch the bag." I barely held onto it. I leaned forward and then backed out of the airplane swiftly, and, surely enough, the bag came out. The rope stopped the bag. The string on the bag broke, the chute came out, and opened beautifully!

There was, however, too much weight on the old parachute we were using, and "BLOOEY" it tore open and exploded into a thousand pieces. We were in the same spot as a week ago. Again we were forced to get separated in order to open our parachutes, and fall very closely to the ground. The net result of our double jumps was that no one took us up to jump without looking in the back of his airplane to

Ray nor I ever smoked - but Ray wanted a picture similar to mine " thumbing my nose"

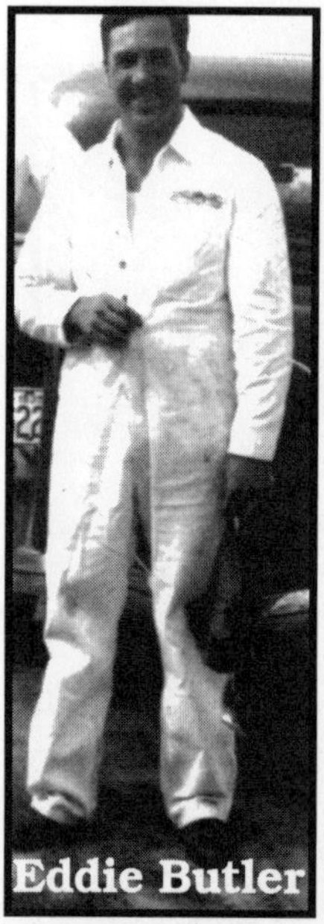

check for any hidden or strange looking parachute bags and harnesses.

Our mentor, Eddie Butler, had moved to New Jersey where he worked for the Switlik Parachute Company. Though he was not a professional pilot, he did drop tests for the company. Ray and I kept in touch with him and were aware of his work. While developing a drop test slide device which would enable him to make a series of drops in a single flight, he made a basic error in design and rigging. In his plan he sought to execute a slide device on the lower wing of a biplane which would hold several parachute dummies to make a multiple drop of chutes. In review of his plans, I had a concern that the slide device would destroy or affect the elevator tail surfaces of the aircraft, and, perhaps, inhibit his control of the airplane. While on a visit with him I recommended that he never slow the airplane down. Unfortunately, while drop testing parachutes, Eddie lost control of his plane which went into a spin, and he was killed.

CHAPTER FOUR

STRANGE OCCUPATIONS

Ten jumpers in each of the two trimotor planes- one trimotor Ford (below) and one Stinson (above).

"Kim, last one out of the trimotor Ford gets to take movies!"

Chapter Four

At the 1938 Cleveland Air Races, Ray and I hit upon another brainstorm for trying to make some extra money for our jumps. I had noticed that at the air races all of the major newsreel companies were represented with their camera teams taking action pictures of the races or any happenings there which would be of interest to the movie going public. I went to the local Pathe Newsreel manager, and suggested he allow me to take a newsreel camera on one of the tri-motored Ford planes to take motion pictures of the parachute jumpers. My plan was to carry a camera, taking motion pictures as I fell and after my parachute was open, to continue to take movies of the other jumpers until we landed on the airport.

He was astonished that anyone would suggest such a wild thing, but immediately inquired, "How much money would you like to be paid for this?" I told him I would take the movies for $50. "Sold," he snapped. I answered too quickly, I should have asked for $100.

Thirty-one jumpers were set to make a mass jump that morning to open the air show, with three teams of us jumping from the two Fords and one tri-motor Stinson. Prior to the jump I was carefully briefed by the Pathe representative on the camera equipment. The camera was operated automatically by a switch, and the focus was set for infinity. It had a handle which, as a trench camera, allowed me to hold it with my left hand, and a leather strap which was fastened around my left wrist.

It was obvious that I could not just jump holding the heavy camera, then open my parachute. It would most likely fall toward the ground and injure me terribly. Those concerns were voiced by the cameraman from Pathe, and for each I had an answer. I explained that I would jump, pull the ripcord, open my chute and hold the camera on top of my emergency chute to absorb the shock of the opening parachute. With the camera constantly running, I would then hold the camera in position and take pictures of the jumpers surrounding me as we descended. He accepted my plan and released the equipment to me.

When I told the other nine parachute jumpers of this plan they all laughed, but agreed to help me. As we marched out to board the tri-motor Ford, a Bureau of Air Commerce inspector walked up to me to inquire what I was doing with the camera. When I told him of my plans he screeched, "Are you crazy? The opening shock of your parachute will cause that camera to drop and it might hit and kill somebody!" I offered a contrite, "Yes sir!," and took the camera back to Pathe Newsreel. Quietly, I explained that I could not take the camera that day, but would be able to do so the following day.

On the next day, as we walked out to the airplane to depart for our mass jump, I saw the same Bureau of Air Commerce inspector standing by the door looking at me carefully. "No camera today?" he asked. Smiling, I replied, "No, none of that." When I climbed aboard, I retrieved the hidden camera from under the pilot's seat, where I had placed it earlier in the day, strapped the camera around my left wrist, and mounted it on top of my emergency chute as we took off. At 800 feet, the three airplanes proceeded in a line formation directly in front of the grandstands. I yelled back in the cabin for the master jumper to jump, and to make certain that he jumped early enough so that I would have time to land on the airport. He laughed and waved his hand in agreement.

I asked the jumpers to pose looking in my direction, waving just before they went out of the open door. Standing in the aisle, I flipped the switch and started the camera, aiming at the first jumper to leave the plane. All the rest followed suit moving rapidly down the aisle and out of the airplane. There was no problem in being too close to the jumper in front of me, because, as each jumper fell below the tail of the airplane, he slowed up so much that he had enough separation to open his parachute immediately. We were so low there was little chance of the jumpers drifting into the stands. The low altitude provided the incentive to all jumpers to open their chutes early enough to be able to use their emergency chutes if the first one failed.

As I ran down the aisle and reached the doorway, I did not hesitate. I vaulted out with the camera taking movies, did a quick one and one half turn and pulled the ripcord. Out came the parachute, up went the canopy, and my chute

In my first shot as cameraman, I caught a great picture of the jumper as he stepped out of the plane.

After I jumped out of the plane, the only thing I got was a great shot of my feet. However, a shoe shop in Washington displayed this photo, and I got a new pair of shoes.

popped open with a violent snap taking the camera away from its position on top of my emergency chute. The camera went straight toward the ground. It was, however, still attached to my left wrist. It tore my arm from my shoulder, but continued taking pictures at my foot level.

I could not move my arm at all. The pain was awesome, and the camera, on a swivel, was slowly turning around taking motion pictures. I could in no way control the parachute and landed on a paved concrete runway. In about a 20 mile per hour wind, I was dragged along the runway with the camera bouncing up and down, and its lens trickling out. The camera was still attached to my wrist which, surprisingly to me, was still attached to my distended left arm.

As I was being dragged along the runway on my back by the wind in my inflated chute, I could see a bent over driver on a motorcycle, with a side car, coming down the runway to my rescue. He stopped ahead of me, grabbed the canopy of my chute, brought it into the wind, and stopped me. After detaching my parachute from me, he loaded me, my chute and the camera into the side car, and roared off to the same hospital I had visited before when I had crash landed into the Ford in the parking lot.

I received $50 from Pathe Newsreel Company for carrying their camera and taking pictures. I received $20 for the jump itself. It cost my father about $150 to pay for the work on my shoulder. I doubt the camera was ever used again. Later, Pathe used the motion pictures I had taken for a short subject film called "Strange Occupations". Since the camera was hanging down near my feet turning itself on a swivel, the majority of the film showed pictures of my feet. Once in a while other parachute jumpers in the air appeared.

During this time, Mr. Mark S. Willing, a retired, well to do banker from Chicago, had been following Ray's and my aerial exploits in the newspapers. He phoned me one day at my home asking us to lunch with him to discuss a new device which he had invented, and on which he had a patent

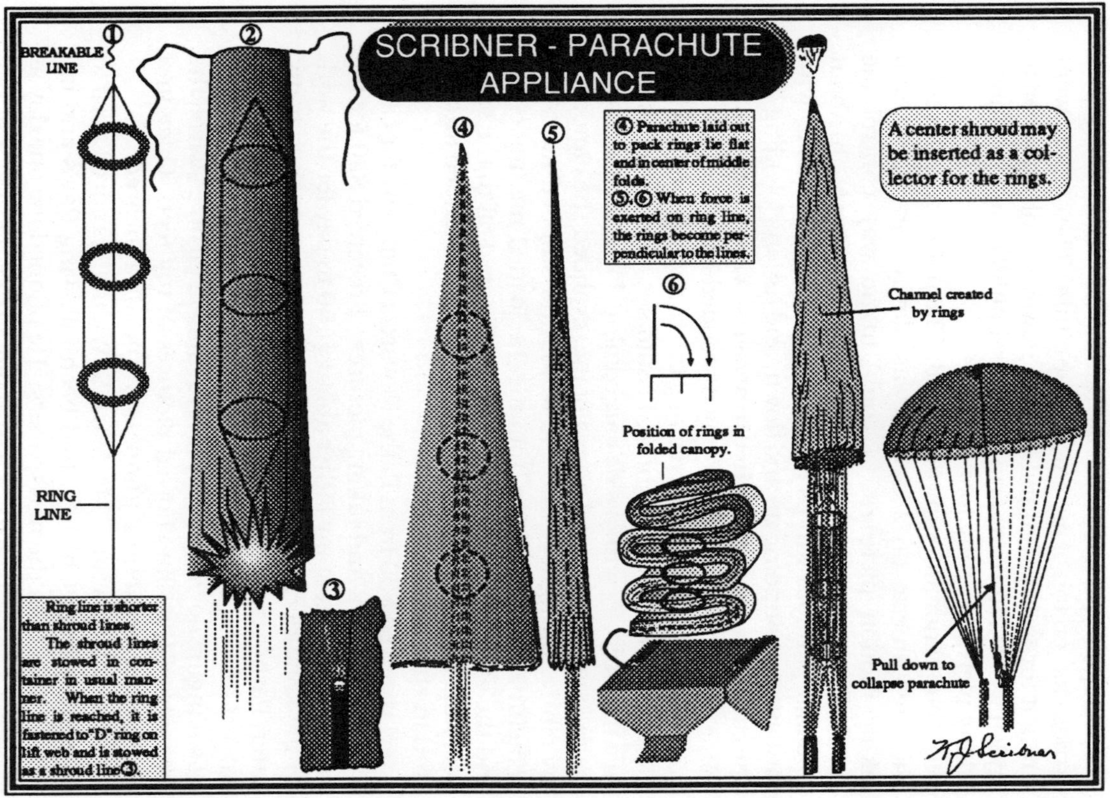

SCRIBNER - PARACHUTE APPLIANCE
①
BREAKABLE LINE
RING LINE
②
③
④
⑤
⑥
Ring line is shorter than shroud lines. The shroud lines are stowed in container in usual manner. When the ring line is reached, it is fastened to "D" ring on lift web and is stowed as a shroud line③.
④ Parachute laid out to pack rings lie flat and in center of middle folds.
⑤,⑥ When force is exerted on ring line, the rings become perpendicular to the lines.
Position of rings in folded canopy.
Channel created by rings
A center shroud may be inserted as a collector for the rings.
Pull down to collapse parachute

pending. He was reticent to give explicit details of his invention over the phone, saying only that it involved a means of mechanically opening a parachute faster than was then possible, thereby saving lives of parachutists who had to jump at low altitudes. Our invitation was for lunch at the Willard Hotel in Washington, D.C. An invitation for lunch at that hotel was enough reason for Ray and me to meet to discuss anything with anyone.

We met and introduced ourselves to this most gracious elderly gentleman, and, as luncheon was served, we listened most attentively to his discourse on his newly invented device. It was quickly apparent that Mr. Willing did not know anything about parachutes. It was equally apparent that, if he were going to pursue his invention, he really did need our assistance. We really did need his money.

His device was quite simple. It involved three rings made of lightweight quarter inch thick aluminum alloy, with each ring measuring twelve inches in diameter. The three rings were to be spaced about two feet apart from one another, and joined by parachute shroud lines, so that as the parachute was drawn from its container by the pilot chute, the rings would be withdrawn at right angles to the canopy. As the canopy was drawn over the rings, they were held in a manner so that they did not extend very far above the pilot's head. The canopy's being withdrawn over the rings would separate the silk at its opening position where the shroud lines were attached to the canopy. The spreading of the silk would permit air to enter inside the parachute before it normally would have, since the parachute had to be fully extended before it would begin to open in the ordinary way a parachute functions.

As we listened, I could visualize jumping with such a string of rings above me when that parachute opened. Now, to my mind, the parachute opened fast enough already. In point of fact, I should have liked to see it open more slowly to reduce the opening shock. Regarding his invention, I de-

Drop test of parachute that failed - static line to open chute got caught.

University of Maryland released me to go to Wright Field

December 15, 1937.

Dean Steinburg
Engineering Department
University of Maryland
College Park, Md.

Dear Dean Steinburg:-

Confirming my telephone conversation, may I ask you to allow Kimball Scribner to go to Wright Field, at Dayton, Ohio, shortly after the first of the year in order to oversee experiments on my device for opening parachutes in the handling of which Kimball is an expert, and whose services for that purpose I need.

The Army cannot get the tests made at Langley Field which they want and the Navy of course are working on their own line independently at Lakehurst, N.J.

Kimball and I have tried to explain to you the need of such a device and I think that you thoroughly understand our point of view.

With kind regards, believe me,

Yours very truly,

Mark S. Willing.

duced that, when the parachute opened with the rings above one's head, the fast opening shock would slam the rings down on the cranium. I glanced at Ray. When Mr. Willing was looking away from us I touched my head and winced. Ray knew my meaning.

At length, we spoke about testing such a device, discussing test drops with weights attached in comparison with one without this ring installation. Mr. Willing proposed no hourly or daily rate, instead he offered Ray and me a percentage of interest in the device. This agreement left us no choice, since Mr. Willing would pay all our expenses. We proceeded accordingly knowing the device might be of no real value, but fearful that he would get someone else to test this plan if we did not agree to do it.

We had two sets of rings made, threaded them together, and placed a set of three connected rings into a parachute with a singular shroud line holding all three rings fastened to a fitting where the regular shroud lines were attached. The plan was to have the canopy withdrawn over the rings, causing the parachute to open before it became fully extended in the usual way. We then rigged a dummy with lead that weighed 200 pounds, and arranged with Harley Clapsaddle, our pilot friend, to rent his biplane, and to carry the dummy on his wing next to the pilot's position.

Ray went along with the pilot to cut loose the dummy with the experimental parachute attached. As it fell, a static line attached to the plane would pull the release pins on the parachute for it to open, as I was shooting motion pictures from the ground. As they came in sight at about a 45 degree angle, Ray tripped the release, the dummy fell off the wing, the static line pulled the pins out of the chute, and out came the parachute. The rings spread the canopy at its skirt and "WHAM", that chute opened with the speed of summer lightening. They flew around, landed, loaded on a parachute without the rings installed, and went up again. On this drop, the dummy fell and spun a bit, catching the static line. This snapped the line. The dummy and our parachute fell just shy of the airport into a swamplike heavily overgrown area. We could not find it!

Mr. Willing lamented our loss and asked us the worth of the chute. We indicated the value to be about $100. Without hesitation he wrote us a check. However, we still had to have a dummy, so after the airport was closed that evening, Ray and I returned with flashlights, and scoured the swamp and heavy brush. We located the dummy with the chute still packed and attached to it. We took the chute and dummy home. I called Mr. Willing and told him we could save the dummy. I referred only to the chute's being filled with water and mud. He made no request for a return of his money.

After washing the chute in my mother's washing machine, and hanging it up to dry, we packed the same chute up again for a test two days later. This test, with no rings installed, went off without a hitch. Our motion pictures showed a definite slow opening. Mr. Willing was ecstatic at the prospect that we really had something that would save lives, and, of course, he would be recognized as the inventor. In his excitement, he asked us to do an actual "human" test at an altitude of 2,000 feet or higher and wanted to know how much we would charge for such a jump. We asked for $25.

Ray and I set about to remedy the incipient problem of injury to the jumper with those rings packed in the parachute. I showed Mr. Willing a sketch of my solution. I planned to utilize a center line to be installed in the parachute which would serve as a "collector" of the rings. My proposal ran counter to the established policy of never putting a center line in a parachute. This policy had evolved because in the early years of parachute development, a center line had been installed to permit the jumper to pull down the center of the chute in order to dampen the swinging oscillations. In using this design, several jumpers had been killed because, after pulling the ripcord, the pilot chute came out between shroud lines when the jumper was not face down, and the parachute would turn inside out. With the center line installed, the canopy would fail.

My solution was that the center line would be longer than the other lines. In the event the parachute opened inverted, the center line would now lie along the top of the parachute canopy, and come down to the same place to which all other lines were fastened to the parachute harness, thus allowing the parachute to open inside out. When I presented this design to Mr. Willing, he immediately engaged his attorney to prepare and submit an application for a patent in my name for this center line. Since the attorney was at a loss to describe a parachute, I had to write the proposal for him to put in legal terms alongside my drawings.

As an afterthought, I envisioned jumping with the center line attached inside the parachute, providing a longer line which would not prevent an inverted opening. I could pull down the center line, and begin to collapse the parachute. I could then keep on pulling it down, reducing the area of the chute which was holding me until I could pull it all the way down, allowing for a slight portion of the chute to be open in order to produce enough drag to barely restrain my body from tumbling. I would fall feet first toward the ground, then by simply releasing the center line, the parachute would pop up to its normal full open position and stop my fall immediately.

The more I thought about this, the more certain I became that it would have practical applications. Not only would it serve as a superb demonstration for people to watch; it would have certain military usefulness. If a pilot were to jump in a manner that he would be blown out to sea by a strong wind, he could collapse his parachute at will, and increase his descent so rapidly that it would be as if he were falling with no parachute open. Falling so close to the ground he could stop his rapid descent by simply releasing the center line, collapsing his chute on the way down as often, to any degree as he wished in order to avoid overshooting his target

Two of the cameramen who received "exclusive coverage"

area. I felt fully protected for my invention of this device utilizing a center line, because I establishing a patent pending. Only in later and wiser years did I realize that an application of a tool is not patentable.

How to demonstrate my invention in the most favorable way? Well, it is important to remember that I had not tried out the center line application at all. I had, however, great confidence that it would work as I had described it. I felt certain that I could jump at 3,000 feet, open the chute, and play with it. I would pull the center down a fraction at a time and release it until I could completely collapse the parachute, drop like a rock, and reopen it by releasing the center line I was holding down.

Of course, the best way to demonstrate this center line was via the newsreel companies. I set about making telephone contacts with all of the newsreel companies. I required five cameramen, each from a separate company. Each of the cameramen I approached was enthusiastic to cover this interesting event with the provision that he would receive exclusive coverage. Without hesitation I assured all five exclusive coverage, and committed each to say nothing to anyone of this most secret project. Each agreed.

I engaged my friend, Harley Clapsaddle, to fly me. Ray and I had packed a backpack parachute with a center line installed. It was free at the bottom, and curled up so that when I inserted it inside the vent at the top, and tied it securely to the center top of the parachute, it would, upon any opening of the chute, stay there for a moment. The high pressure of the incoming air held it there. Once the chute was fully inflated, the pressure holding the center line against the inside top of the canopy would drop, and the center line would fall down into my hands, or near enough for me to reach it.

Even if it landed in the shroud lines, I could pull the shroud lines in to take hold of it. With this in mind, I waited for the cameramen to arrive. The first one was the most

Before newsreel jump (left) and actual newsreel footage (below)

College Park, Maryland

friendly. As each subsequent cameraman arrived, the individual and collective anger grew. I played dumb and suggested that word must have gotten out about my jump. I reasoned with them that since they were all there, we could produce a much better film presentation if each one took a part of the filming, then combined their films to produce one good film with a copy for each. Somehow I pierced through their exasperation with me, and we set about making plans for the best coverage.

With three cameramen on the ground at various positions on the field, one on the plane with me, and one in another plane to cover me after I jumped, I felt we had a fine piece of film making set up. When everybody was in position a chute fitted on the cameraman going with me, we took off and climbed to 3,000 feet. In great anticipation, I directed the pilot, good old Harley Clapsaddle, right over the airport. The rented Stinson plane carrying the other aerial cameraman was beside us several hundred feet lower. We were all set, waving to each other.

All went well. I climbed out onto the wing. The cameraman in the plane with me began taking movies. I seated myself on the trailing edge of the wing, looked down and, then, nodding to Harley, I rolled off and opened my chute straight away. As the opening shock subsided, I looked above me to find that the center line had fallen within my grasp. The canopy above me was in perfect position as I dampened the swinging by pulling down on the regular shroud lines to stabilize the chute. All cameras were rolling. Everyone was waiting for me to collapse the chute, drop, and then reopen it.

I took a strong grip on the center line, and began pulling it down toward me. The center of the parachute came down, but not far. The line was a single shroud line and it began to slip through my bare hands. It was if I were trying to climb a single clothes line fastened to the top of a gymnasium. The cameramen were taking pictures of me all the way down until

I landed on the airport.

What had been anger turned into exasperation. The cameramen could be best described as a small mob with murder on its mind. Each had spent a great deal of time and money. They had jointly rented a plane with a pilot, and had nothing to show for it. I explained to them about the center line slipping from my hands, and that I believed the problem would be solved if we braided three shroud lines together and put knots in them. They agreed to give me one more chance.

We climbed to 3,000 feet again with all cameras shooting away. After rolling off the wing, I opened my chute. Down came the center line, with real vigor I grabbed hold of it, and began to pull it down. The canopy began to collapse. I could feel that I was falling as the parachute collapsed until very little of the chute remained open. I let myself fall, almost free, then released the center line. It flew straight up, and, with a loud bang, the chute was again fully opened. I repeated this several times. Upon my successful landing, all was forgiven. Within one week the film, with voice over, describing the collapse of the parachute, was shown all over the country.

Chapter Five

VENTED CHUTE DEVELOPED

Government test - opening chute after 10,000 ft. free fall to have the emergency chute break loose and fall to the end of the shroud lines. It is a good thing I didn't need it as there would have been no way to use it.

Chapter Five

Parachute jumping continued to consume my time in the '30s. The only dark moments were caused by my being injured on my landings, due to lack of directional control of the parachute. While I studied engineering at the University of Maryland, I solved this difficulty by designing and building the first steerable parachute with my partner, Ray Morders.

The conventional design for a parachute includes an open vent, or section, at the top of the chute to allow air to escape to provide a steady vertical descent. We covered this area over with silk. We made two tail like vents for our parachute canopy through which the air coming into the parachute could flow out of the vents imparting a forward directional movement for the jumper as he descended. If he chose to close one of the vents, it produced a turning movement. Holding a control line attached to each vent, a jumper could close either one of them, giving himself a right or left turn. He also could close both vents just before reaching the ground to provide for an easier landing.

Our successful design led to our establishment of the Eagle Parachute Company of Lancaster, Pennsylvania. We took over the failed Folmer Clog Parachute Manufacturing Company which had all the necessary facilities and sewing equipment for the production of our parachutes. Ray and I were absolutely certain we would make a million dollars.

In order to secure an approved certificate for this parachute, we had tremendous challenges involving live jumps and drop tests. I made one jump from 10,000 feet to reach maximum speed in order to prove this parachute could sustain the opening shock. In this jump, the shock was so severe that my emergency chute broke away and kept on going. I was fortunate that I did not need the emergency chute because it remained on the end of the shroud lines below me. In addition to trying to obtain a Civil Aeronautics Authority certificate for our Eagle Parachute, we were busily pursuing potential marketing prospects for this new parachute. Of course, the real market for our parachute was the military.

On one of my frequent visits to the CAA in Washington, I was introduced to two Air Force representatives from Peru who were immediately interested in the Eagle Parachute. I explained that CAA approval was pending performance tests, structural design and manufacturing examinations. However, I offered to provide them a demonstration using an experimental parachute. They were elated at the prospect of a demonstration to show their Peruvian commission. Their one requirement was that the demonstration be given in New York City area so that their commission might attend. There was no problem making the jump except our concern about exposure of the Eagle Parachute to the public, press, and other competitive manufacturers before we had it accepted and licensed to be sold.

Ray and I located a small airport in Valley Stream, Long Island, which had been closed to all flying by residents who had generated enough pressure for local ordinances to be issued forbidding all flying at the airport. The airport had one short runway with an "X" painted at both ends. We had no

THE SUNDAY NEWS - SUNDAY, APRIL 16, 1939

Men Without Wings Meet Problem Of Steering Themselves Through Space

Against a Lancaster skyline, Raymond Morders shows the training outfit of two chutes, front and back. At right, he demonstrates the way the new parachute flips up over the jumper's head as he falls. Shown below, the completed parachute is given its final look-over before its folded into a package no bigger than a soldier's knapsack.

Sailing down toward the Lancaster Municipal airport, parachute jumper Morders steers his chute around a right-hand corner by pulling down on the "tail" at the right, leaving air escape through the one showing above the chute at the left. He's facing the camera in this remarkable action shot by Walter Hallowell.

THE SUNDAY NEWS - SUNDAY, APRIL 16, 1939

intention of landing a plane there, only a parachute jumper.

We rented an airplane which I was to fly while Ray made the demonstration jump from over the center of the closed airport. On jumping, Ray would was to make a series of turns and land just in front of the Peruvian dignitaries. I would then return the rented plan to its home airport, and drive to Valley Stream to pick up Ray.

On a gorgeous windless morning, Ray and I approached over the closed airport at 10:00 a.m. At 1,500 feet, Ray eased himself out of the rented Fleet biplane to sit on the trailing edge of the wing step area beside me. I made a gentle circle and came over the center of the field just over our Peruvian delegation. Ray released his hold on the side of the cockpit, fell a short distance, and opened the Eagle Parachute. I put the plane in a steep turn, closed the throttle, and began a spiral down to catch up with him to see his maneuvers. Ray made a splendid jump, did his turning and steering performance, and landed just in front of the observing military people from Peru.

People in the neighborhood, hearing the plane circling above, were shocked when they saw a body fall away from it, and the plane appeared to go into an uncontrolled diving spiral. They rang the police and patrol cars were swiftly dispatched to the closed airport. Just as Ray was bowing to receive his accolades, and was, via an interpreter, answering the Peruvian's questions, police cars entered from both ends of the field, lights flashing, and sirens wailing. Seeing the parachutist shaking hands with the military men left the police undecided on what action to take. Ray greeted the police, shook hands with them, and gathered up his parachute, seeking to give the impression that the police were his escorts. He then, in a bold and grand manner, saluted the Peruvians in a grand farewell gesture, climbed into the back of the police car, and was driven off to jail!

I observed all the activity from the air and quickly decided to fly back to the Flushing airport from which I had

Assured Security for Pilots and Passengers with the Improved EAGLE Parachute

AIR SCOOP PREVENTS TUMBLING

An outstanding new safety feature of the **Eagle Parachute** is the method provided for **controlling the position of a jumper's body during a free fall.**

This simple but important improvement makes it impossible for the wearer's body to spin or tumble before the ripcord is pulled. The Eagle Back Pack is designed so that the pack will swing above and behind the wearer's head immediately after his jump from the plane. The pack maintains this position by means of the AIR SCOOP (Pat. Pending) which is built in the back of the pack. This AIR SCOOP produces a drag which holds the packed parachute in a correct position for positive opening and keeps the wearer's body in an **upright** position which is **ideal** for falling and absorbing the opening shock of the parachute. Most important of all, it eliminates all possibility of the wearer's legs fouling the shroud lines of the chute as it opens. It also prevents blanketing and streamlining at high speeds.

The EAGLE Air Scoop which Prevents Spinning or Tumbling.

For Your
Security
An EAGLE
PARACHUTE
Steerable
Non-Oscillating
Comfortable
Proven

STEERS TO SAFE LANDING

Genuine ability to steer himself to a desireable landing spot is another new safety feature provided to the wearer of every type **Eagle Parachute.** The shape of the canopy is directly responsible for its steering characteristics.

This feature has been perfected to the point where even the inexperienced can, on his first jump, guide the parachute to a safe landing.

Eagle's improved safety features have removed the hazards which have attended parachute jumping in the past.

Steering to the Left

Due to the improved design, the full opening of the chute is much quicker, thereby making it safer for use at low altitudes. A controlled free fall, positive opening with no danger from becoming entangled in the shroud lines and steerability are the features which give unfailing confidence to all persons who wear EAGLE PARACHUTES.

❑ ❑

EAGLE BACK PACK

Designed for a positive opening, comfort to wearer and to fit in an **extremely thin** pack or container our back pack gives to pilots and passengers a parachute which is easy to wear, does not hamper walking, allows freedom of movement, and relieves the wearer of its weight when in a sitting position.

The parachute itself is 27 feet in diameter. It is made of the finest of pure white silk and is packed in a light gray water-proof container. The harness is made of **soft** webbing of great strength designed for comfort and quick release.

❑ ❑

EAGLE SEAT PACK

The Seat Pack contains the same size parachute as the back pack and has the same operating principles. This pack is designed primarily for those persons who find a seat pack most applicable to their type of aircraft. The pack itself forms a seat cushion and provides for maximum comfort.

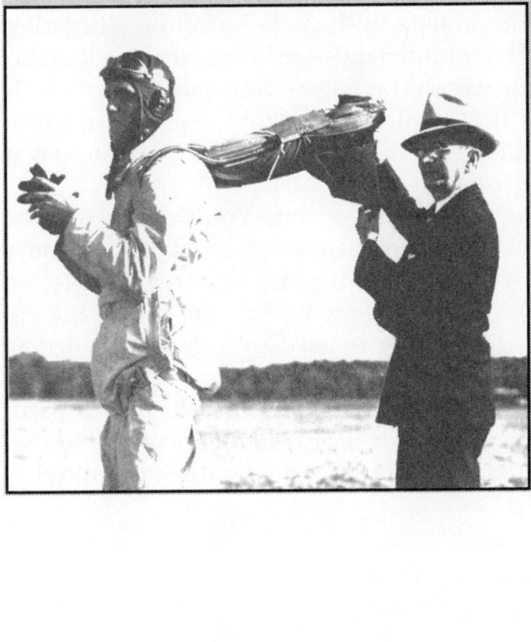

In all EAGLE packs the ripcord is easily accessible and there are no protruding or exposed parts; thus eliminating the possibility of the parachute catching in cabin or cockpit.

rented the plane. I landed the plane, finished the business of paying for its rental, and jumped into my car to head for the Valley Stream police station. Enroute, I worked on the best way to make a subtle approach to the police in my inquiries regarding the whereabouts of Rigger Morders.

After entering the police station, I saw Ray in a cell block just beyond the main office. His parachute rested beside him, and he was wearing a big smile. When the police had arrived at the scene of the landing they had asked Ray a barrage of questions, "Who are you?" "Why did you jump out of that plane?" "Who and where is the pilot?" "Did you have permission to make this jump?"

To protect us and not reveal any specific information to anyone, Ray decided to give them dumb answers and withhold everything. He answered that he was given an airplane ride out of some little airport on Long Island. He said he was a college student from Washington, D.C., that he didn't know the name of the pilot or the airport, and that he fell out of the plane by accident when he leaned too far out to view the area. The police did not believe a word of his story.

I introduced myself as a friend of his who could not understand how he got here in the police station. The police assumed Ray had telephoned me to pick him up. I asked Ray the same questions which the police were asking. It quickly became apparent that, without specific witnesses or information about the plane or pilot all they could hold Ray on was a charge of trespassing.

The police chief finally said to me, "Your friend has been most uncooperative. We don't believe either of you. We have been advised to release you with the understanding that when you leave you will not come back." We seized the opportunity, thanked them, grabbed Ray's gear and fled to Lancaster, Pennsylvania.

In our continued pursuit of the certification of our parachute by the CAA, we had to deal with stringent and demanding requirements which were as rigid as those required to license the building and selling of airplanes. One of the major requirements was to provide a structural test of the parachute using a six hundred pound weight in the drop test. This required locating six hundred pounds of lead ingots and threading them to two steel rods to make up the dummy unit to which we would attach the parachute. We could not lift the dummy unless we separated the ingots, and reassembled them on the wing of the airplane.

We rented a standard biplane which had a front cockpit for four passengers, in addition to the pilot's cockpit seat, and set up arrangements for the CAA engineer witnesses to observe the drop test at the airport in Hagerstown, Maryland. Ray was to climb out of the front cockpit, and when the airplane was over the center of the airport at 500 feet, cut loose the 600 pound dummy, and have the static line pull the ripcord pins for the chute to open. I was to stand with the CAA representatives to observe the chute opening, and its descent. After its landing only the CAA people could take the parachute off the dummy and inspect it for damaged harness, torn silk or tattered seams.

On the morning of the test, as Ray came over the center of the airport at 500 feet, he cut the rope holding the chute and dummy on the wing, and pushed it off with his foot. However, in shoving the unit off the wing, it turned, and the static line became caught on the dummy. The line broke and the 600 pounds of lead with the unopened parachute fell straight down, and buried itself very deeply in the runway. Late into the night while Ray and I were "getting the lead out", we discovered that the parachute was demolished; the lead ingots were bent in such a way that we could not take them apart. We had to rent a tow truck to raise the 600 pounds of lead up onto the runway. With crow bars we were able to take it apart and rebuild the dummy.

On the next day with the CAA observers on duty and our dummy rebuilt, we went through the same procedure. This time the chute opened. There was no damage to the chute as a result of the heavy weight. Following careful and exacting examination of the harness, shroud lines, and all sewing, it was declared satisfactory by the CAA. Soon we received an "approved type certificate" allowing us to build and sell the Eagle Parachute.

At our company, in addition to Ray and me, there was our president, Mr. Beech Gill, who provided the capital to finance the company, Frenchy Fortune, our engineer, and several women seamstresses. Mr. Gill was not qualified in any technical way, yet, he was the business brains, and had money to help us establish our firm, enabling us to do some absolutely terrific things in our experimentation and development of some solid, important designs and approaches to parachuting. Frenchy was a marvelous instructor who taught us to lay out the silk, sew it, place the canopy on top of a large cutting board, mark and cut it. Using two, three and four needle sewing machines, as well as the large harness machines, we sewed away. Help from Frenchy Fortune actually prepped me for later CAA written and oral examinations for seven ground instructor's ratings.

Our Eagle Parachute Company, even with its CAA approved certificate, could not stand the pressure and actual threats of pending patent violations and law suits from other parachute companies. We went out of business. We could not sell the parachute on the open market because, in the process of manufacturing our parachute, we had to use someone else's ripcord, someone else's pilot chute, someone else's harness, and someone else's connecting links, all of which were, at that time, patented. In addition, we were receiving protests from other parachute companies, claiming we were violating their rights by using portions of their parachutes. We should have approached existing parachute companies, and sold them on using our steering design for their parachutes. We did, however, have a contract with the Forest Service to fight forest fires with our steerable parachutes and, today, every steerable parachute utilizes the basic principle for steering that we developed. So at 19, with the Eagle Parachute Company forced out of business, Ray and I returned to Washington, D.C. to pursue our flying careers in 1937.

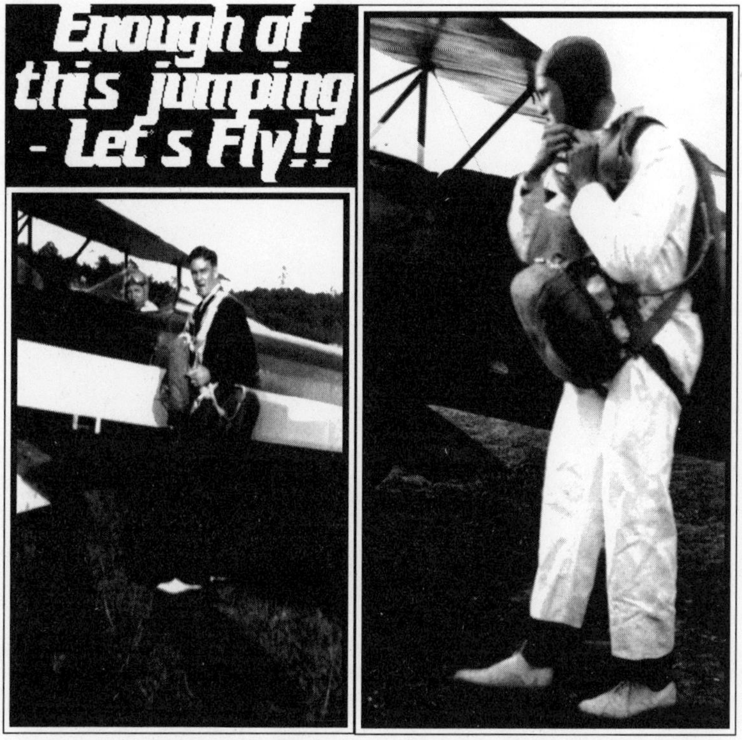

Chapter Six

LEARNING TO FLY RIGHT

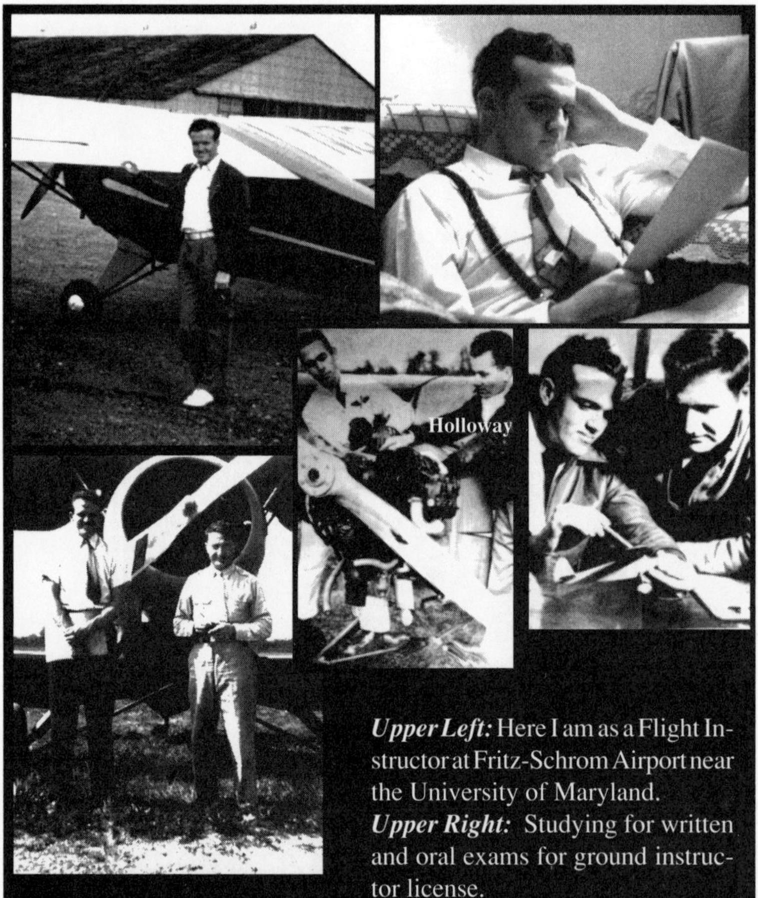

Upper Left: Here I am as a Flight Instructor at Fritz-Schrom Airport near the University of Maryland.
Upper Right: Studying for written and oral exams for ground instructor license.
Lower Left: I flew everyday in a cub from Congressional Airport to Baltimore, MD. to obtain training in acrobatic flying so I could teach advanced or secondary Civilian Pilot Training for George Washington University and University of Maryland students.
Center and Lower Right: Bud Holloway and I in "Civilian Pilot Training Primary Program" (CPTP) - Congressional Airport, Rockville, MD.

Chapter Six

In August of 1937, I was issued my private pilot's license. I began at once to study for the written exams to apply for a commercial pilot's license, and on May 16, 1939 I obtained that credential. Two month's later, I obtained a flight instructor's rating. In all, I had garnered a total of 244 hours flight time. Within a week of receiving my flight instructor's rating, I was employed as a flight instructor at the Fritz Schrom Airport near the University of Maryland, where I was paid an hourly rate for flight instruction.

Fritz Schrom Airport was owned by a farmer who had built a runway and hangar on his farm land, and purchased a single Cub airplane. While waiting for my students to appear for flight training, I used my time floating on an inner tube in his small lake, studying for my next exams. I was able to use the spare time to complete the written, oral and flight exams to be certified for the re-rated flight instructor rating to qualify me to teach flying for the new civilian pilot training program just being initiated by the federal government.

In August, 1939, in a new position at Congressional

Airport in Rockville, Maryland, I began training a 16 year old boy to fly a Funk, the newest airplane on the market. The Funk, built in Akron, Ohio, was a gorgeous little two place, side by side airplane, powered by an inverted four cylinder Ford engine. My student was equally enthralled with the new plane and his father decided to purchase one. My boss, Arthur Hyde, an agent for the Funk, was most happy to sell him one. The Funk was purchased with the understanding that Arthur would arrange for the plane to be picked up by the student and me at the the Akron plant, and we would fly it back to Congressional Airport in Washington, D.C.

On our arrival at the Funk plant, the plane was brought from the hangar and delivered to us, whereupon I eagerly checked it over, boarded, and began my flight plan to Sistersville, West Virginia to land, refuel, and, depending on the time of day, perhaps stay overnight. Enroute, the engine developed a rough sound, so I landed at Sistersville for an engine check. After cleaning the plugs, the engine run up seemed smooth, and although the sun was going down, the weather to Washington was forecast clear. I felt certain I would have no difficulty landing the plane at Congressional Airport once I could see and recognize Washington, D.C.

I had never flown at night, never flown on instruments and never flown over the Allegheny Mountains in the dark. However, in considering my options, I decided that with no navigation problems, fine weather, and a new plane I would takeoff and fly over the mountains. Too late, I discovered that I did not have a flashlight, and that the battery had not been connected to the generator.

We were in a black cockpit only able to see outside the airplane. The moon was on its way up in the east, in the direction we wanted to fly. I felt all would be well if I continued east over the mountains until I could pick up the welcoming lights of Washington. I was petrified though, experiencing my first fear ever flying an airplane. My great confidence in my flying suddenly reverted to condemnation of my poor judgment. How could I be so dumb as to fly a single engine new airplane at night without having, at least, checked the electric system, without even bringing a flashlight? I couldn't even turn back because I was unfamiliar with the country behind me.

Time was now becoming a critical factor. We couldn't see our watches, didn't know how much gas we had, and couldn't find the lights of Washington. I maintained my altitude as best I could, even though I could see, only by moonlight, the dark, ominous mountains below. Flying on and on there was, in the distance and a little to the left, the glow of city lights on the horizon. They were, of course, the lights of Washington. I reasoned that I would fly toward them, turn left for about twenty miles, and follow the streets I knew well past Bethesda, and on to the airport. Even without light I wasn't worried. I could land successfully in the

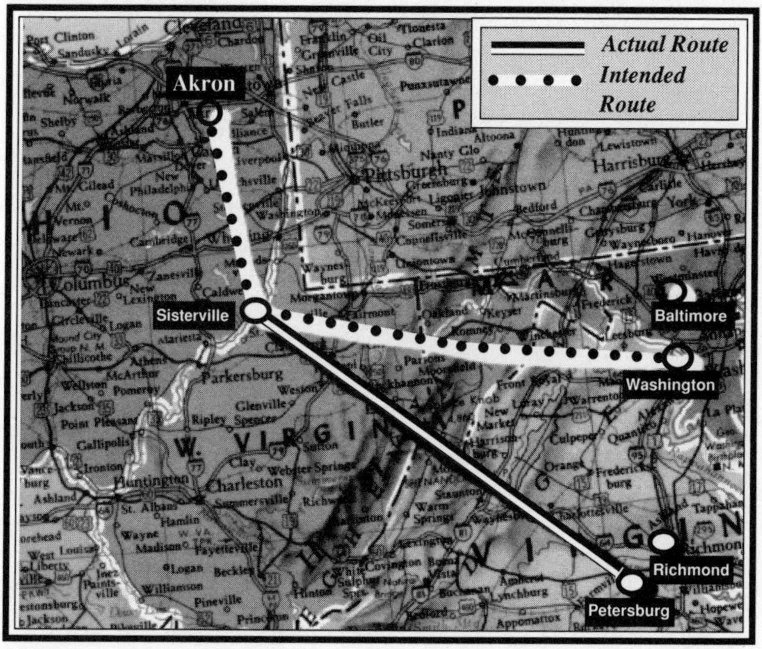

Flying above the engine of a well lit passenger train , I was able to see ahead of the train and land the Funk in a field just south of Richmond - a long way off from my intended destination.

moonlight. Suddenly, as we flew closer I realized, with twinges of panic and a shot of adrenaline, that this city was not Washington, D.C. I couldn't see the Washington Monument, the Capitol or the White House. Where were they?

I realized, after calming myself, that the city lights when we first saw them were to the left, our easterly heading toward the moon. Aha! It must be Baltimore, north of Washington! All we had to do now was to turn right, and forty miles south would be Washington. We proceeded away from the city of Baltimore for only a few minutes. I realized quickly if this were Baltimore, then where was the Chesapeake Bay? All of the street lights were uniform away from the center of the city. No bay!

I did not know what to do. I had a gnawing feeling that we were running out of gas. Quickly, I decided that I must land. With reduced power, still heading south, I began a slow descent, looking every where around us. At about 1,000 feet, and flying along above a highway loaded with fast moving traffic, I glimpsed a sight which made me gasp. A train below was going our direction near the road, and its great headlight was showing not only the tracks ahead of it, but open fields. All I had to do was fly over that engine, stay with his speed until the train lighted up a field of any reasonable size, and I would land the plane there.

It was a passenger train. I could see the lights from the passenger cars. That was good because its speed would be above my stall speed. I didn't get too close to the train because of crossing power wires, but I had a good view of the woods and various fields as we came toward them. On a slight turn in the railroad tracks, there was a pasture-like field straight ahead. I pulled back the throttle, dropped the flaps, and headed toward the field. The train went on ahead, but with the moonlight I could see the field with woods on the far side. Just before we were about to land, I felt a bump (later I discovered we had hit the top of a fence). I held the yoke back and we landed. I put on the brakes, and we were almost

FUNK - Built in Akron, Ohio. I flew it at night over the Allegheny mountains - landed at night in a field near Petersburg, Va. (near Richmond) out of gas.

DEFUNKED - I flew it across the Atlantic in one hour and fourteen minutes. ***I really did!!!***

stopped when the wheels dropped into a dirt ditch, and the Funk went up on its nose.

With the ignition off and no telltale smell of gas, we carefully unbuckled our safety belts, and eased ourselves out onto the ground. As I stood there wallowing in gratitude to the fates, we heard someone coming toward us. From a short distance across the field, two men were moving rapidly toward us with flashlights. As they came up to us, puffing from being out of breath, one of them drawled a syrupy, "Hey! It's a Funk! Well, whadda ya know? Why, I used to work in the Funk factory on these airplanes. Maybe I can put this one back together!" The speaker introduced himself as Frank Kavetco. He and his companion had heard us while we were tracking the train.

My first question was, "Where the hell are we?" Frank answered "Petersburg, Virginia, south of Richmond." No wonder Richmond didn't look like Washington. Frank said he would take care of the plane, and assured us that it wasn't damaged. He urged us to go to the end of the field where a lady would take care of us. I couldn't believe our good fortune when Frank took us into the house to introduce us to a very nice elderly woman who insisted on feeding us, and offered us her guest room upstairs. After a welcome shower, we fell into an exhausted sleep.

As soon as we awakened the following morning, I went, at once, to the window overlooking the field where we had landed. It was surrounded by a fence, but there was no airplane there. It had disappeared. We dressed hurriedly, and went downstairs to be met by the smell of frying bacon, and the pleasant woman who had sheltered and fed us. I asked, trying to be casual, "What happened to our plane?" She replied, "Oh, Frank and a group of his friends came back last night, lifted the plane over the fence, and the last I saw of them they were pushing the plane down the road. How would you like your eggs?"

After a delicious breakfast, and many thanks to our

hostess, we walked on down the road leading us to U.S. Route One, looking and asking locals if they had seen a plane go by on the ground. As we made a turn in the road we could see the Funk parked in a gas station, with our new found friend, Frank Kavetco, on his knees putting finishing touches to the wheel pants that he had removed, cleaned and painted.

The plane looked as new as it had the day before at the factory. Frank had, of course, filled the tank with high-test Amoco gas, washed it, finished off the wheel pants, and cleared approval of the state police for us to takeoff with traffic being held off the road. He would not accept any payment for the gas, just waved us away as we took off over Richmond on our way to Congressional Airport, north of Washington, D.C.

On the flight I carefully explained to my student, and now owner of the plane that, if he told his father or Mr. Hyde what a dumb thing I had done, my name and career would go down the drain. I pointed out that all that had really happened was an adventure for us both. We agreed to only mention that we had spent the night enroute.

Frank Kavecto went on further south to Miami to serve as a mechanic at Municipal Airport. When I happened to see him there, I couldn't believe it. From then on, of course, Frank became my ground crew and chief mechanic, handling the gliders, my SN-J, the AT-9 (on loan to me from the CAA) and my beloved P-38 and Stearman. Every flier should have a forced landing at night, be lost, out of gas, and meet a fine person, and first rate mechanic like Frank Kavetco. Most especially, if he comes out of the woods with a tool kit in his hand.

FLYING PAN AM BOATS

My good friend, Captain
Marious (Lodi) Lodeesen
HOW TO LEARN TO FLY IN 6 EASY LESSONS.

Chapter Seven

While working for my good friend, Arthur Hyde at Congressional Airport in Rockville, Maryland, I met another lifelong friend, Bud Holloway, and I was placed in charge of all flight operations and ground school training. Under Arthur's guidance, we began one of the first civilian pilot training programs in the country. In addition to teaching and flying, I was receiving my own separate instruction in advanced CAA secondary aerobatic flying which was given in a WACO-UPF-7 biplane. Oddly enough, this was the first training I had ever received.

Upon receiving my secondary instructor rating, I enlisted ten students to train them for a commercial license and acrobatic flying. For the period of July 20 through November 4, 1940, I gave fifty hours of flight and 140 hours of ground school training to the ten advanced students. Even though I was flying in winter in an open UPF-7, and had no time

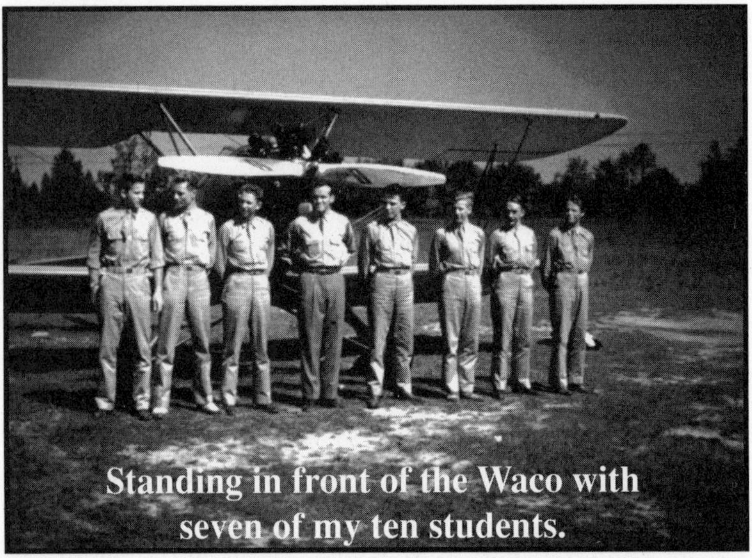

Standing in front of the Waco with seven of my ten students.

off at all, I did acquire 1,445 hours of total flying time.

Allan Rothenberg, one of the more gifted of my advanced students, sought to join the Navy as a pilot. Despite his having completed the Civil Pilot Training Program, his application was rejected. Evaluation of the rejection led to the conclusion that he had been excluded because he was a Jew. On learning of this action, I wrote a strong letter of endorsement of him and protested his exclusion, and, after some haggling, he was accepted as a student pilot in the Navy in June, 1940.

The wise choice of the Navy to accept Al was repeatedly verified by the distinctive service he rendered as a plane commander of one of the 4PBY's which were sent on the torpedo attack against the incoming Japanese fleet the night before the Battle of Midway; his rescue of 72 survivors of Destroyer Meredith, which had been sunk by the Japanese; his being presented the Navy Cross for torpedoing a Japanese cruiser in 1942; and his glide bombing of another cruiser at Tassafaronga four nights later. In addition to the Navy Cross,

Al earned 3 Air Medals, 2 Distinguished Flying Crosses, and the Silver Star. I enjoy reminding Al of his first distinctive service under my tutlelage when he was placed in charge of a rake and clean up!

Allan Rothenberg

My friend, Bud Holloway then moved on to a position at Embry Riddle Flying School in Miami, where he was making almost as much money as I, teaching only half as many students, and in gorgeous weather, no less. My pay of $700 a month just did not satisfy me once I realized the life Bud had created in Florida, spending half a day on the beach.

Bud telephoned to advise me when an opening developed for the position of secondary acrobatics instructor. With my classes completed, and a warm parting handshake with Arthur Hyde, off I went to Embry Riddle to begin training students for their commercial pilot licenses. Several of those students went on to work for Pan American Airways.

Bud and I were employed by Pan American on January 1, 1941. The following day, twenty Army Air Corps pilots were given a special release and employed by Pan American as copilots to ferry aircraft and supplies to West Africa under Pan American's government contract. By only one day, we were senior to those twenty men. To determine our own seniority, we flipped a coin. Bud won, and from then on was senior to me throughout our careers with Pan American.

Part of the employment process was a series of rather intensive physical examinations, including an elaborate eye test for depth perception. We had already taken the test a number of times. The process of the test was that the pilot being examined was seated twenty feet away from a lighted boxlike apparatus which held two black vertical pencil sized rods. One was stationary, the other could be moved back and forth by strings held by the pilot, one in each hand. One could move one rod fore and aft. The purpose was to position the movable rod opposite the stationary one.

The nurse first moved the rod back and forth, and then the pilot taking the test was directed to drop the strings, pick them up, and move the rod back and forth until he determined it was exactly opposite the stationary rod. The nurse would then observe the scale under the movable rod, and record the distance they were apart. This was measured in

Bud and I had a wonderful time living together and flying for Embry-Riddle. We both went to work for Pan American on the same day - 1/1/41

Bud and his wife Clarissa

millimeters. Each person was given six attempts to bring the rods opposite each other, and was scored on each attempt.

After a few minutes of chatting with the nurse, telling her what a fascinating test it was, she agreed to our request to be allowed to watch each other take the test. I was first at the test. No way to cheat. Wrong. As Bud leaned over, with the nurse observing my moving the rod back and forth, he held his hands behind his body clearly giving me hand signals. A little more ahead, now back a bit. With his thumb extended I knew that the rod was exactly opposite the other stationary one.

The nurse was taken aback. It was amazing! She explained it was very rare for anyone to place the rods exactly opposite one another. When we changed places, I gave Bud the same excellent hand signals, and he miraculously duplicated my perfect placements. Two stellar performances were too much for the nurse. She called the doctor in to share the interesting phenomena with him. His face showed that he knew we had pulled some scam, yet our demeanor of innocence rescued us from his commanding an encore performance from each of us.

At the time Bud and I arrived at Pan American, the airline's fabulous successes, innovations and great bursts of growth were at full momentum. Pan Am's service had begun in 1927 with a Fokker F-VII airplane which flew the ninety miles distance from Key West to Havana in one hour at a ground speed of 90 miles per hour. A fabulous plane, the Fokker F-VII had the capacity of floating on water. It had one drawback, however; if the aircraft went down at sea only the wings floated, leaving the fuselage under water.

Under brilliant surveying and technical advice of General Charles Lindbergh, the airline expanded its routes in the Caribbean, South America, Pacific, and Atlantic Ocean areas. Typical of General Lindbergh's expertise, is the fact that his flight route chosen for the Scandinavian countries, Greenland and Iceland is not far from the modern route taken

FOKKER F-10

Following the Fokker F-7, the Fokker F-10 was introduced in January of 1929. The F-10 carried the larger 425 hp Wasp engines, and its maximum takeoff gross weight was 13,100 lbs. The new model carried up to 12 passengers. Fourteen of the Fairchild F-71s as shown below were used by Pan American in Central and South America and in Alaska. The F-71, too, had a Wasp 420 hp engine and could carry six passengers.

today by the Pan American west coast-Europe bound airplanes.

With its series of flying boats, Pan American was able to rise above the obstructions of limited, or no airfield access to important cities around the globe. The very few airports in the world were mostly made of grass, gravel, or cinder strips which inhibited the load level and abilities of anything but the lightest and least complicated landing plans.

The glamour and romance of the flying boats remains for all those who flew them as crew or passenger. Those exciting and challenging days for the pilots have been wonderfully

described by my great friend Captain Marious (Lodi) Lodeesen. Lodi was of Dutch origin, a linguist, author of numerous books, friend and hero to hundreds of people who knew and loved him. His untimely death came just prior to his delivering a prepared, inspiring speech to the Clipper Pioneers on October 27, 1984. With permission, I have included some excerpts of that fine speech which give some of the best and most succinct descriptions of that era in aviation.

> *"Many times I had almost abandoned all hope since I stepped ashore at Ellis Island, an immigrant Dutchman, with a dream in my heart to fly. And here at Pan American's "gateway to the world", I knew*

ACROSS the PACIFIC
IN FIVE DAYS
Via PAN AMERICAN
SKYWAY TO INCA LAND
IT'S A SMALL WORLD BY
PAN AMERICAN WORLD AIRWAYS
The System of the Flying Clippers
HAWAII BY FLYING CLIPPER
PAA
HONOLULU CLIPPER
PAN AMERICAN AIRWAYS SYSTEM

Captain Marious (Lodi) Lodeesen

that my odyssey would really begin.

I had passed that afternoon driving through Miami's portals, a wasteland of abandoned suburbs with shells of houses, billboards and stunted palmetto bushes. A dismal scene as Samarkand, Miami lay prostrate under the blow of the great depression of 1929. The happy go lucky fantasia of the crazy 20's had shuddered to a halt. The world had come to an end, the singing and dancing, the booze and the easy dough. People walked around in a daze.

Aviation was emerging from the era of ocean spanning dare-devils like Alcock, Brown, Byrd, Acosta, Broick, Schlee, Renee Fonck, Nungesser and Lindbergh. Juan Trippe wanted to make his game respectable. That's where we came in.

Pan American's future skippers, so thought Mr. Priester, the genius vice-president of Pan American Airways, should be a cross between the captain of the Queen Mary and a bosun of a tugboat, equally at home in the ship's first class salon as in the stoke hold. I can see us now, a bunch of scarecrows in dirty overalls, scraping, painting, splicing, sweating, doing jobs that no day laborer with a right to unemployment compensation would even consider today.

Federal licenses in various aviation trades fol-

lowed. For good measure we were taught tidbits such as how to drill for oil, to tie nautical knots, name the sails of a full rigged ship, and other things no Pan American ocean flying commander could do without. Only one thing they failed to teach us: how to subsist on $150 a month.

Into the hangars we went under the gentle care of Rich, the hangar foreman, an evil eyed type who acted like a fugitive from a Georgia chain gang squad. At lunch time we emerged from the bilges, washed the coal dust from our hair and ate fried mullet and grits...

...we hurried to 'Bill the Tailor' on South Miami Avenue to buy a double breasted blue serge suit off the hook for 25 bucks, but before we entered the cockpit we discarded this splendor and donned white coveralls and shoved a tool box beneath our seats.

We alternated controls every half hour, we tapped a radio key, we refueled the ship at stops, greased the engine's rocker arms with an alemite gun, and envied the skipper having a cup of coffee with the station master on the barge...

Do you remember your check out to captain? Mine was typical for our period. The flight to San Juan in a P-12 Commodore was the first command of Paul Youngs, a former Marine lieutenant, and it was my first copilot trip. Even in those days scheduling goofed sometimes...

About passengers: not too many cared to fly to Rio in seven days and seven nights. But Havana was around the corner, the tourist paradise with plenty of booze and dancing girls.

Remember the milk run in the S-40, the flying box car with an interior exuding a tough late Victorian elegance? Loaded to the gunnels, we lifted from Biscayne Bay, lumbered over the Florida Keys and over placid lagoons, over the gulf stream of deep indigo. We squatted down on Havana Harbor amidst tramp steamers in whose rigging I left many a trailing antenna I forgot to reel in...

Before dawn we chugged to the barge and climbed into the cockpit, smelling faintly of stale sweat, limp sandwiches, and rubbery chicken legs from the box lunch. A soothing hum of engines, rattling of loose rivets on the bulkheads. Hours of skimming over sandy beaches, over green jungles and endless estuaries, dodging rain squalls, and we hugged the surface when driving rain made visibility almost zero. That was the flying boat..."

Captain Lodeesen's farewell address provides an insight into this magical era of international aviation and the environment in which participants not only flew the airplanes, but were learning, how to build, through trial and error methods, America's first international airline.

Bud and I arrived at Pan American during the heyday of the Sikorsky S-42 flying boat, an aircraft which could carry almost double the number of passengers twice the distance of the DC-3s. A classic airliner, it could carry its full passenger complement over a range of 750 miles enhancing the trans-Caribbean route to Colombia, South America, and reducing the number of stops necessary for a scheduled flight. Its advances paved the way for the Martin-130 which made conquest of the Pacific Ocean possible.

On my twenty-fourth birthday, I flew my first Pan American flight in an S-42. While taking instruction as a junior pilot under the direction of Captain Bob Fatt, I was involved

Sikorsky S-42 - Pan Am's proud American Clipper. Broke all performance records for flying boats.

in ground training where we spent days in the hangar after the airplanes had been pulled out of the bay and rolled into the hangar for overhaul. We each elected to purchase a set of tools at Sears Roebuck which we used to change parts on engines, working alongside the mechanics as part of our training.

While learning to weld, I thought that I was doing so well that I should try welding aluminum. It melted almost immediately into a liquid form, and splashed off the workbench onto my shoe, frying my heel. After receiving first aid, I wore a slipper throughout ground school. I remember learning Morse code (we had to send 18 words per minute) with only one shoe on.

Ten days after my checkout flight, consisting of three

takeoffs and landings, I received a phone call assigning me to my first scheduled passenger flight to South America. I had a commercial license, but no instrument rating. No matter, these certifications were not necessary at that time, because the government did not monitor the airlines as they do now.

In preparation for my big initial flight, I bought a brand new uniform, and appeared at the Dinner Key Marine Terminal one hour ahead of my departure time. Seeking to get off to the right start, I went immediately to introduce myself as the first officer to Captain Alfred F. Dreyer. He made no response to my introduction of myself. Nevertheless, I knew what my duties and functions were, and headed on down to check the amount of water ballast which was in the bow of our S-42 seaplane.

Captain Dreyer marched aboard, seated himself in the cockpit, and I climbed in on the right side. As the radio operator and flight engineer climbed in behind me, I became acutely aware of feeling completely at a loss, nervous because I had no idea of procedures in the cockpit for this airplane. Captain Dreyer looked at me and queried, "Clear to start engines?" "Yes, sir," I responded. The captain then had the flight engineers start the four engines, and barked, "Clear to taxi?" "Yes, sir," came my reply. Then he started to open four throttles and we moved forward. I wonder why we were turning to the right when I could see he had a full left rudder on. I quickly discovered the reason. The airplane was still attached to the dock. The airplane went into the sand. The captain pulled back the throttles, shut the engine down and looked at me, saying nothing.

Men on the dock jumped into the water and fastened lines on the airplane. With tow tractors, they dragged the dock and the airplane back onto position. When we were back into our seat positions again, the captain looked at me and again said, "Clear to start the engines?" Flushing slightly, I replied clearly, "Yes, sir!" I had learned my first lesson: to open my side window and signal to cast off the lines. There

Sikorsky S-36 (Dec. 27, 1927) - operated for two months (only one purchased); superceded by the S-38.

Sikorsky S-38 - Developed by Pan Am, this aircraft opened air travel to Puerto Rico and Central and South America.

Consolidated Commodore - purchased by Pan Am on Sept. 15, 1930. The 22 seater pioneered services down the east coast of South America.

Sikorsky S-40 - The first commercial four engine flying boat. Established the world's record for the longest over-water route - 600 miles.

were many more lessons to be learned.

Later, on the same flight to San Juan, Puerto Rico, with only scattered clouds in our path, the captain engaged the auto pilot, and gave the radio operator a brief position report to transmit to Miami and San Juan. Looking ahead, I could see there was a long row of high dark clouds in front of us which we could not circumnavigate. I was perplexed when the captain ordered the engineer, "Get them out!" Responding to the order, the engineer got out of his seat, went to the closet and returned with four yellow rubber raincoatlike garments which had no opening in the front, and had to be put on backwards. The captain and the radio operator busied themselves putting all papers and maps away. Not knowing or asking why, I put all my papers in my briefcase.

Then, following suit with my mates, I put the yellow coat on backwards. As soon as we entered the black clouds, I discovered why. The rain we encountered hit us with a roar, the air was rough, and water started to leak in around all of the front windows. Completely unconcerned, the captain would occasionally wipe his glasses with his handkerchief. Soon, we burst into bright sunny skies, removed our rainwear, and the engineer hung them up to dry.

During the flight, when the captain desired to change course to avoid flying into a cloud, he had to lean forward and turn a small knob left or right on the autopilot. To offset this burden, he reached into his briefcase, took out a roll of string, and, using scissors, cut a length of string about two feet. He then took out a stick which was doubled with a metal sleeve in the center. When rigged into one long stick, he now had a four foot length which had a rubber nipple on one end. Then I knew what he was up to.

He tied a small loop in one end of the string, tied one end overhead to a handle, sighted its length to be opposite that turn knob, inserted the stick, fastened the end with the nipple to the turning knob on the automatic pilot, and leaned back in his seat. He could then turn that airplane from his

Sikorsky S-43 - built as an amphibious twin-engine flying boat, capable of landing on both water and land. Carrying 18 passengers, it was faster and more flexible than its predecessors.

Boeing 307 "Stratoliner" - first pressurized cabin landplane ever used in regular commercial flying - could literally leap over troublesome weather. The 307 made a comfortable 185 mph with 33 passengers.

The Douglas DC-2 introduced in 1934 had the capacity of 14 passengers. It was the warm-up for its successor, the 21 seat DC-3 that would revolutionize commercial transports.

Douglas DC-3 - earned its nickname of "workhorse" by carrying more than half a billion passengers, in all, not counting millions of servicemen during the war. In 1943, Pan Am had 53 of these DC-3s operating on overland routes.

leisurely position by a slight twist of the stick with his fingers. With it suspended between us, he handed it over to me and said, "Wanna' fly?".

This was not the kind of flying I wanted to do. As soon as the captain elected to have his lunch, I turned off the autopilot and flew the airplane. I had never had any training in instrument flying, never been in a Link Trainer, but I had been reading a book on instrument flying. I thought I was doing very well, I kept the heading, and altitude, and had the radio operator send position reports. There was a cloud ahead, not too deep, but I thought it would give me a chance to fly on instruments instead of going around it, as I had been instructed by the captain. As soon as I entered the cloud, without my seatbelt on, the first good bump put me in the ceiling.

I knew that the captain was going to be fiercely angry. I looked back to see if he were coming toward the cockpit. He was! We came out of that cloud in a dive, not too critical, but heading and altitude were off, and with lots of speed. Now back in my seat, with a bump on my head, I recovered with a climbing turn. I saw the captain seat himself as he was wiping off his soup stained uniform. Fortunately for me, we were on a six day trip and there were other days I could use to reduce his considerations of my idiocy.

Chapter Eight

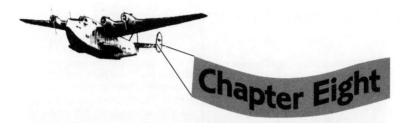

FROM FLYING BOATS TO LINA ROMAY

Sikorsky S-42 - the Hornet-powered S-42 was the first true Clipper. It paved the way for over-ocean flights that would carry pasengers and cargo throughout the world. A considerable improvement over its predecessors (the S-40 and S-41), the S-42 entered Pan American Airways on August 16, 1934.

Martin M-130 - The *"Hawaii, Phillipine and China Clippers"* was built to a Pan Am specification. It opened a mail service across the Pacific on Nov. 22, 1935. On Oct. 21, 1936, the M-130 carried the first trans-Pacific paying passengers.

Boeing B-314 - Pan Am's *"Yankee Clipper"* not only inaugurated the first scheduled transatlantic service in 1939, it also introduced a new concept of luxurious flying. The 74 passengers could relax in overstuffed chairs and sofas. The spacious state rooms even included a bridal suite.

PAN-AM CLIPPERS (1934-1945)

	S-42	M-130	B-314
NUMBER BUILT	10 (Sikorsky)	3 (Martin)	9 (Boeing)
GROSS WEIGHT	38,000 lbs.	51,000 lbs.	82,500 lbs.
EMPTY WEIGHT	19,000 lbs.	28,000 lbs.	50,000 lbs.
WING SPAN	118' 2"	130'	152'
LENGTH	69'	90' 10"	106'
HEIGHT	21' 9"	24'	27' 7"
TOP SPEED	182 mph	180 mph	193mph
CRUISING SPEED	157 mph	157 mph	183 mph
RANGE	3,000 miles	3,000 miles	3,500 miles
NO. OF ENGINES	4	4	4
HORSEPOWER (EACH)	700	800	1200
CREW	4	5-7	7-10
PASSENGERS	32-44	46 (18-30 night)	74 (36-40 night)

** These figures changed with variations of each flying-boat.*

Chapter Eight

World War II erupted in Europe just three months after the start of Pan American passenger service across the Atlantic. With the United States entering the war two years later, Pan American was in a unique position. In cooperation with the American and British governments, the airline developed a new Africa Orient Division (A.O.A.) which provided air transport services to Africa, across the continent to Egypt, and provided ferry services to deliver military planes to the Middle East. Almost 12,000 miles of ocean, jungle, and desert routes were established in just 60 days, which normally would have taken years to develop.

The need for airports was so desperate down the east coast of South America to Natal, Brazil, that some were used before they were completed. In Africa, Pan American built 14 air bases, including runways, hangars, barracks and power stations. Over 16,000 tons of equipment was transported to outfit them. On the eve of the first global conflict, the world was depending increasingly on the airplane.

Bud Holloway and I were transferred to the Atlantic Division of Pan American in New York in December, 1941. We

Martin M-130

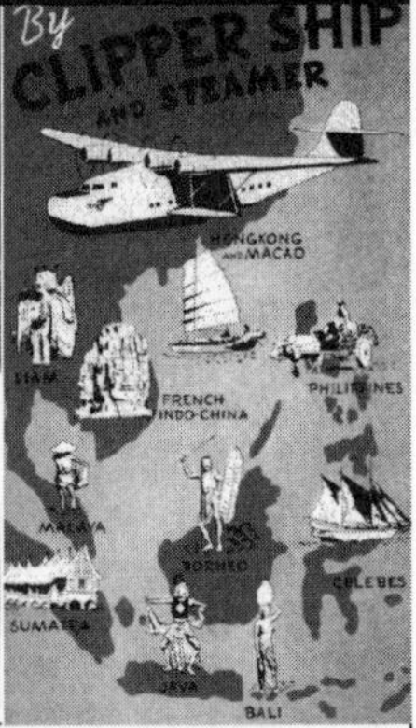

Interior Views

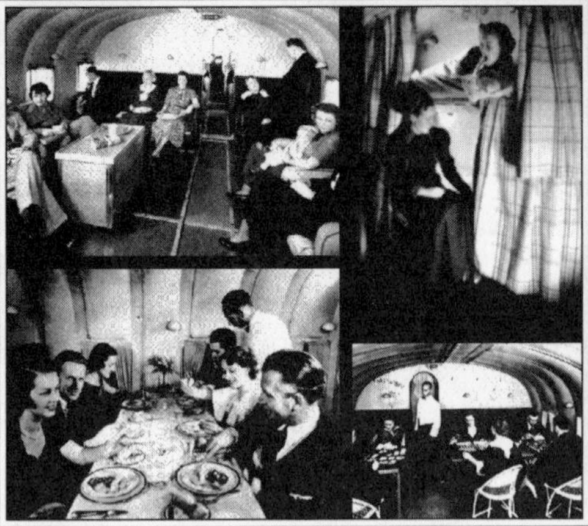

The M-130 Cockpit

Passenger compartments doubled as sleeping quarters, and the tables in the lounge area provided a place to play cards, write letters, and dine.

The Boeing 314 Clipper

With a bomber's wings, a boat's hull and a liner's luxury, the 314 had everything except speed.

One of the most luxurious airliners of all time, the Boeing Model 314 Clipper, came very close to never being built. The airline already had scheduled transpacific flights but needed larger and faster airplanes to increase the essential payloads and to speed up its flight schedule.

The pilots, radiomen, navigators and flight engineers enjoyed the roomiest control cabin of any airliner. The six to ten man crew was accommodated on a spacious upper deck accessible from below by a spiral staircase. There were even sleeping accommodations for the off-duty crew members carried on long flights. Cargo and mail compartments totaling 1,036 cubic feet were on this deck as well.

The 314 was the largest production airplane built in the major assemby building of the old Boeing Plant I, which had been built in 1917 for World War I aircraft production. Final assembly took place on a wooden ramp outside of a factory, after which the airplanes were launched down a slipway (the factory had been a yacht works) into the river. It was too dangerous to taxi the airplane down the river to Seattle harbor for take-off, so they were tied alongside a barge, which was towed to the harbor. After the first take-off, further shakedown flights were made from a Boeing base on fresh water Lake Washington.

As originally designed, the 314 used vertical tail surfaces based on those of the XB-15. These proved to be inadequate on the first flight, due mainly to the increased side area of the huge hull. Test pilot Eddie Allen had to resort to differential power settings in order to turn the craft on its first flight. A new double tail was designed and built, but it, too, was inadequate. Finally, a center fin, equal in area to the original fin/rudder combination, was added and the directional control problem was resolved.

rented a room on the third floor of a home known as Mrs. Chapin's Chateau, and drove to and from our work at the La Guardia Marine Terminal each day. Having received our instrument, multi-engine, and seaplane ratings we were to fly on the Boeing 314 "Yankee Clipper" flying boat as fourth officers. In addition, we were assigned as copilots on local B-314 training flights with captains being checked out as master pilots of ocean flying boats, training under the tutelage of Captain Harold Gray.

Boeing B-314 "Yankee Clipper"

The Boeing 314 was the largest flying clipper ship Pan American operated over world wide routes. Its sea wings, the relatively short wing stubs to be seen under the engines at the water level, served several purposes. They provided stability to the flying boat when it was on water, and acted as a loading ramp to the entrance doors. It carried the bulk of fuel required for an ocean crossing.

Nine B-314s were built for Pan American. Capable of flying any ocean route, they were still relatively slow compared to modern transport planes. Carrying 74 passengers and a crew of 12, all were unpressurized, and limited to a normal maximum altitude of eight or nine thousand feet for passenger comfort. The operation of this aircraft, with its limited power, was so limited that many westbound flights had to be turned back to Ireland.

Prevailing westerly winds across the Atlantic meant almost certain completion of eastbound flights. Westbound flights were another matter, and were made at very low levels with some as low as 100 feet from the ocean to avoid the stronger winds which increase with altitude. Routes were taken on individual flights to establish least time tracks where advantage was obtained from wind direction and velocities.

Position reporting while flying many hours over water was not easy. Flights were made at night to utilize the stars and planets. Celestial observations to obtain lines of position were taken by the navigator, captain or first officer, who would plot celestial fixes to best determine position. From these calculations, ground speed, wind direction, and velocity were computed, and an estimated time to arrive at the next reporting point was determined and indicated on the navigation chart.

The estimated time of arrival was based upon the expected winds to be encountered along the route ahead. Flight progress was plotted on the "howgozit" chart to graphically display fuel being consumed. From this the captain would determine the range of reserve fuel limits to make a decision if the flight should be continued or turned back.

Hair-raising and interesting experiences were the order of the day on these flights, with each journey being unique. Sometimes there were delays of many days in the Azores, waiting for wave conditions to subside to allow a takeoff. Flights into Africa, the Azores or Lisbon often resulted in landing on a lake requiring flares to be dropped from the airplane. The captains encountered such obstacles as a hippopotamus in the landing area in Africa, and a holding in

Natal, Brazil, while waiting for the sun to come up, so a landing could be made on the river among many small fishing boats.

During January of 1942, I flew on several Yankee Clipper local training flights in New York, serving as fourth officer for captains being checked out as master pilots of ocean flying boats. In flight, I was an observer looking out for other airplanes while the student pilot or captain checked was under a hood put up just before takeoff. The hood was used to assure that the pilot being checked would fly only by reference to instruments.

The only way to fly across the ocean was to utilize celestial navigation. Radio bearings, at best, could only be used within 200 miles of a coastline, or within the same range of a weather ship. The navigator would drop flare lights on the ocean surface on the various headings, taking drift sights on the floating flares, and computing the wind direction and velocity. From this information he could determine the ground speed, and by dead reckoning, compute an estimate of the airplane's position.

A celestial fix was required to determine the flight's real progress. We were reluctant to rely on anything except a celestial fix, unless radio bearings on coastal radio stations or a weather ship were available. We often did not know where we were out over the ocean. It was up to the navigator to persuade the captain to climb to an altitude above the clouds in order to obtain celestial observations, because, at high altitudes, the navigator might get an observation of the

North Star to establish latitude to determine if we were on the right ocean crossing track.

The navigator would try to get a two or three star fix, then plot his "howgozit" curves to determine how the airplane was progressing, with reference to time, distance, and fuel to destination or alternates. It was imperative that we obtain accurate navigation fixes because of our marginal fuel reserves on all westbound flights, so each flight across that ocean was a carefully planned, carefully executed expedition.

Standing on the flight deck behind the pilots, where takeoffs and landings were made, we copilots watched for other air traffic, and assisted with the bow line when we returned to the Marine Terminal to secure the 314s. By constant observation of the check captain in charge, we learned about the proper way to start, taxi, take off, and make instrument approaches.

In an intense ground school instruction, Blackie Blackburn, a professional sea going navigator, took pains to indoctrinate us into all phases of ocean navigation on the surface of the sea, a history of navigation, chart design and the utilization of the Mercator Chart used by our aircraft ocean navigator. Our curriculum included emergency procedures in the event of fires, engine failure, ditching, and surviving at sea in life rafts. Navigation studies continued with heavy emphasis on the stars, planets, and their relative position to constellations.

As students, we had to learn old established historical methods of navigation updated to meet the problems of an airplane flying at 130 miles per hour while the navigator attempted to take a three-star fix. We measured the altitude of a celestial body, utilizing our hand held octant which fitted into an observation port through the ceiling of the plane. We took our sight over a two minute period, averaging the observed altitude and averaging the time. It was a cumbersome system, but it worked.

On completion of our written and oral exams we were scheduled as fourth officers to fly to Bermuda and back in order to keep up with our navigation studies. We served on ocean crossings to make up the multiple crew allowing the captain or first officer to sleep, while keeping two pilots in the cockpit at all times.

The pre-war flying boats such as the B-314 required a very large crew. Not counting the stewards (air hostesses were not employed by the airline until after World War II), a crew consisted of at least eight, a captain, first officer pilot, second officer pilot navigator, third officer pilot, fourth officer, an engineer officer, a radio officer and a junior flight engineer.

The engineering and radio officers were specialists long trained in operation of power plants and radio, and equipped with ample theory and shop experience to enable them to trace trouble, rectifying it, where possible, in flight. The second officer pilot navigator was in direct charge of charting the plane's position by celestial navigation, by dead reckoning, and by radio bearings taken on the plane by surface

Crew on Transatlantic Survey Flight
March 26, 1939

stations.

The first, third and fourth officer pilots shared the bulk of the flying duties with the captain, while the junior flight engineer officer helped the engineer officer by inspecting fuel tanks, fuel lines, and the big engines themselves, both in flight and on the ground. This was more than a mere subdivision of continuous labor. Five, all except the engineer and radio officer, were pilots fully qualified to take off, fly the ship and land it.

There was no royal road to a captaincy. Most pilots entering Pan American service were college graduates and graduates of Army or Navy flight training centers with a year or two of active duty. Their first rank was that of apprentice pilot working in maintenance shops, and duty in the offices to acquaint them with the work of all departments. All had to qualify for navigator or flight engineer certificates.

During this time they began courses of study toward examinations for advancement in grade. Most took correspondence courses prepared for their special benefit by the Pan American technicians, administered through one of the big correspondence schools. As one specific objective, each had to qualify for a second class radio license. Then, after handling a stiff set of written and practical examinations, the apprentice graduated to the rank of junior pilot navigator.

As one checked out in dead reckoning celestial and radio navigation, basic meteorology, the Link trainer, and amassed flying time, he could move up to first officer class. At least one year later, he had to face another set of examinations for rank of senior pilot or captain on twin engine DC-3s. His subjects including international law, basic celestial navigation, seamanship and the history and cultural background of countries served by Pan American.

Even then the applicant was not finished. After 2,500 hours in command of an aircraft (at least 500 in flying boats of more than 17,000 pounds gross) he sat for further examinations in navigation and another eighteen subjects. If he had an excellent record, and showed outstanding ability as a leader and manager, then he might be awarded a rating of "Master Pilot of ocean flying boats". Only with technological advances, and after these procedures became a burden on the airline, were these rigid procedures discarded. Records indicate they were followed on our seniority list - down through K. J. Scribner. I was the last PAA pilot to qualify as a "Master" pilot in this manner.

Passengers arrive in Lisbon after 24 hour and 3 minute flight from Port Washington, Long Island. The total elapsed time included a one hour, 36 minute refueling stop in the Azores. The flight continued on to Marseille, France.

On June 28, 1939, man's greatest steps toward shrinking the size of the world in which he lives, took place.

On that date in 1939, the Dixie Clipper of Pan American World Airways lifted off from the waters of a Long Island marina, circled and headed eastward over the Atlantic. On board were 22 men and women for a flight that would take them to Marseilles, France, 42 hours and ten minutes later, after brief stops in the Azores and Lisbon. The aircraft, a 42-ton flying boat built by the Boeing company to Pan Am's specifications, actually spent 29 hours in the air.

Apparently, based on reports from the distinguished passenger complement, the flight was smooth to the point of being "humdrum." Others compared the trip favorably with remembered luxury voyages on the great ocean liners *Normandie* and the *Queen Mary*. Obviously, the fact that the airline had hired Waldorf-trained chefs to plan, prepare and serve the inflight meal service, which was presented with a wide selection of Champagne, wines and liqueurs, paid off. When it was time to retire, equally luxurious sleeping accommodations were ready with "...dressing rooms that would be the envy of many a fine hotel."

Passengers were also very impressed with the fact that the craft was "perfectly vibrationless and insolated to the point where you (could) speak in an ordinary voice."

Ironically, just two days before Pan Am's historic Atlantic crossing, the new liner *Mauretania* steamed into New York harbor at the end of her maiden voyage - six days, 18 hours and 15 minutes out of Liverpool.

Training on the B-314 was engrossing and filled with hard work. It was a huge flying boat which took tremendous care and technique to taxi, takeoff and land. The propellers were not reversible, creating a real problem when taxiing. Floating bow lines attached to anchors, or buoys, had to be picked up by a copilot, usually the fourth officer, standing on the bow hatch which opened outward and down to make a platform. The copilot would toss a line with a hook on it to pick up the looped end of the floating line, then place it over one of the bow posts which he inserted into the top of the bow of the Boeing.

Meanwhile, the captain attempted to use the water current, wind direction and velocity, engine power, and flight controls (including flaps) to position the flying boat near the floating bow line to establish minimum forward speed. Using a combination of all these factors, and cutting the ignition on and off to keep the engines operating at minimum possible power, still resulted in frequent missed approaches and go arounds in the water trying to pick up the bow line.

To taxi the B-314 in a cross wind represented a real problem as exemplified in the photo below. The seaplane did

not have wing tip pontoons to keep the wing tips and outboard engines out of the water when cross wind gusts would lift the up wind wing. Efforts by the pilot to keep the wings level with his flight controls were not enough. Crew members were sent out inside the up wind wing to keep it level by using their weight to hold the wing down. The wing

Little did the high priority passengers of this flight realize that the Boeing 314 was anchored to a WWI German bomb hidden in the buoy. Surviving countless dockings, the buoy finally expoded - killing two maintenance men - when ignited by cleaning torches.

Prior to US involvement in WorldWar II, Pan American was flying into neutral countries and Captain Holloway and I were flying as copilots (fourth, third, second and first officers) on the Boeing 314 Clippers. Bud was on a flight, as first officer, from Bermuda to the Azores, then on to Lisbon.

The Captain made the landing at the Azores without incident and taxied into the harbor. The third and fourth officers proceeded to lower the hull section beneath the cockpit area; lowering the door afforded an area for standing; and throwing the bow line that was used to pick up a floating line attached to a buoy anchored to the bottom of the harbor. Holloway, as first officer, was seated next to the Captain.

Holloway did notice that the buoy was a different color, new and seemed to float higher in the water, but everything was normal. The line was picked up and placed over the bow post to secure the Clipper, and the passengers were taken ashore.

Upon reaching the dock where the launch unloaded its passengers and crew, Holloway spoke to the station manager about the new buoy. The station manager beckoned him aside and in a very quiet manner said,"Don't tell anyone about this but - remember the old float was floating a bit low. It was leaking so I had two of our maintenance men uncouple it, bring it ashore and take it up to our maintenance shack up on the hill.

The men towed the heavy metal buoy up there on a flat metal platform, placed it inside the building, obtained blow torches, and began to rid the buoy of its rust.

"What happened then? It blew up, killed both men, destroyed the building, and left that big hole!" It looks like the Germans had placed it there during World War I to destroy any ship that bumped into it.

No one spoke about this incident until I telephoned Captain Bud Holloway, now retired, to ask him about any unusual experience he had observed on his Boeing 314 flights. This was one of them.

could hold up to six men, with the smallest crew member going in first because the inner wing passageway became narrow and a bit restrictive the farther one ventured out into the wing.

Flight training with Chief Pilot, Captain Harold Gray, was thorough and required commitment, for Captain Gray was a most formidable person. Very technical and very strict, he held meetings with each captain before and after each ocean crossing flight. Periodically, he would take a regular flight to Europe or Africa via South America, and each first officer and second officer navigator would cross his fingers and hold his breath when word emerged that Captain Gray was due for such a flight. It could last a week or several weeks.

In May 1942, I was navigator on our flight from Horta to Bermuda; I was able to obtain good celestial fixes, and found the winds were strong, causing our progress to be marginal, fuelwise. Captain Gray made several visits to the navigator's table to take a few fixes himself, agreed with our progress, and announced he was going to sleep, leaving me orders to wake him in time to dress to come to the flight deck to make the landing.

If my estimated time of arrival were correct, I should wake the captain at the top of our descent, about twenty minutes before landing. I focused on my estimated time to begin our descent to land at Bermuda, but clouds had developed, and no fixes were available. All of a sudden, a call came from the cockpit, we looked down, and we were over Bermuda at 8,000 feet. I put my finger to my lips, and with hand signals to the two pilots in the cockpit, requested them to make a slow 180 degree turn. The captain was still sleeping.

I gave the pilots a heading to go back the way we had come, and told them not to descend. When we had flown away from Bermuda twenty minutes, I requested the pilot to turn around again and begin descending as soon as we were inbound. I waked the captain by saying, "We are about to descend, and should sight the island in eighteen minutes." As he put on his shoes and glanced at his watch he replied, "Well, we shall see what kind of navigator you are." In eighteen minutes the lights of Bermuda were straight in front of us. He tapped me on the shoulder and commended my work. Years later when Captain Gray was president of Pan American, and I was Chief Pilot, I never bothered to mention the navigational assistance I had required from the two pilots in the cockpit.

On another memorable flight with Captain Gray, I was tagged for a long fourteen day journey flying under U.S. contract to fly shuttles between Natal, Brazil, and Fish Lake, Liberia. This flight was the inaugural one of a series, and required the Chief pilot to inspect all of the facilities at each station where subsequent Yankee Clipper flights would stay overnight.

Among the crew there was a capricious, friendly, and fun loving pilot named Al Deposo. Al's sense of humor was larger than his practical or common sense, and he lived off the joy of playing pranks, using his cover as fourth officer for his fun. Despite my best efforts and numerous admonishments, Al insisted on spending his flight time performing pranks such as tripping the seat mechanism which would drop one down hard to the bottom level of the cabin, a jolting and memorable experience.

On the return flight to Natal, from Africa, my schedule required that I should wake the captain (the Chief Pilot) to assume a flight shift with Al. At half an hour before the captain was to be awakened to come to the flight deck, I went to the galley to make a sandwich, leaving Al on the flight deck alone. As I was finishing making my sandwich, the captain came out, announced he was rested and would go on duty early.

When Captain Gray arrived at the flight deck he opened the cockpit curtain to find two empty seats. THERE WAS NO

ONE ON THE FLIGHT DECK! The plane was on autopilot. I heard a strange noise upstairs. While still munching my sandwich, I started up the stairway. When I reached eye level with the flight deck floor, I saw the chief pilot dragging Al by the foot out from under the navigator's table where he had been pretending to be asleep. The staged event was to have been a great joke on me. Al had not expected the captain for another thirty minutes. The captain was not amused: he fired Al Deposo on the spot.

When America entered World War II, I wanted to join to become a fighter pilot. I was refused, along with other trained airline pilots, because it was determined that we would need as many trained commercial pilots as possible to ferry the cargo for the war effort. Pan American enlisted its resources early on in the war. It was my task to fly big Navy flying boats over the North Atlantic, to Ireland and other neutral countries delivering materials needed for the war effort. I was appointed senior grade Lt. in the Navy - duty but only when I flew as Captain on the Navy flying boat, the PB2Y3-R.

Navy PB2Y3-R

My brother Bourdon F. Scribner, a spectroscopist at the National Bureau of Standards, and I were together in New York on the day Pearl Harbor was bombed. He left immediately to return to Washington, D.C., but he was casual about his swift return and down played the matter. At various times during the war, I questioned him about what he was doing to assist the war effort. Always, he would shrug and mutter something about his serving on the Civil Air Patrol and as an air raid warden, or talk about his occasional turn at serving at the Washington Stage Door Canteen. I commented a couple of times that all efforts were important, be they large

Bourdon F. Scribner

or small.

Only after the war was over did I discover that what he had done in the war was to work on the Manhattan Project. His part of preparation of the atomic bomb was the development of methods for the analysis of uranium for impurities. His work in this area solved a basic problem in the production of the pure uranium required for the bomb.

On return from an ocean crossing in June of 1942, I found a message waiting for me at the flight operations office informing me that my father was attending a convention in New York City. I phoned him at the Waldorf Astoria and made arrangements to get together to celebrate.

Rather excitedly, I arrived for my first visit to the Waldorf. I turned over my fire engine red Pontiac convertible to the parking attendant, uncertain I had enough money to pay for parking. I phoned my stepmother Miriam - she advised my Dad was sleeping when I arrived, so I wandered about the lobby passing time. In my ramblings, I came upon a poster advertising Xavier Cugat, his orchestra, and a singer named Lina Romay. The poster was displayed outside the Wedgwood Room, heralding the opening night of a new musical review.

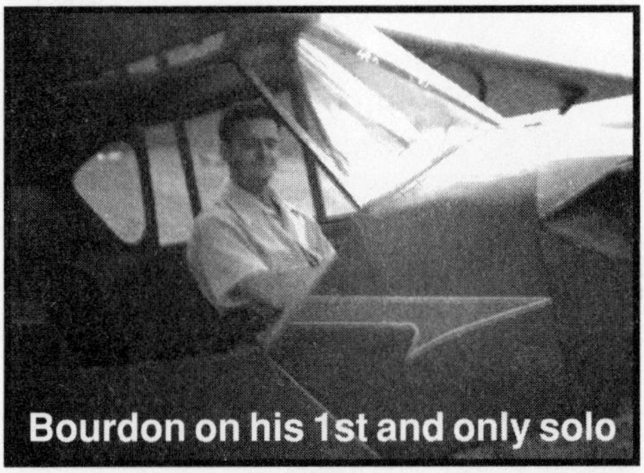
Bourdon on his 1st and only solo

I was elated. Cugat's music was superb, and dancing was, and is, one of my passions. My only problem was to get access to the ballroom. All of the other men entering the room were presenting their credentials and invitations prior to being admitted. I had neither credentials nor an invitation. Those being admitted were critics from various newspapers and magazines. The first class treatment they were accorded certainly appealed to me.

My own high school experience as a gate crasher inspired me to look for options. I spotted a palm tree between the desk where the invitations were being taken at the entrance way. By that palm, there was minimum space available for a person, with care, to slide through. I eased myself into the ballroom. Casually, I walked over to the bar, expecting at any moment to feel a tap on my shoulder, and to be unceremoniously exited from the room. I requested and was handed a gin and tonic. To my delight no bouncers came my way.

The seated music critics had secured writing pads at the entrance way. I strolled over, picked one up and headed back to the stage. Quickly, I had to decide whom I would represent as a music critic, so I chose *Life* magazine. Standing off to one side, I observed Mr. Cugat speaking with a reporter. When the reporter left, I walked over, shook hands, and introduced myself as Kim Scribner, *Life* magazine.

Mr. Cugat was charming and, at my request, introduced me to the beautiful young singer, Lina Romay. Taking notes all the while, I learned that she was born in Flushing, New York, daughter of a Mexican attache and an Irish mother, and she had just returned from filming a movie in Hollywood. She explained that her mother came to chaperone her each evening for her performances at the Waldorf. It seems Mrs. Romay stayed in a courtesy room provided by the hotel. My own chivalry was offended when I heard that she had not been invited to come to the ballroom to hear her daughter's opening night of a new show.

Getting more grand by the moment, I insisted that her mother join me at "my table" for the performance. Just as I

had seen in the movies, I beckoned a waiter and requested a telephone. When he returned with the phone, I used it to invite Mrs. Romay to join Mr. Scribner, *Life* magazine, at his table. She seemed delighted and headed on her way.

Now the problem was to get a table. I called for the waiter again and informed him that, "Mr. Cugat would like to have a table for six set up down front for special guests." The head waiter was notified immediately and a lovely table was quickly arranged. One more call to make. I rang my parents room and informed them to ask for Kim Scribner, *Life* magazine, when they came down to join me in the Wedgwood Room, to play along with me, and just follow my lead.

Wonderful music filled the evening. At the end of the performance, I escorted my parents to the train station for their trip home, and confided that I had crashed my way into the ballroom. Waving good-bye to my bewildered parents, I rushed back to the Waldorf, picked up Lina Romay and her mother, and drove them to their home in Flushing.

Soon, I was a nightly guest at the show at the Waldorf Astoria. After explaining to the head waiter that I did not have enough money for the cover charge for the evening, we made an arrangement that I could sit at any vacant table so long as I did not order anything. To handle the costs of my parking fees, I arranged with the head parking attendant to exchange some small carved ivory heads which I had purchased in Africa.

In time, I revealed to Lina Romay that my work was not with Life Magazine. She took my mischief all in stride and shared her own glamorous life style with me on our many evenings together. With Lina Romay, I became accustomed to meals at the Stork Club provided by people like Walter Winchell, the columnist and radio personality, and Sherman Billingsley, owner of the Stork Club. I quickly found the high life at low cost extremely enjoyable.

Throughout this period of high life I continued my training and flight instruction. At the time I received my captain's rating, Walter Winchell announced Lina Romay's and my engagement in his column. However, Lina had choices to make. Go back to Hollywood, be in another movie or go to Miami to be the wife of a DC-3 captain. Lina went to Hollywood, I went to Miami.

Chapter Nine

BACK TO LAND-BASED PLANES

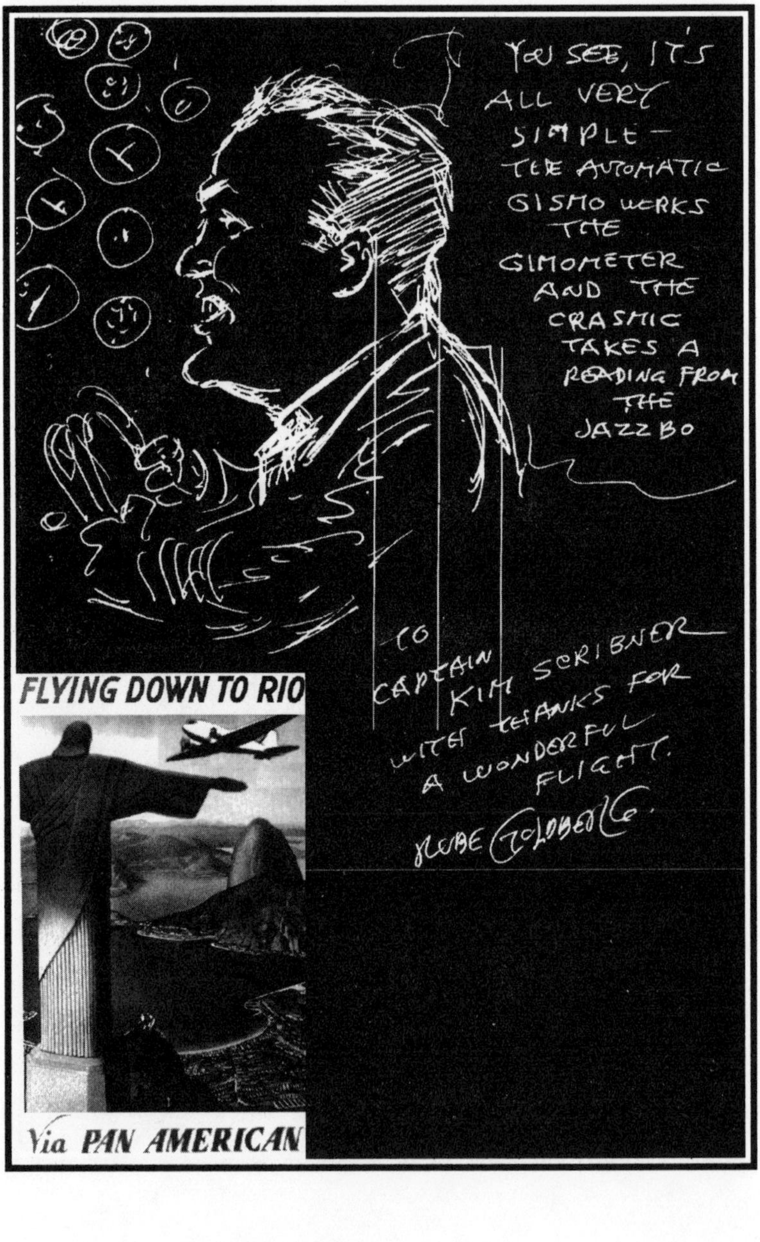
YOU SEE, IT'S ALL VERY SIMPLE — THE AUTOMATIC GISMO WORKS THE GIMOMETER AND THE CRASMIC TAKES A READING FROM THE JAZZBO
TO CAPTAIN KIM SCRIBNER WITH THANKS FOR A WONDERFUL FLIGHT.
RUBE GOLDBERG.
FLYING DOWN TO RIO
Via PAN AMERICAN

Chapter Nine

After being transferred back to Miami, I found the transition from seaplanes to landplanes not too difficult. I had flown as a copilot on a DC-3 in 1941, and was able to put energy on advancing my ratings. In February 1943 I was given my first command flight on a route check to Rio de Janeiro.

All of our flights to South America were made during daylight hours because there were no night landing facilities available at the airports, meaning that a flight from Miami took five days with layovers in San Juan, Trinidad and Belem. After arriving in Rio, we frequently had a five day layover before returning to Miami. What holidays those were. With the exchange rate at the time, a night on the town of dinner and dancing cost $5 for two.

Flying the DC-3 into Rio on instruments was most unusual, and could prove to be a dicey bit of business. Radio operators were a part of the crew because we did not always have VHF (very high frequencies), direct or line of sight radio communications available. At that time, we did not have the automatic direction finder with a needle to point at the ground transmitting radio station.

The radio operator, using a loop antenna, was required to take manual bearings for the captain. The operator would listen to the radio signal, turning the loop back and forth, to receive a null, or no sound, then read and call out the bearing to the captain. The aircraft had no sense antenna to indicate a station was ahead or behind, so one could fly over a station, and the relative bearing would still show the station was ahead. With only the loop antenna available for navigation purposes, approaching Rio, with its surrounding mountains, was a problem.

Flying unpressurized at an altitude of 12,000 feet, we

had to first overhead Santos Dumont Airport. To insure against overheading the station, and not being aware of it, the radio operator and the captain established a heading to fly, keeping the radio station slightly to the left of the airplane. Using this technique, the radio operator could determine when we went by or abeam of the station.. At this point, the captain would start the time clock, stay for one minute on the same heading, then turn to a heading going abeam again, each time flying one minute, descending below the mountains during the boxing of the station.

By observation, the captain could determine the relative wind direction as he continued to box the station and descend on instruments. On any side of the box patterns, if it required more or less time to get back and pass abeam again, he had one direction of the wind determined. As he continued on the other side of the box pattern, he could, by observing the time to go abeam, and establish another wind direction factor.

After descent to a certain level, the captain would fly away from the station, make a turn to bring him toward the active runway, and continue down to a minimum altitude to make the landing. All of the instrument approach was accomplished by the radio operator's calling out relative bearings to the captain. If the approach was missed and no landing was possible in Rio, the captain would utilize tail bearings called out to him to fly out of the area, following the harbor channel used by ships coming to and from Rio.

This flight path was established between high mountains out over the ocean to enable all the flights to proceed to an alternate airport to land. With concentrated teamwork, we managed quite well, however, when the automatic direction finders were installed on all our aircraft we were much happier, flying with much greater confidence.

Pan American pilots flying to and from Rio faced constant change and adaptations in flight procedures. Utilization, in flight, of the metric system of measuring altitudes in an airplane was one significant barrier. Using this system required the pilots in all American built airplanes to have a conversion chart in hand to convert meters to feet to hold, or fly to altitudes which they could only read on their altimeters in feet measures. What a mess it was until the Civil Aeronautics Administration was able to correct this burdensome and unsafe practice.

It was only through vast changes, standardization of procedures, improved navigational aids, weather reporting, and improved airport facilities initiated by our government that safety and advanced procedures were developed. Colonel Cloyce J. Tippett, Senior Civil Aeronautical Authority in South America, and later head of the International Civil Aviation Organization, is credited with leadership in spearheading these most important advances in aviation.

Rio based pilots could never be accused of being humorless. Quite the contrary. On one occasion, two captains, Ned Avary and Gordon Wood, each flying a DC-3, one northbound and one southbound, were flying toward each other with

1,000 feet of altitude separating them. On the same radio frequency, both pilots reported, at the same time, an unidentified flying object.

The story of the pilots detailed the sighting of a huge, hovering, saucerlike vehicle with strange lights emitting from its portholes. Their descriptions were identical, reporting

Colonel
Cloyce J. Tippett

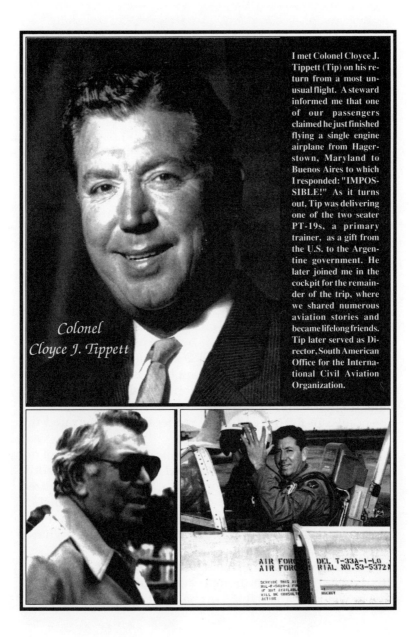

I met Colonel Cloyce J. Tippett (Tip) on his return from a most unusual flight. A steward informed me that one of our passengers claimed he just finished flying a single engine airplane from Hagerstown, Maryland to Buenos Aires to which I responded: "IMPOSSIBLE!" As it turns out, Tip was delivering one of the two seater PT-19s, a primary trainer, as a gift from the U.S. to the Argentine government. He later joined me in the cockpit for the remainder of the trip, where we shared numerous aviation stories and became lifelong friends. Tip later served as Director, South American Office for the International Civil Aviation Organization.

that the vehicle suddenly left its hovering position in a tremendous burst of speed. It may be noted that upon arrival at their respective destinations, newspaper reporters were awaiting them. In detail, the two pilots related identical tales of the unidentified flying object (UFO) in appearance, position, size, color and shape as well as the direction in which it departed.

Anyone may discount these identical observations by Captains Wood and Avary. They were, after, all, neighbors, great friends, and both known for their sharp sense of humor. In the area where the UFO was reportedly sighted, there were no other witnesses who came forward. No Pan American pilot, before or since, has reported strange unidentified objects of the type described by Gordon Wood and Ned Avary, though such stories continue to be reported of sightings elsewhere.

Under a special U. S. Air Force investigating program which has continued to collect data from persons claiming to have seen a UFO, most observations have been explained as imaginary, or the observer's having been exposed to a natural phenomenon in the sky which he interprets as a UFO. No photographs have exposed a UFO, because those submitted have been of poor quality, and appear to be photographs of normal, but unusual cloud and light formations. There is, to date, no hardware, or positive evidence that a foreign flying object (except for meteorite substances) has penetrated the earth's atmosphere and landed.

It was on a flight from Rio to Miami that I met one of my most memorable passengers, Colonel Hubert Fauntleroy Julian. With the cockpit door open, I noticed and recognized Colonel Julian. Up the aisle came a very tall, distinguished looking black man who was dressed in all white clothing, topped off with a large plantation owner type hat. What a figure he cut.

After reaching our cruising altitude heading toward San Juan, I left the cockpit to approach Colonel Julian in hopes that he would be amenable to a chat with me. I had read about him, the Black Eagle, in one of H. Allen Smith's wonderful books.

Colonel Julian showed no resistance to being recognized. He openly discussed several of his career exploits with me, confirming the story of his challenge to Hermann Goering, head of the Nazi Luftwaffe, to meet him at ten thousand feet above the English Channel to fight an aerial duel. The challenge had been issued as an effort of Colonel Julian's to avenge the vile and cowardly insults to the black race made by both Hitler and Goering. Goering had begged off that challenge, claiming war duties precluded his participation.

Colonel Julian was from that magical era of barnstormers and performing aerialists. He and other courageous minorities broke the barriers which stood in the way of black people who wanted to be part of the developing world of aviation. Through their pioneering efforts, flying clubs for black people were organized, first in Los Angeles and Chicago, promoting airmindedness, organized air shows, and flying instructions. The daring exploits of Willie "Suicide" Jones, Dorothy Darby, Ken Hunter, Colonel Julian, and others sparked aviation interest from black Americans across the country.

Colonel Julian laughed with me about another story of his first and only parachute jump at Roosevelt Field, Long Island, New York. It seems that the famous ocean flyer, Clarence Chamberlin, in his big biplane Condor, was making every effort to fill his aircraft with local passengers for rides at Roosevelt Field. In the belief that once they were at the airport it was not too difficult to sell them airplane rides, Chamberlin and other pilots were doing their best marketing to attract people to come out on weekends to watch acrobatic flying and parachute jumps.

Someone hit upon the idea of bringing hundreds of black people from Harlem to the field by special train to see Colonel Julian make a parachute jump. Not only would he perform the jump, he would play the saxophone on the way down. His own reputation was enough of a draw for the tremendous crowd which arrived to witness the jump at Roosevelt Field.

Colonel Julian had been briefed carefully on the ground. He was shown how to climb out between the wings, holding onto the flying wires and struts, being careful to step only on the top of the main spar as he made his way out on the wing. The parachute was packed and mounted on the wing. He would wear only the harness. After reaching the outer portion of the wing, he was to snap the parachute risers onto his harness, face into the wind, hold onto the outer strut, and watch the pilot who would spot him.

All went well, he was in the correct position, all he had to do was pull the rip cord on the parachute when signaled to do so. As he lined up with the thousands of people watching, the pilot flew low and in front of them. At the correct moment, the pilot looked at the Colonel, nodded his head, and gestured with one hand for him to pull the rip cord.

Right on cue, Colonel Julian pulled the rip cord. The saxophone was still held to his cheek, having been tied to the harness. Was it a last second change of mind? Was his hold on the strut too tight? Did the Colonel know and realize he must let go of that strut when he felt the parachute open behind him? Whatever the reason, Colonel Julian held onto that strut for dear life.

The parachute opened with a bang and Colonel Julian was swinging below, floating to earth, but he was still holding the wing strut in his hands. The airplane, one strut short, flew in a somewhat wobbly manner, and was carefully landed. Though never confirmed by witnesses, it was allowed that, just prior to landing, Colonel Julian gave a bit of a toot on his saxophone. The Colonel, a man with a dare devil, provocative history, laughed heartily as we shared the story, and told me of his plans to organize an all black operated airline. Among the annals of the early international aviators, Colonel Julian remains one of the most interesting and memorable figures I ever met.

Meanwhile, back in Georgetown, my good friend , Harry Conway, was conducting a most unusual form of flying trapeze. As a representative of All American Engineering Company, Harry would allow himself to be snatched off the ground by a nylon line suspended from a military transport plane going at a speed of over 130 miles per hour. These tests were being conducted as an aid to quicker air rescues of seamen and pilots who might be shipwrecked at sea.

Harry remains a good friend of mine and fellow member of The Explorers Club. Currently involved in corporate flying, he was the second man to demonstrate human pick-up. Lt. Doster, an Army Air Force engineer at Wright Field, was the first.

HARRY CONWAY AND HIS FLYING TRAPEZE

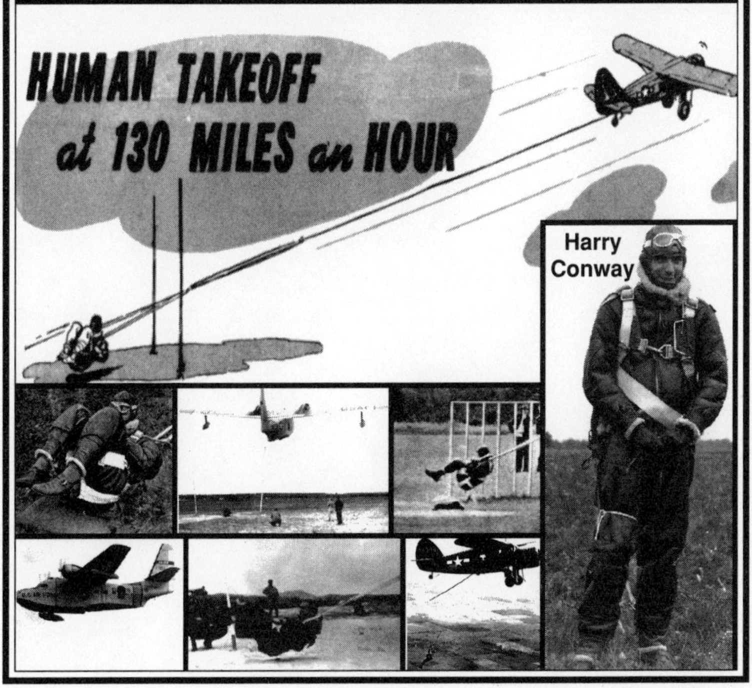

Chapter Ten

INSTRUMENT PROBLEMS

Chapter Ten

After 1,097 hours of flying in command as a captain in Miami, I was transferred back to the Atlantic Division in New York to become a master pilot of ocean flying boats. This was no small maneuver, for there were numerous route checks, exams to take, and a check out on the flying boats again.

Prior to my beginning the program for this qualification, I was requested by the Army Air Forces to visit their Parachute Development Department at Wright Field in Dayton, Ohio, in February 1944. This invitation came as a result of my sending a letter to the Congressman Jennings Randolph (D-West Virginia) relating my concern with the failure of the Air Forces to use my method of collapsing and reopening a parachute at the jumper's discretion.

Mr. Randolph shared my concern and began a discreet inquiry into the matter which could affect the safety of the thousands of parachuting fighting men engaged in the war effort. The Air Forces response to Mr. Randolph's inquiry was "... never heard of such a thing". No one had seen the newsreels of jumps I had made.

Pan American had released me for the month of Febru-

Senator (former Congressman) Jennings Randolph

ary to perform a consultation service with the Air Force, demonstrating my method, with the understanding that I would not make any parachute jumps. I was surprised that the Air Force established my parachute collapsing device as a secret project which no one was to discuss. I tried to explain that thousands of people had observed my using the collapsible parachute. To which they replied, "We understand that, but no one knows how it was done do they?".

Though I was tremendously excited about the project, I was advised that to collect any compensation for the use of my patented "secret device," I must sue the government for infringement. Out of my own sense of patriotic eagerness, I promised that the Air Force could utilize the parachute device in any manner they wished for free.

Years later at a Wings Club party held at McDill Air Force Base Airport in Florida, I was seated at an Air Force demonstration to review a mock invasion by paratroopers. The jumpers all left their aircraft too soon, and with their static line openings they drifted over the airport missing their target area. I kept waiting for them to collapse their chutes and be able to avoid the wind drift. Even with their steerable mechanisms they overshot their target.

I spoke with the general in charge, asking why the parachutists did not collapse their chutes. He said he had never heard of such a thing, and he invited me to submit my invention in writing. I did just that. I am still waiting to hear from the Air Force who have kept my parachute device such a secret.

In 1944, well into the war, preparing for my master pilot checkout, I was still a civilian. However, I was assigned to fly the PB2Y3-R Coronado, the Navy's largest flying boat. Pan American had received a Navy contract for this flying because the Navy did not have enough pilots experienced with the new seaplane.

Almost every pilot flying for Pan American at that time had a commission of some kind with one of the services. Since I did not have the required military commission for the captaincy of the Coronado, I was advised to join the Navy. I went down to Church Street in New York and enlisted, checking in with about twenty other men who were going to be sailors. In due time, an officer came into the room asking for me. He explained that I was not going to be a sailor, I was to follow him upstairs for testing.

After extensive interviews and exams, during my swearing in by a commodore, he stopped suddenly, stared at me and barked, "This is not the Boy Scouts!" I had my Boy Scout salute hand held high with my right thumb holding my little finger.

Since I was too young to be given the commission of lieutenant commander, I was commissioned a senior grade lieutenant, flying the Navy PB2Y-3-R Coronado plane which leaked fuel, was difficult to take off, and took a very long time

to pick up enough speed for the aircraft to rise out of the water. Lifting the 44 passenger load, 15,000 pounds of cargo capacity, took all the power available to get into the air.

It was a converted military airplane equipped with wing tip pontoons which were retracted by the pilot when the plane was airborne, a feature which worked well. However, on takeoff the plane had a most unusual characteristic. If I wanted to take off on a heading of 90 degrees, or east, on a river or bay, the normal procedure was to point or place the airplane on a 90 degree heading, open the throttles and go. Not so on this aircraft.

The desired takeoff direction had to be adjusted so that the nose was pointed 15 degrees to the left of the real desired takeoff path. After applying takeoff power to all four engines, and holding the yoke fully back to get the nose of the airplane up out of the water, it took a while for the speed to pick up and the ship to rise far enough out of the water to allow the nose to drop down leaving the airplane on its step (the after portion of the hull which permits maximum speed to be obtained on the water). However, when pressure was released on the yoke holding it back, and forward pressure applied to keeping the airplane on its step, a turn to the right of 15 degrees took place.

It was most disconcerting. One had to look ahead for sailboats or anything in the way, trying to visualize where that 15 degree turn was going to take place, and attempting to see that the second path on the water was clear. We could not do the obvious thing of reducing power on the left outboard engine to offset the turn, because with 44 passengers, or 15,000 pounds of cargo, we needed all the takeoff power available to get into the air.

In hot climates, the takeoff power demanded maximum thrust. When applying all of the available thrust, the cylinder temperatures became very critical and rose to such a degree we had to open wide all cowl flaps to cool the engines. Doing this prevented the acceleration we needed to become airborne, especially in still and quiet water.

Unique coordination was required between the captain and the flight engineer to get the airplane flying. At the critical point in the takeoff, after it had made its 15 degree turn on its own, the airplane refused to accelerate any more, and the captain would command the cowl flaps to be closed. The temperature of the airplane rose, but so did the speed of the airplane, allowing us to take off.

After takeoff, the flight engineer would sneak open the cowl flaps slightly on the most critical engines, while the captain kept the plane just out of the water, increasing speed but not climbing. Eventually, we climbed slowly, increasing the air speed as the engine temperatures slowly decreased. The cowls on each engine would then be opened to the free position for the climb.

In July 1944, after all pre-command checks were completed for my master pilot of flying boats requirements, I made my first flight from New York to Ireland to be checked out as a master pilot by Senior Check Captain Chili Vaughn. Pan American continued to fly the PB2Y3-R throughout the war in both the Pacific and Atlantic. Following termination of our Navy contract, I flew Air Force planes with a Navy, commission being paid as a civilian.

My final assignment under military contract required my being transferred back to Miami to our Africa-Orient Division to fly the Douglas C-54 Skymaster for the Air Transport Command. The unpressurized C-54s, with their wing span of 117 feet, length of 93 feet, and fuel capacity of 3,500 gallons could fly at 215 miles per hour covering 2,000 miles without refueling. On our round trip, (Miami, Bermuda, the Azores, and destination stop at Casablanca) we required two weeks for a tour of duty.

We all understood that prevailing traffic of passengers or cargo was governed by the capacity at which the aircraft could fly safely loaded between the Azores and Bermuda, the

Navy PB2Y3-R - utilized by Pan Am Navy contract. Provisions made for 44 passengers, 16,000 pounds of cargo, or a combination of both. Used in Atlantic and Pacific Divisions of Pan Am during World War II.

least favorable pay load segment of any of the trans-Atlantic routes. Having flown this route in the C-54 continuously from November, 1944, through May, 1945, and still facing unlimited round trips to Casablanca, I became very concerned, not regarding the safety of the flight operations, but for the lack of justifiable cargo being flown.

I was consistently flying empty all the way to Casablanca, but that was understandable since the war with Germany was over in April of 1945. However, out of Casablanca, I found that all we were carrying was used jeeps all the way back to Miami, with their destination being Trinidad. At first, I thought that this might just be an isolated case of a flight with no cargo. I discovered it was not. After checking six flights behind me, speaking to their captains, and checking their manifests, I verified that we all were carrying the same cargo: one or more broken down jeeps.

I wrote to my friend, Congressman Jennings Randolph addressing my concerns as a private taxpayer. The congressman began an investigation which drew the complaint of Assistant Chief of Staff Colonel A. W. Ireland that the charges were unwarranted. Citing remarkably high pay load statistics, Colonel Ireland insisted that the complainant had not considered the cargo which might have been stowed in the nose or belly of the aircraft. Not so. I had seen all the manifests of the aircraft I had investigated, nothing was on board except the few jeeps and leaden window sash weights.

Flights, once the war was over, were a waste of manpower and machinery. However, in this case certain types of useless flight activities were enabled and covered. Controlled by the scheduled military echelons and reported accordingly to those responsible for civilian airline contracts, these flight activities involved unacceptable waste in movement of cargo and passengers.

The Air Transport Command had its problems in justifying east or westbound flights since the war was over! My whistle blowing efforts had some effect. Congressman Randolph used his position with the Military Affairs Committee to precipitate a general inspection of airline contractual traffic performance with the Air Forces Air Transport Command.

To my delight, in November 1945, I was transferred over to the Latin American Division of Pan American in Miami. After a fast re-check in the DC-3, I resumed my flying to Rio, and all went well until I suffered an attack of malaria in San Juan, Puerto Rico, enroute to Miami. On landing in Trinidad, a few days prior to the malarial attack, I opened the door and discovered a swarm of mosquitoes filling the cockpit. I yelled to the purser to get his mosquito gun to spray the cockpit and cabin. When he did not move to his briefcase, I asked why. He drawled, "Aw, Cap'n Ah jes' hate that ole stuff and ah didn' brang any wi' me."

Just after the five day incubation period, preparing for boarding, wearing my uniform in a tropical climate, I complained to a public health inspector about how cold it was that day. Seeing my coloring, instantly summing up the situation, he led me away to a hospital. Once hospitalized, my adventure continued. They did not have an area in which to quarantine me, so they cordoned me off with improvised nets around the bed. Awakening from a stiff shot of morphine, I became delirious, thinking I was being buried alive.

After some difficulty with treatment, the doctors discovered I was allergic to the usual cures of quinine and atabrine, and had to increase my hospital stay to seventeen days. The extra time there did not contribute toward any improvement of my spirits; for I then developed shingles and jaundice. Once recovered, I was off to the enjoyable assignment of flying the Douglas DC-4, the lead off plane for Pan American's post-war parade of aircraft.

Flying a Pan American DC-4 from San Juan, Puerto Rico to New York, my first officer Jack "Lefty" Leftwich and I made a routine takeoff at night on a direct flight to New York with approximately fifty passengers. About twenty-five miles to the northwest there was an intense electrical storm. The lightning indicated that it was a major tropical front with huge clouds being constantly illuminated by light flashes. We had no radar at that time to aid our penetration of storms, so we had to "eye ball" our way through them.

We made a standard climbing departure at an indicated air speed of about 150 miles per hour. As we approached the storm area, we could see it was not possible to circumnavigate it. Our best bet was to cut through it at right angles. Seat belt and no smoking signs were still on, and the flight attendants were advised to remain seated with the passengers.

In the storm penetration, I was utilizing all available instruments, primarily the artificial horizon. I turned all cockpit lights to full bright to avoid being blinded by lightning. We did not use the automatic pilot because it would over control the plane in rough air. During our climb into the extremely rough air, the thunder and heavy rain made normal communications among the crew impossible.

I focused my attention on instrument flying, looking ahead to see a better path to fly. I concentrated on holding the proper altitude with respect to the artificial horizon to maintain a constant climb air speed. While climbing through 5,000 feet with heavy, pounding rain, extreme turbulence, lightning and thunder, suddenly, my artificial horizon showed the plane to be in an extreme attitude with the nose too high and wing down. My gyro controlled artificial horizon had failed. Yet, no warning light had come on.

My turn and bank indicated we were flying straight with wings level. Both my gyro horizon and the copilot's indicators were not in accord with my primary instruments, making both gyro artificial horizons unbelievable, however, there was no vacuum pressure failure warning light on to indicate lack of air pressure to operate gyros.

To maintain the desired attitude of the aircraft, and climb, we had to keep a constant air speed of 150 miles per hour. During our climb through this altitude, the ball indicator showed the wings to be more or less level between extreme air bumps, because gravity kept the ball centered in its curved holding rack.

I observed an obvious increase of air speed. With this increase in air speed. The altimeter, and the rate of climb indicated we were descending rapidly. I was keeping the wings level. With the turn needle straight up, indicating no turn, I carefully moved the control yoke back to slow down. In addition, I kept rolling the horizontal stabilizer wheel nose up.

Instead of the airplane's slowing up as it should, the air speed increased, going to over 200 miles per hour. We were descending very rapidly now toward a direct dive. I closed all four throttles, we did not need any power on with that speed. The airplane went over 250 to 300 miles per hour indicated air speed, far exceeding the limitations of the airplane.

I was still convinced that with no instrument vacuum failure warning to indicate a turn needle failure, the airplane was flying straight ahead with wings relatively level. However, my raising the nose to slow up the airplane seemed only to aggravate the situation. The increase in air speed was an indication of a malfunction of some kind, because as it increased we were rapidly losing altitude, and now were diving toward the ocean!

The needle was still straight up, ball centered. At approximately 1,500 feet, I made a very loud call to the first officer, "What does your turn indicator show?" "Full right turn," he yelled back. This automatically meant my turn indicator had failed without any warning. Based on my glider flying experience, I now knew we were in a diving spiral, I had to believe his turn indicator, not mine.

I called for his help to stop the spiral dive, but, because the air speed was so high, the controls became extremely rigid. They felt locked, but, together, we were able to raise the right wing, and stop the diving spiral. As I continued to pull back on the yoke the elevators started to raise the nose toward the horizon, and the wings were approaching a level position.

The stabilizer change I had been applying earlier to raise the nose now took effect. Below 1,000 feet, as the nose began to rise in the heavy rain, the rate of climb indicator showed zero. This meant the nose was passing upward through the horizon. As the nose came up, we felt great relief to observe from all working pressure instruments, that we were going into a climb. The air speed decreased very rapidly. It indicated we were now in a steep climb, but we could not tell where the nose of the aircraft was with reference to the invisible horizon.

The flight controls began to feel very sloppy as the air speed was reducing. We knew we were about to stall, so I slammed and held the yoke all the way forward, and pushed the prop controls all the way into full low pitch. I then pushed four throttles all the way forward against their stops. With a terrible roar, the airplane nose dropped over forward into another steep dive. Fortunately, we did not drop over backward, because we could never recover from that position.

We let the nose drop to dive, the altimeter began unwinding again as we began to recover from the stall and get air speed. We then brought the nose back up again to find and hold it in a position. First up, then down, trying to find a stable air speed in order to reduce the total power I had applied to all four engines.

Unexpectedly, we came out of the storm into quiet calm air heading south at approximately 1,500 feet, looking at the bright lights of San Juan in the distance. We were now able to make our way visually back to land. After a few minutes, I advised the first officer that I had better go back in the cabin to visit the passengers.

I opened the cabin door and saw the flight attendants still strapped in their seats, looking petrified with fright. Almost all of the passengers had slipped down in their seats with their seat belts under their armpits, due to the violent recovery from our diving spiral. One of the passengers, a small elderly Puerto Rican gentleman smiled and said to me. "Some storm, eh, Cap?"

After landing, we addressed the problem of our loss of instrumentation. How could it have happened? As soon as the passengers were unloaded, the maintenance staff checked the airplane. We required an inspection not only for the failure of instruments, but a structural check of the airplane to ascertain if there were any damage resulting from the excessive speed and loads imposed on the airplane from our recovery from the diving spiral.

After inspection, the chief mechanic advised us that there was no structural damage, and that we had our minimum instrument pressure required. He declared that we could not have lost our instruments, that both vacuum pumps were operating in a normal manner.

Of course, Lefty and I insisted that I had lost my gyro instruments, the artificial horizon and my turn indicator. To prove this, we insisted the maintenance chief start all four engines and taxi the airplane in a circle to observe my turn indicator. He shrugged, arms in the air, and, with a negative head movement, he and one of his mechanics walked off to start all four engines. They taxied the airplane in a full left hand circle. My turn indicator stayed straight up while the copilot's indicator showed a full left turn with no warning light to indicate any loss of instrument vacuum pressure. The chief mechanic could not believe it.

We reviewed the aircraft manual, and discussed the possibility that, because there was a split in the source for air flow for all gyros in the cockpit, it could have become restricted or clogged. We noted in the manual that the copilot instrument air intake source was in a clean area of the nose wheel section, and the air intake on the captain's side was above the drag brake for the nose wheel.

Inspecting the nose wheel section, we found that the air

The Consolidated Convair, built by Consolidated Aircraft Company and delivered in June, 1948, was designed and built for relatively short haul and short field operations. It had twin engines, seating capacity for 40 passengers, and, in the minds of the pilots who flew it, "it flies like a fighter." It proved to be a very dependable and air worthy airplane - being phased out only because of the small version of the jet transport.

Curtiss C-46 - Developed during World War II, this aircraft specialized in cargo and could carry twice the load of its more famous competitor, the C-47 (DC-3).

intake on the captain's side had mud, rubber, and grease which had blocked the air intake. It was so blocked that, instead of a flow of air through the system, we had static air pressure trapped in the lines which did not allow the low pressure warning light to come on to indicate instrument failure.

The maintenance staff agreed with me that to correct this they could make a strainer with a piece of gauze and place it sealed over the rear air intake valve of the turn indicator instrument. This would allow relatively unfiltered air to flow through the system, in place of the air from the intake in the nose wheel section, and give us gyro action.

In a sailplane I owned, I installed full primary instruments which were operated, not by a vacuum pump, but by a French horn bulb which I would squeeze to create enough air flow through the gyro impellers to keep them functioning and allow my turn needle to function. It was not very accurate, of course, but it was enough to let me know if I were in a turn. I could hear the gyro turning, and, once in a while, pump it up with the bulb.

On the intake rear side of the turn and bank indicator, I placed a piece of gauze to filter out dust and dirt from the floor. I recommended we do the same thing to all DC-4s, bypassing that air intake source above the nose wheel drag brake. We did this, checked that all instruments were operating properly, loaded all the same passengers back on board the DC-4, and flew without incident through the same storm to New York.

All of the airlines took our recommendations based on my incident report to the chief pilot. They removed the source of the air intake above the nose wheel brake on the DC-4 to a clean area in the nose wheel section to relocate the source of intake for all gyro instruments on the captain's side of an aircraft.

In looking back to that period of instrument flying development in the industry, we must remember that when an instrument failed it did not have a fail safe provision incorporated in its design. When the instrument failed, only the source of power to operate the instrument had a warning signal for the pilot. The instrument itself continued to give its last prevailing indication. The last indication may have been wrong, even if it indicated what the captain expected. Today's electrical instrument systems have fail safe characteristics or designs incorporated in them. If an instrument landing system fails, the instrument automatically clears itself of all indicators, wipes itself clean, and provides an instrument failure flag on the face of the instrument, providing protection for passengers, crew, and the aircraft.

Chapter Eleven

Can't wait to hear this one.
FOOLS OF THE AIR
Ok, Scribner! Let's Hear it!
Well...Uh...Uh...On Sunday, I was chased by an Air Force P-51...dove from 10,000 feet, passed Matheson Hammock ...kinda low and fast...but didn't violate any altitude regulations...that is, over water... and I didn't return!...
CAA

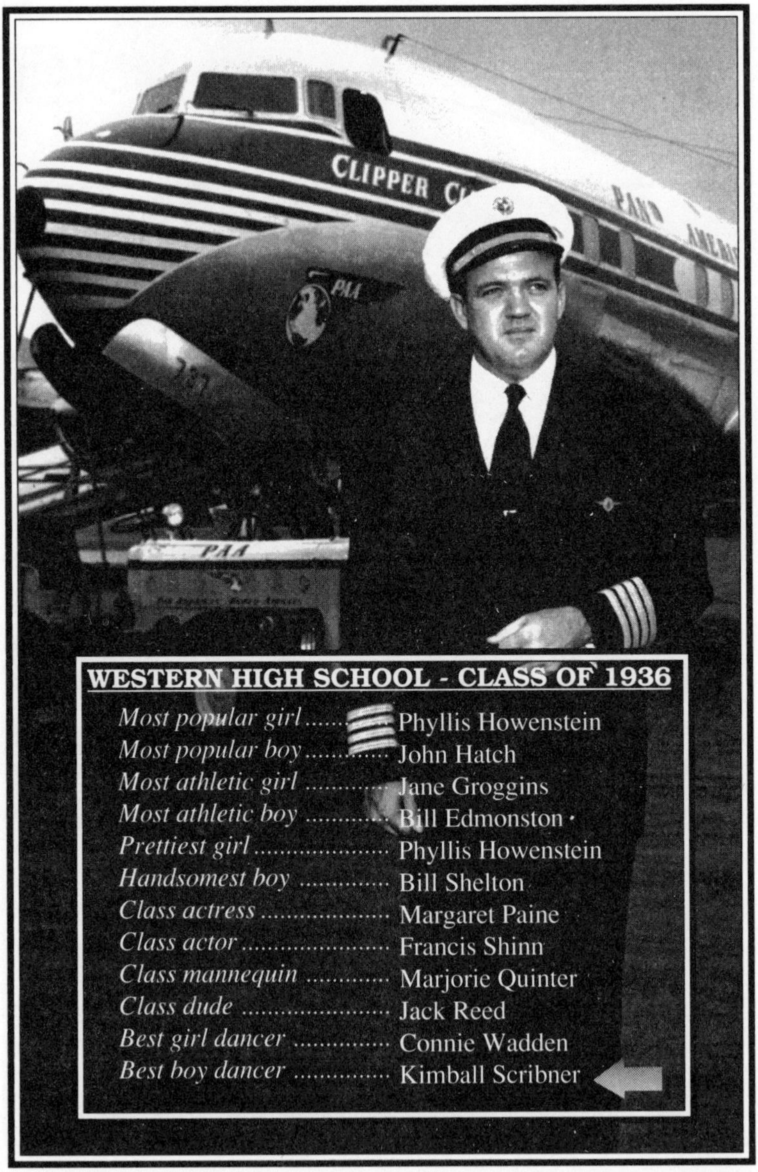
PAA
PAA
WESTERN HIGH SCHOOL - CLASS OF 1936
Most popular girl .... Phyllis Howenstein
Most popular boy .... John Hatch
Most athletic girl .... Jane Groggins
Most athletic boy .... Bill Edmonston
Prettiest girl .... Phyllis Howenstein
Handsomest boy .... Bill Shelton
Class actress .... Margaret Paine
Class actor .... Francis Shinn
Class mannequin .... Marjorie Quinter
Class dude .... Jack Reed
Best girl dancer .... Connie Wadden
Best boy dancer .... Kimball Scribner

Chapter Eleven

In his book *Prairie Wings,* Edgar M. Queeny describes man's eternal desire to take part in the fascinating realm of silent soaring flight with birds:

> *"Bird flying has always fascinated man. He has envied their independence, their ability to travel in three dimensions and soar by taking advantage of speed imparted by their own strength to move their wings and then to glide. He has wanted to experience the ecstasy of being lifted upward to the heavens by warm rising air, or soar along ridges where deflated air movements allow the birds to continue to fly unaided by their own wing movements other than to control their direction of flight."*

There is a group of glider and soaring pilots, the Soaring Society of America, who truly know these feelings. Since World War II, soaring has grown, bringing into its scope men and women who realize their ambition to see through the eyes of a soaring hawk, gull or lazy buzzard, all the beauty that is to be seen from the flying position of a bird. To fly quietly, soaring from one thermal to another, climbing without power, without vibration, realizing the thrill of competing with the soaring birds, to thwart the ever present pull of gravity: that is the ultimate thrill of every pilot. Imagine joining up with a buzzard to work a thermal, flying within a few feet of the feathered one, and having him or her give a slight turn of the head. The least one can do is wave hello.

In June of 1946, I convinced my friend, Bud Holloway, to split the purchase costs of a sailplane glider and trailer which I saw advertised in a newspaper for $600. Available at a fraction of its original government purchase price of $4,000, the sailplane was purchased during the war for glider flight training, and now was declared surplus by the government.

She was a beautiful training type sailplane made of wood and fabric; certain to be air worthy since all her parts were entirely new. Neither Bud, I, the seller of the sailplane, nor anyone else we knew, had any knowledge of glider flying. We assembled the glider in an open field, flipped a coin and Bud won the first turn in our newly licensed Leister Kaufman (LK-10A).

With the tow line fastened to the rear bumper of my car, we were set to go. The plan was for me to tow Bud into the air, or so we thought. At about 150 feet of altitude, he was to release the tow line, fly around, and land in an adjacent field. At the signal for me to start the tow, I drove as fast as I could over the bumpy field. The sailplane never left the ground, it chased me to the end of the pasture where I turned, and then continued to chase me until I stopped. Towing by car was out, we had to have an airplane.

We bought a fine new surplus Stearman biplane, attached the tow line, and Bud again won the toss for first try at Brown's little grass airport south of Miami. Having read all we could find on soaring, we towed each other to 5,000 feet, released the line from the tow plane, and on the way down learned to fly the sailplane.

The LK-10A, had a wing span of 51 feet, empty weight of 400 pounds, maximum dive speed of 126 miles per hour, and a glide ratio of 25 lateral feet to one foot vertical. One of our earliest lessons was that, unlike airplanes, the sailplane did not always have to be landed into the wind. We learned to land downwind with the sailplane, using the spoilers to allow us to touch down any place we wanted along the runway. Then the single wheel's brake would begin to function and slow us down until we came to a stop. Landing this way, we could continue down to the end of the runway, lift the tail around and be ready again for takeoff into the wind.

I was enchanted from the beginning. A loop, for example, could be made by keeping the same wing loading of 1-G. The same applied to slow rolls. It was not long before I thought of inverted flight as a possibility, though I realized that I had to strengthen the glider before I tried that project.

After purchasing Bud's half interest in the sailplane, I set about promoting the glider, contracting with the 14th Annual Miami All American Air Maneuvers to put on a demonstration for $500 a day for each of the three days of the show. I rebuilt the sailplane, strengthening the gussets, had the wings rib stitched much closer than in the original wing covering, refinished, and repainted her white.

Having never been one to do things the simple way, I worked on an outside loop which would require an inverted dive beyond the maximum allowable speed limit of 126 miles per hour, something that, to my knowledge, no one had done before. Slowly, I began inverted flying, increasing the inverted dive, and attempting to raise the nose toward an inverted loop until I was finally able to go over the top, and complete the outside loop, provided that I dived to 150 miles per hour.

As I choreographed my maneuvers thoroughly, knowing the speed required and altitude lost, I worked out a pattern of various maneuvers from 3,000 feet, to then land, stopping in front of the grandstands on a newspaper. With a brake on the wheel, landing fast on a taxiway, and applying the brake carefully, it was easy to pull off stopping on a

newspaper. My wife to be, Gloria Dickinson, agreed to stand on the newspaper until I was close enough to see it, and then as I came up to it she would step back. With an announcer describing it, one would think that I had adjusted all my flying exactly from 3,000 feet to end up on the newspaper!

My first day's performance at the show went exactly as planned, except the arrival of Miss Aviation for 1946. Just as I was climbing out of the sailplane in front of over 8,000 people, lovely Miss Maxine Herik stopped in front of the announcer's stand. I thought the resounding applause was fantastic, until I turned around to see the beautiful girl for whom it was intended. With no other gracious recourse, I joined with hearty applause.

Next, I agreed to put on my sailplane aerobatic flight for the Air Pageant in Tampa, Florida at Drew Field. The pageant was held to honor both the twenty-fifth anniversary of the National Aeronautical Administration in Tampa, and the beginning of commercial air flights from Drew Field. My only obstacle was towing my sailplane from Miami to Tampa.

After locating a pilot to fly the Stearman, I arranged for Gloria to be his passenger, and for me to be towed in my sailplane. I carefully briefed the pilot to tow us from Brown

Field, south of Miami, following the Tamiami Trail, a direct highway from Miami to Tampa. Only after takeoff did I realize that he thought I meant to follow the trail in the event he became lost, and he dragged us across the Everglades toward Tampa. Gloria had a fit about flying so low over the Everglades. I was not a bit happier, but there was nothing to be done about it. For years she laughed and regaled me about remembered visions of "...alligators snapping away at me all the way across Florida." We made the journey safely, landing with only vapors of fuel remaining.

Still flying with Pan American, I filled my leisure hours with gliding. However, a rival passion evolved for the military surplus P-38 fighter, which I purchased in November 1946 for unusual high speed aerobatics in the coming 15th All Annual All American Maneuvers. The P-38 was a steal at eighteen hundred dollars because it was a surplus item. It was available because the fuel consumption costs were prohibitive for private owners of moderate means. I was not to be dismayed, I convinced Standard Oil to sponsor me with the proviso that they would handle the fuel costs.

My not knowing how to fly the P-38 led me to enlist John Yandell, the former CAA inspector from whom I had purchased it, to check me out. Using the operations manual, and one flight riding on John Yandell's back, I then flew solo. Immediately my thoughts went to being able to do stunting aerobatic movements with the plane. Luckily, I located two excellent P-38 mechanics who were delighted to prepare the plane for aerobatic flying. We readied the P-38 with an auxiliary hydraulic accumulator, so I could roll it with both engines off and propellers feathered, still being able to extend flaps and landing gear, land and stop with the nose wheel on a newspaper.

To avoid being seen flying low with the P-38 inverted in the Miami area, I flew it over the Everglades to practice. Gloria would drive my convertible to the end of a long road nearby to watch my flying and give me her comments. On one flight out, I took off at the 36th Street Airport flying low toward Gloria's position, rolled upside down, and, suddenly, my right engine failed. I pushed the nose upward, rolled upright, and seeking directional control, reduced the power on the left engine.

As I was about to feather the propeller on the right engine, everything reversed. The bad engine came back, the good one failed. All too suddenly, I realized that I had not changed my tank selector after takeoff as I should. With climbing, almost out of control, rolling inverted, engine power changing, I was busy. Change tanks, boost pumps on, change trim again and again, and maintain flying speed. I took that P-38 back and landed it in a full sweat. It took me a week to recover from that stupid maneuver, but Gloria thought the flying was great!

An editorial article in the *Miami Herald* in October, 1946, read as follows........

The Miami Herald

PAGE 6-A TUESDAY, OCTOBER 22, 1946

As We See It—

Fools of the Air

Isn't there some authority that can stop the three fool fliers, who endangered the lives of thousands Sunday at Matheson Hammock, from repeating their murder-packed stunting?

Three planes, one a two-motored job, flew at times over the park and the bathing beach at altitudes of not more than 100 feet, frightened holidaysmakers reported. The ships were privately owned. No punishment could be too severe for these potential killers. They are worse than a drunken auto driver.

I bought this P-38 (in mint condition) for $1,800.00

There were two planes, not three. I know because my P-38 was one of them. Now, hear me out! I could not explain then to the CAA what really happened, but since I am retired, and with the statute of limitations in mind, I would like to explain how I happened to dive my P-38 at over 300 miles per hour at what I thought, from 10,000 feet, was a bit of land sticking out into the bay south of Miami.

At the time of the incident, I was single, sharing digs with my friend Frank T. Donahoe, a Pan American first officer with whom I had gone to high school. At my suggestion, Frank had come to work at Pan American, after leaving as a commander in the Navy. He still belonged to a Navy Reserve unit in Miami, and, of course, we had great debates regarding the fighting capabilities of the Navy Corsair Fighter versus the Air Force P-38. I deliberately needled him with suggestions that I could knock him out of the sky if I were in my airplane and he in a Corsair.

His Irish dander was up one day and he said, "All right,

Scribner, there is only one way to resolve this." His plan was to use the next Sunday which we both had free until afternoon, to meet at 10,000 feet over Biscayne Bay south of Miami at 12:00 noon. We would pass each other at noon on the dot, and then the fight would be on. We were to use the same VHF radio frequency, free of other communications, and whoever got the other in his sights to shoot would call out "gotcha" to claim having a "hit the enemy".

Sunday came. I spotted him. We communicated over

the radio and the fight was on. My first mistake was going too fast as we passed each other, and going into a tight turn. Frank followed me. The result was my radius of turn was wide, his was inside mine, and it was only a short time until he was able to cut me off. I heard him simulating machine gun fire "da-da-da-da-gotcha!"

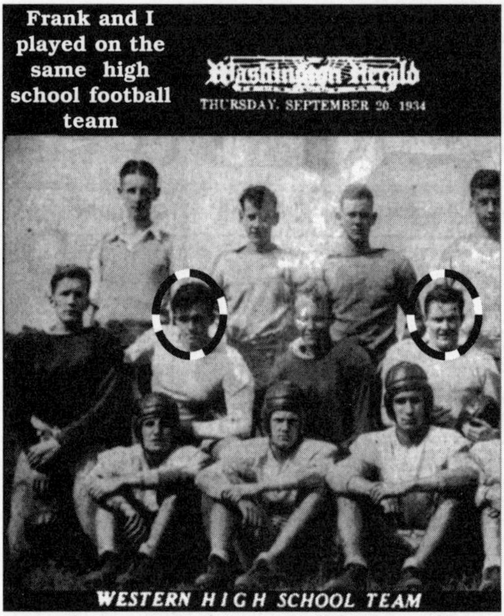
Frank and I played on the same high school football team
THURSDAY, SEPTEMBER 20, 1934
WESTERN HIGH SCHOOL TEAM

I engaged in all sorts of acrobatics trying to shake him off my tail, rolling climbing, looping, and all I got was "da-da-da-da-gotcha!" Thinking I could get him by pulling a maneuver he had told me the Navy used, I rolled the P-38 over on its back, pulled the nose down straight toward the bay. Wrong! One does not dive down on water, because even though the altimeter is unwinding to give one altitude, it is behind in its indications, and there is nothing to look at to give one the depth perception needed to pull out of a dive.

My plan had been to dive down with any point of land extending into the bay as my target, then stay over the water, level out close to the water, relying on my peripheral vision to keep the land in sight. I would then pull straight up, with the "enemy" following me. Then, I would be in a position to chase and shoot him, provided I let him pass me when I climbed the P-38.

Frank guessed my strategy, reduced his speed as he

Western High School - Class of 1936
Frank T. Donohoe Kimball J. Scribner

followed me down, and signaled another direct hit over the radio. I managed to chase him a bit more for a few feeble attempts to get a shot, but we called it a day, and off I went to ferry a DC-4 back to New York.

On my return the next day, I came down the stairway of the DC-4 to find my mechanic waiting for me. "Have they got you yet?" he frantically whispered. I blithely replied, " Has who got me and for what?" He told me about the newspaper editorial, and warned me that the CAA representatives were waiting for me for questioning. Flashing back I remembered my peripheral vision revealed a lot of bathers sitting in the sand as I flew my P-38 by that bit of land.

When I entered the government conference room, I saw six seated CAA inspectors and department heads, most of whom I knew. After being invited to be seated, the spokesman intoned, "Captain Scribner, before you tell us how high you were flying when you buzzed Matheson Hammock on Sunday, I want to tell you something. It was a hot sunny day, and I was sitting there with my wife in the sand on the beach near the water when you buzzed by." Well, they had me there.

Frank Donohoe as a Pan American DC-8 Captain

Not knowing how much they had seen, I began with a defense, explaining that while I was out for a bit of flying on a sunny day, I was suddenly attacked by an Air Force P-51 Fighter who kept diving at me. Trying to outrun him, I explained, I had dived at the water, but near enough to a bit of land to avoid the mirror effect of the water, and avoid hitting the water.

I admitted that when I flew by that I did see people off to the side, but reminded the investigators that I did not return, rationalizing that if I had intended to buzz the beach that I would have made more than one pass over it.

I asked what civil air regulations I had violated, since there were no regulations regarding minimum altitude allowable for flight over water. I pleaded the circumstances again which had provoked my flying so low. Verbally dancing as fast as I could, I reminded them of my clean record clear of violations, and my sworn statement that I would never have flown over the beach if I had know people were there. I escaped without violation points, and no mention of the other plane was made.

My wife to be, Gloria Dickenson, sitting on the beach at Matheson Hammock as Frank and I flew by.

Four years later at the Miami Air Show

I had always been fascinated by "Sky Writers" so I bought a Navy SN-J, similar to the Air Force AT-6 and made it into a Sky Writer.

I had to learn all about it and it was fun. I rigged a tank for "Corvis low grade oil" in the rear seat area of the cockpit including the addition of a pilot controlled valve. When I opened the valve, oil was allowed to flow into the extended exhaust stack on the side emitting a cloud of white smoke.

After many experimental flights, I learned the following:

A) Ideal conditions for sky writing required no clouds and a temperature inversion in the air (i.e., Instead of become cooler, the air retains its warmth with altitude)
B) The size of the letter was based on a tight circle release of smoke. (i.e., This established the size of the letter " O" or the number "0").
C) For the letter to remain continuous, the plane must climb slightly to avoid blowing away the established letters.
D) Writing is done upside down and backwards for it to be legible on the ground.

I had a contract to sky write for an orange drink, but could not afford the idle plane usage from inclement weather. Nevertheless, I had a great time.

Dick Diamond, a former student and friend, flew the "sky writing" SN-J with me.

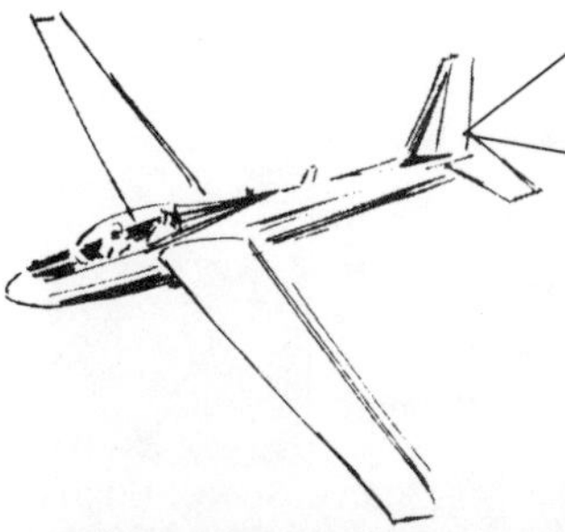

Chapter Twelve

UNUSUAL FLIGHTS

★★ EXTRA ★★
July, 1947
Yaeger breaks sonic barrier for first time
Scribner marries Gloria Dickinson
Odom flies around world in 73 hours
Spruce Goose, Hughes plane, flies briefly
I DIDN'T TOUCH YOUR EGG MONEY!!
WE HAD CORN BEEF HASH YESTERDAY!!
THE SCREWDRIVER?
WHAT'S FOR DINNER?
I DON'T WANT TO READ BETTER HOMES AND GARDEN!!
DID YOU PUT GAS IN IT?

Chapter Twelve

Pan American was terrific about allowing me to fly in the air shows. Many of the pilots and crew members attended the shows, sitting in a rooting section for me, and the airline was most generous in allowing me to keep my P-38 in their hangar

For the 1947 All American Air Maneuvers, I made a gentleman's handshake agreement with the show's manager, Jiggs Huffman, agreeing to fly my sailplane, and P-38 each day, and race the P-38 on the final day of the show. For my efforts I was to be paid $500 per day for the sailplane flying, and $1,000 per day for the P-38 flying, for a total sum of $4,500 for 45 minutes of flying.

Practicing during off hours as a captain at Pan American, I continued my preparations for the show. My real challenge for this show was qualifying as a racing pilot, for which, in addition to flying the closed course race, I had to prove my capability to withstand a dive recovery of 6-Gs, or six times my own 200 pound weight.

I had watched the other pilots in preparation for such dives and wanted to avoid making a common mistake. The pilot first was required to install a sealed accelerometer in his plane, climb up to 6,000 feet, dive and pull up to show 6-Gs being indicated on the G-meter. In recovering from the dive, the pilot would black out, and, because he was unconscious, he could no longer pull back on his stick. Afterward when the load on his body was reduced, and blood circulated back to his brain, his eyesight returned, and his regained control of the plane, he would check the maximum reading to find only 4 to 5-Gs recorded on the meter. I felt the problem was that they were bringing the nose up from the dive too slowly.

With this in mind, I dove the P-38, and instead of smoothly pulling the nose up to recover, I snapped the stick back, imparting a sharp G-load on the plane and myself. I did not really feel it at all, but the G-meter registered a 7. On landing, I quietly passed my discovery all around to the other qualifying pilots. In no time all had their required readings.

Only three days before the opening of the coming show, during practice, a coolant fluid line on the right engine burst on my P-38, causing an engine fire. In accordance with my study of emergency procedures, I eased back the throttle on the left good engine and feathered the propeller on the right engine. I flew around the airport and called the tower to request emergency fire equipment to stand by for my landing.

P-38

After landing, while closing all fuel valves and cutting off ignition switches, I did not see the fire truck which was following me down the runway. The engine let go with a big blast of CO2 from a boom which extended above me, and since I had the hatch open after landing, I was covered by the CO2. What a cold explosion!

Uninjured, I climbed out and slid off the airplane as it

came to a stop. The fire had totaled the plane I was to fly in three days. I had to find another P-38. The plane that I located was rented to me with the provision that I install an automatic direction finder. I found one and installed it.

My next problem was that I had to qualify this new P-38, since it had no position on the line of airplanes for the start of the race. I met with all nine of the other race pilots and secured their agreement to allow me to race the rented P-38, provided that I took last position at the starting line up of the $10,000 classic trophy race. Racing aerialist competitors are not known for their generosity, and since I was making the request, I had no other choice.

With my rented plane in the worst position, I climbed on board. Looking straight ahead in my line of flight for takeoff, I saw a tree! I knew I could not make a climb over that tree in the distance allowed, so I jumped out of my plane, and, after waving frantically to the starter, I got some help. Condescendingly, he offered me a position two hundred feet behind the Corsair which had the pole position. I accepted.

At the drop of the flag, the starter of the unlimited race moved out of the way. I had my two engines pulling me at maximum power when I released my brakes and almost caught up to the Corsair ahead of me before we were off the ground. At the scattering pylon, I was in the lead, but from then on I was being passed from right, left, and above.

The P-38 was flying heavy, it still had its armament protective shield, turbochargers, etc. However, the other planes pulling maximum power had failures. One upset on takeoff and several caught fire. Of twelve starting the race only five were left to finish it. Since I was now last, and could not miss taking the $500 for fifth place, I eased the engines back into long range cruise. The first four airplanes landed. People went home. I cruised around the track, and after making certain I had completed the required number of circuits, I flew an extra one. I could have taken 5th place in a Cub on that day!

For the last day of the show, there was a cloud ceiling of about 4,000 feet. With my flight program set for a high speed dive toward the center of the airport in front of the grandstands, then going into a high altitude loop, I had a problem. In my rented heavy P-38, on which I could feather only one propeller, and with no open sky above me in which to fly into a large high loop, I faced the problem of making the loop inside of the overcast cloud coverage.

As I dove down at the center of the airport to go into the loop, I tried not to fly too fast to avoid being unable to close the loop inside of the 4,000 foot ceiling. So, as I brought the nose of the P-38 up, I began to apply more and more power to those two roaring engines.

Climbing toward that cloud ceiling, I realized I was going to enter into the cloud. All I could think to do was tighten up the loop, and stay below the cloud base. Any P-38 fighter pilot knows what happened. I put that plane into a high speed stall. All of a sudden, while going onto my back as I tightened up on the loop, it went into a violent snap roll! It continued to snap around, and I found myself in a violent spin with all the engines on full roaring power.

I had no control, all movements of the control stick and rudder were without response, they were limp. As I spun around, I looked at the thousands of people below me. Realizing my error, I pulled the power off of the outside engine, and the spin stopped.

I was now in a steep dive at the people seated below me, and as I recovered from the dive, I turned the plane to just avoid flying over the stands. To save face, I feathered a prop, continued around the grandstands, landed, rolled up to my target newspaper, and brought the rented P-38 to its final stop. As I opened my cockpit hatch and stood up, I received a fantastic ovation, people stood up, waved and applauded.

I felt sick. I knew I had almost killed myself, and had endangered all those people there. As I was walking toward the stands, an officer in the Air Force, no doubt a P-38 pilot, walked over to me and said, "I am amazed. I didn't think you were going to make it out of that high speed stall." He recognized my deep feelings without my saying a word.

Days prior to the air show, my good friend, Jiggs Huffman died, and with his passing went my handshake agreement for the thousand dollar per day for the P-38 flying. The new manager had no knowledge of our verbal agreement, and before I could gather evidence to support my claim, the new manager was killed when his car was hit by a train. For this exhibition of "how not to fly a P-38", I received nothing.

In my search for a new sailplane which could meet my growing requirements for acrobatic flying, I drew up my specifications, and had it built by the Schweitzer Aircraft Company in Elmira, New York in 1947. The all metal sailplane offered me unique high performance developments in soaring. It allowed all the acrobatic demands I placed on it, and could dive over 200 miles per hour through use of its special water holding wings.

With the weight of water in its wings, I could convert rising air to give me greater forward speed to compete in soaring con-

tests where speed was essential. The water made the glider heavy, and enabled me to fly over 80 miles per hour straight ahead, then slow up to circle under a cloud to climb. In this manner, I did not lose time searching for the thermals and was able to fly faster across country. I had the additional capability to fly acrobatics at high speeds, then jettison the water when I wanted to reduce the weight for my final maneuvers, and land.

1947 was a remarkable year for me. Most importantly, I married Gloria Dickinson, secretary to the Latin American chief pilot. We rented a beautiful home on Sunset Island Number 4 in Miami, complete with a charming live-in couple to assist us.

In October of that year, we had a remarkable flight together. It was brought about by one of the infamous hurricanes which sometimes strike Florida. At the onset of the hurricane, I had made arrangements with a Pan American employee to move my new sailplane out of the predicted route of the hurricane to the safety of an Air Force hangar south of Miami.

Gloria and I were settled in our new honeymoon home planning to wait out the hurricane when our telephone rang, and an anxious Pan American employee began to tell me, over heavy wind and noise, that while all of the other airplanes had been evacuated earlier in the day to Camaguey, Cuba, there was a Pan American DC-4 still parked at the 36th Street International Airport.

I was requested to fly the, already deep in water, DC-4 to Cuba. With permission for Gloria to accompany me, we threw a few things into a suitcase, and headed off in our convertible in intense rain. Water was so deep in the streets that our car motor stalled, and we had to abandon the car. We took off our shoes, hailed a bus, and, after rushed explanations of why we wanted a ride to the airport in a hurricane, the driver took us there.

Coming into the airport in heavier rain, I could see a DC-4 sitting next to a hangar with water fully covering the landing gear wheels. We ran from the bus and saw the copilot who had been called out to assist the flight. With water over the wheels there was no way to be driven close to the plane, so the copilot and I removed our trousers, stuffed them under our raincoats, and waded with Gloria in our arms through the water up the steps to the main cabin door of the DC-4.

After dressing again inside the airplane, we prepared for takeoff. I signalled the ground crew to remove all lines, and that I was ready to start the four engines. Our problems were compounded since there was no control tower, all the operators had gone home. There were no runway or taxiway lights, and the airport was entirely dark, except for the moments when a great purple flash illuminated the opposite side of the airport as another transformer blew.

I moved swiftly to apply takeoff power and released the brakes. With the air speed now reading seventy miles per hour from the wind, we hardly moved ahead on that taxiway before we were airborne. Though it was rough at first, the air became smooth as we climbed. We had no flight plan, but the hurricane forced us to focus on the assurance that there was no other air traffic.

Heading for Cuba, at 8,000 feet, we flew into the calm quiet air above clouds in the center of the hurricane, but we soon encountered rough air again. After establishing contact with the Camaguey radio, we landed at the airport, and parked among airline transport planes of every description.

There were no hotel accommodations, so Gloria, the co-pilot and I improvised sleeping arrangements in the DC-4 for the night. We were awakened at sunrise by the Camaguey station manager who delivered a hand message requiring me to ferry the DC-4 to Havana to pick up a charter of aged male Chinese passengers who were returning to their homeland to die. We were to ferry them on the first leg of their journey home to China.

Loaded with our passengers, we flew out of Havana on a beautiful day. As we flew low along the keys to Miami to see damage done by the hurricane, we came to where the huge Air Force hangar had once stood. It was demolished, and, of course, I knew instantly that my new sailplane was destroyed as well.

In Miami we turned over our Chinese elders to another crew, and Gloria and I headed home. Just inside the door at home, I picked up the ringing telephone to receive a message from the Pan American employee who was to move my sailplane for me. He was profuse in his apology for not having been able to tow the sailplane as he had promised. It seems the wind force was so strong that he had to resort to storing it in the nearby Pan American hangar. He was somewhat cheered when I reported to him that the Pan American hangar was the only one of the two hangars still standing.

In December that year, I was designated flight examiner by the CAA; and the first month of the new year brought my appointment as senior check pilot for Panagra pilots flying DC-6s on Pan American routes into Miami from South America. However, before I could complete the ground and flight training on the DC-6, I was appointed sector chief pilot and senior operations representative for the Latin American Division pilots based in New York.

As senior representative in New York, I was given the responsibility of representing Pan American at Air Transport Association meetings in Washington, D.C. This allowed me to

DC-6

The Douglas DC-6 purchased in February, 1952 followed the DC-4. (A DC-5 was actually built, but not on a production basis.) The DC-6 became the work-horse of the "pressurized fleet." Its reliable engines, its flight characteristics and capacity for carrying 44 to 88 passengers made it one of the most desirable types of transport planes. It provided sleeping accommodations for passengers and crew. Many supplemental airlines (the former non-scheduled carriers not limited to specific routes and types of airline operation) find the DC-6 very much to their liking. They were purchased from the major airlines as they became surplus due to transition to DC-7s and jet transports by the regular scheduled carriers.

operate as a committee of one for the three divisions of Pan American. The three divisions had no interest, at that time, with what they considered to be minor domestic airline problems. No one seemed to realize the influence that the Air Transport Association could have on the CAA and the CAB regulatory groups, nor its great importance to international carriers as well as domestic airlines.

Following my continued interest and development of various projects such as obtaining changes, and/or interpretation of civil air regulations, I was elected by the Air Transport Association to be chairman of the chief pilot's committee, an assignment which allowed me to be a part of many projects seeking to improve flight operations for all airlines.

Chapter Thirteen

WORK AND PLAY

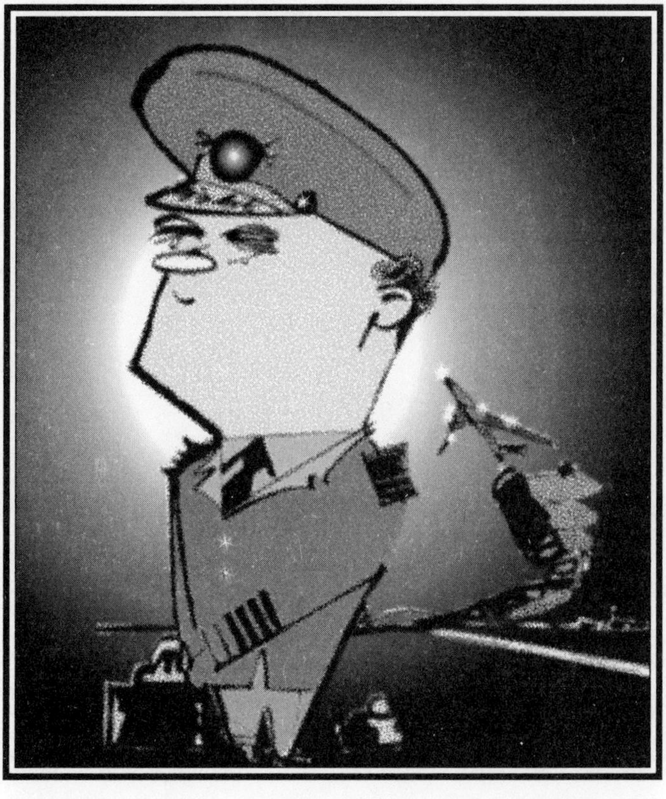

...AND THEN YOU CAN MAKE YOUR SNOWMAN

Chapter Thirteen

Stationed in New York, and functioning as sector chief pilot, I was able to take on many research and development projects. One of those primary projects concerned the New York-San Juan route of Pan American. From its inaugural flight via Bermuda in March of 1947 through May 1948, more than 3,000 flights had been made flying between New York and San Juan. The route of the flight over Bermuda was more than one hundred five nautical miles farther than that required over a direct route.

Saving time and money were the objectives of our efforts, so I started a research and development project to develop a new system of navigation using regular commercial broadcasting stations along the eastern seaboard states, instead of the old system of use of celestial navigation. For Pan American to fly in a more direct manner under existing conditions, a celestial navigator would have to be on each flight, and qualified in celestial navigation at a very dear price. As it was, a three pilot crew was required, because It usually took between eight and a half or nine hours to fly the distance, exceeding the two pilot, eight hour limitations.

During the two years of flights via Bermuda. there had been many improvements in radio navigation aids along the coast of the U.S., namely, the reclassification of principal marine radio beacons to Class A stations, and modification of the radio transmitting station at Bermuda, and throughout the Caribbean area. The changes greatly increased their reliability and operating ranges.

My project was to develop a new system of navigation which would use regular commercial broadcasting stations along the eastern seaboard states, replacing the celestial navigation options.

My ideas represented a direct departure from normal, recognized, and approved over ocean navigation procedures. In order to calm the advocates of the "old world " systems, I called the commercial stations we would use "secondary navigation aids".

After several experimental flights to determine the best radio stations to use, I drew up a proposed radio navigation system, utilizing regular broadcasting systems in New York, New Jersey, Maryland, Bermuda, etc. Any station could be used, but the important point was that any station tuned in properly and identified could not be changed. The pilot would plot the average bearing on a station after hearing the FCC station identification call letters which were broadcast every fifteen minutes.

The plan utilized all regular approved radio navigation aids such as range stations, low frequency marine coastal stations, the transmitting stations aboard weather ships, and the regular commercial broadcasting stations along the eastern seaboard of the U.S. Through close coordination between captains, dispatchers, and meteorologists, the weather reports from different aircraft flight coverage were sufficient to maintain a constant watch on the movements of weather fronts and changes in wind direction and velocities.

After five months of studies, and a preliminary survey to establish reliable radiation of all radio facilities, Pan American was granted permission to fly DC-4 cargo aircraft on eight round trip survey flights over the New York-San Juan

route.

Various routes were considered to determine one which would afford maximum utilization of navigation aids in the zones on the extremities of the proposed route. With the assistance of the U. S. Coast Guard headquartered in New York, air sea rescue considerations were carefully studied. The Oceanic Airways Traffic Control Center was questioned regarding the effect a direct route would have on its related services, and pilot meetings were held to discuss the plans for the proposed route.

Pan American submitted a request to the CAA in Miami for a proving flight on the direct route. Upon receipt of the request, the CAA local authorities took immediate action to transmit this most unusual and unheard of type of request to their regional headquarters in Atlanta, Georgia. There again, the request was reviewed with such negative response that it was transmitted to the CAA at Washington, D . C. levels.

At CAA headquarters in Washington, it was decided that the request for a proving flight could not be denied, but strict conditions were imposed on the experiment: government observers would come from the top regional and Washington offices, the CAB would have an observer on the flight, and the captain must be a regular captain selected along with two regular copilots from the New York division.

I was not permitted to be a part of the proving flight crew and 17 observers which took off from Miami on March 23, 1948. Upon the arrival of the flight in New York, Captain Bob Jocelyn, the crew, and all the observers came up to the observation deck area for food and coffee. Not one word was said about the progress of the flight. However, the captain smiled and surreptitiously nodded his head, so I knew that all was going fine so far. I asked the observing group if they had any objections to my riding along as a passenger if I restricted myself to the cabin. There were no objections, so off I went to San Juan.

There was no qualified navigator among the group of observers. All they did was to go up to the cockpit, one or two at a time, to inquire about the progress of the flight, asking very serious questions in very somber tones. The key CAA man asked to be advised when we were abeam of Bermuda. The captain, meanwhile, was covering the chart with radio plotted fixes.

When we came abeam of Bermuda, the captain advised the group over the public address system, informing the observers how he was averaging his bearings before he plotted them, and, of course, the chart reflected excellent fixes. From the abeam fix, the head CAA man asked the captain one question, "At what time will we arrive over the San Juan Airport outer directional fix?" The question was the key to the capability of the flight crew to navigate the direct route.

Bearings began to show the San Juan area ahead of us, and averaging them put us right on track. The main, and only, problem Captain Jocelyn had was to make his estimated time of arrival over that radio station at San Juan as accurate as possible. He told the observing team his estimated time of arrival, and asked that each of them synchronize their watches and write down his projected time of arrival. In keeping track of the plane's ground speed, with bearings coming in from various islands, it became evident to the captain that we would arrive well ahead of his projected time.

Very carefully, he began to reduce power on all four engines to slow the plane down. Seated in the back of the plane, I could tell what he was doing, because, after about an hour, with almost two hours to go, I could feel the DC-4 noticeably vibrating as he speeded up. He kept this up, going fast, slowing up, almost to the point of stalling the airplane. But, when we passed over the radio station, Captain Jocelyn was right on target with his estimated time of arrival. We got approval for the direct route.

There were literally millions of dollars at stake with this development. We Immediately increased our schedule frequency from five to six round trips a day. When we put faster airplanes on the route, direct flights between New York and San Juan were all made in less than eight hours, reducing the amount of crew required with the two pilots doing all of the navigation.

When Eastern Airlines was given CAB approval to fly New York to San Juan, they, of course, planned to fly the direct route. Even though Eastern had excellent domestic airline pilots, they had never been ocean navigators, and did not have a clue as to how to fly that route. I was afraid that the best they could do was to follow Pan American airplanes enroute, and, before long, be lost, miss their estimated times of arrivals, and jeopardize our approval to fly the direct route.

I met with Eastern Airline's Chief Pilot John Gill, explained to him all aspects of our operation, and turned over all our radio navigation ground school material and charts for him to copy. The Eastern pilots went to work, concentrated on our material, took tests, and were route checked in the identical manner of Pan American pilots over the direct route. This effort was made to assist Eastern, and to illustrate an example of not being competitive at operational levels in the airline industry, even though we were all trying to exceed one another in passenger carrying capability.

My work as sector chief pilot did not preclude my being able to pursue my participation in soaring contests. Using my wonderful all metal high performance Schweizer 1-23, I won the National Aerobatic Championship at the Fifteenth National Soaring Contest at Elmira, New York in 1948, and collected $50.00 prize money. In addition to the acrobatic contest work, I received the Stroukoff Award ($25.00 prize money) for my record for miles distance, altitude, and hours duration soaring in the cross country race of the competition.

The special cross country soaring contest interested me because it involved a specific triangular course to fly in a race against time. Each sailplane was released over Harris Hill at a specific altitude to cross the starting line to be timed for the race. This type of contest is very challenging and requires extensive planning. It can be very expensive when the sailplane is damaged upon landing in some barnyard, golf course, or tree. I am only one of many glider pilots walking around with scarred results of abrupt landings.

It is most important, when soaring cross country, to go the greatest distance possible to be awarded points for miles flown. However, certain precautions must be undertaken by the pilot to always keep in sight and mind a site to glide to and land. No matter how high one is flying, the site one has selected to land on must be safe to do so.

With only one shot at landing, one can't go around again for a better approach or landing. Being careful to avoid telephone lines, tall trees, rough ground, and great slopes is absolutely essential. On landing near a house, one, hopefully, meets the people in the house, explains his presence on the host's property, and requests permission to make a collect call to get his crew out to help.

When the crew arrives the pilot is already at work taking apart the sailplane to load it onto the trailer, and tow it back

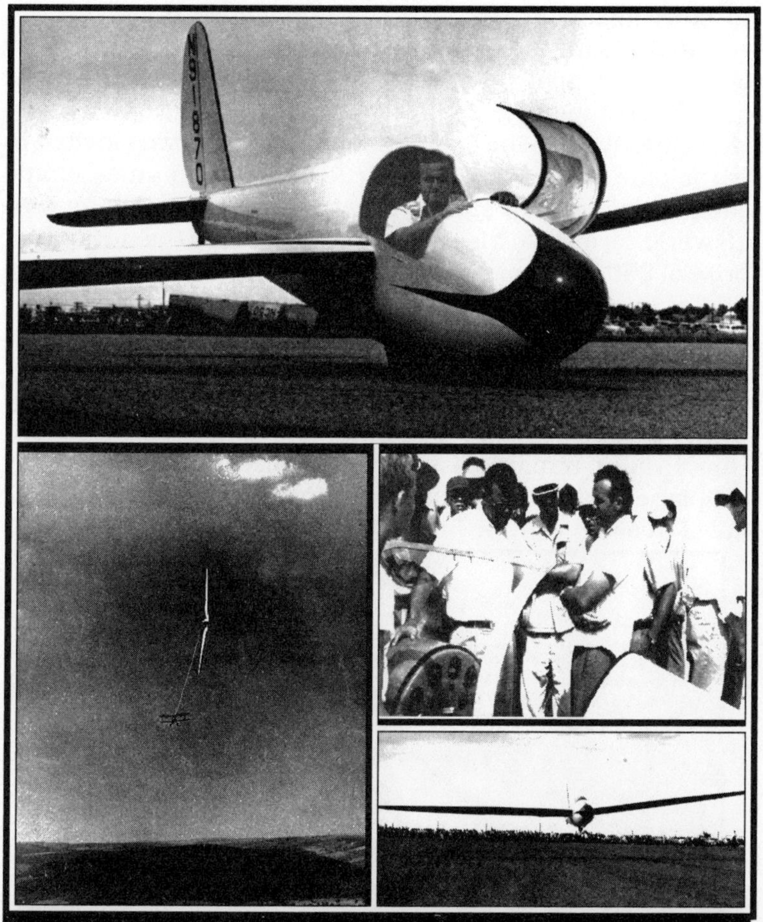

My all metal sailplane was capable of diving up to 200 mph with water stored in the wings. The water could be released by opening dump valves.

to start again on the next day's extended flight. Cross country soaring is not for the impulsive, impatient or in any way hurried pilot. Good as we may become, we are not qualified competition for birds, the real soaring champions.

Shortly after the competition at Elmira, I was invited to participate in the Cleveland Air Races to fly in an aerobatic competition against Marcel Doret, a French champion with 18 world records to his credit. In addition, to the meaty first prize of $500.00, this three day competition determined the title of International Sailplane Aerobatic Championship. I accepted the opportunity with relish.

On the last day of the races, on takeoff, and at 100 feet, I was in fine position below the airplane, in low tow with plenty of speed. I rolled inverted around the propeller blast. How I did it remains a mystery to me, but I released my sailplane from the tow line. My tow line device may have failed in some way, or I may have inadvertently released it.

In any event, there I was upside down, close to the ground without being towed any more by the airplane. I simply raised the nose of my inverted sailplane, rolled to an upright position, flew around the inside of the airport and landed. My scheduled performance time was gone. I did not have time to have the sailplane positioned again for takeoff.

I met with the air race officials who suggested that since Marcel Doret was scheduled to fly soon that I be towed up with him behind the same tow plane, be released at the same time, perform some aerobatics together, separate, complete our own maneuvers, and land to await the judges' decision.

Through an interpreter, Marcel Doret agreed. However, I had a problem. With our language barriers of not speaking any of the other's language, how could we be coordinated to fly together? It took several hours to work out the details, including who would fly on whom, what maneuvers we would perform, and how we would separate to do our individual flying. I wanted to fly on him so that I could determine how closely I would fly to him. He finally agreed, and we made his tow line shorter than mine so I could fly off of his position.

After flying a few maneuvers together, we were to compete in aerobatics, and, in the process, avoid running into each other. As all aerobatics pilots know, when two pilots dive at each other they leave quite a bit of space between one another in passing, because at the angle from which the people seated in the grandstands are viewing, they cannot see how close the planes are to each other.

I thought my French competitor knew this, would govern his dive accordingly, and dive to pass me with at least 100 feet between our wing tips. Not so! After we released at the same time, he dived in one direction, and I in the other. We then turned to dive toward each other and cross at the middle point of the airport. The good French ace, however, was going to do the real thing!

We passed very closely, because he kept edging his beautiful all white sailplane toward me. It was not too bad when I could see him, but since we were each to go right into a loop, where would he be at the top of my loop? I could not see him at all after passing him and starting my loop until, sure enough, at the top of my loop, there he was, his great smiling face looking straight at me. We barely missed each other again!

Straight away, I did a half roll after passing him at the top of our dual loops. I dived away from him, went inverted, did an outside loop, rolled out, and flew toward the grandstands. There I flew inverted again, and, by making gentle S turns in the strong wind, I flew upside down and backwards across the airport.

I then flew away from the airport, turned, and flew fast back toward the airport. With its hangars between me and the grandstands, I kept a steady rate of descent down so the audience would believe I was landing off the airport, or flying into the hangar. Instead, I pulled up sharply, fairly close to a hangar, went over it, put on my spoilers, flew directly at the grandstands, landed on a taxiway, crossed over some grass, and there, in front of the center seating for special guests, was my wife, Gloria, standing on a newspaper. I rolled along the

ground applying slight brake action to my one center wheel. As I came up to Gloria, she stepped back from the paper so that I could see. I let the sailplane sneak up and stop right on top of the newspaper.

As I was basking in the applause of 50,000 spectators in the grandstands, my competitor ran out of luck. He landed closely behind me, caught his wing tip on a runway light, ground looped, and was standing out by his sailplane waiting for his ground crew. As a result, the judges awarded the status of World Aerobatic Sailplane Champion to me.

Establishing records and winning competition helped take out some of the sting of my being ostracized by the soaring society. My putting on aerobatic exhibitions received good sums of money from major air shows. Staying in the best hotels, having my own tow plane, buying the latest sailplane, and, yet, not going in for soaring great distances to establish points for international recognition was contrary to their religious pursuit of soaring.

Most of the soaring pilots worked hard at their jobs, utilized their vacation times to enter the soaring contests,

**BOEING 377
STRATOCRUISER
(1949)**

- . 95 ECONOMY CLASS PASSENGER CRUISE AT 25,000 FT.
- . LOWER DECK LOUNGE
- . PRIVATE STATE ROOMS
- . SLEEPERETTE SERVICE FOR ALL PASSENGERS
- . JOINED PAN AM IN 1954
- . (4) 3500 H.P. P&W ENGINES
- . LENGTH 110' WEIGHT 147,000 LBS.
- . SPEED 275 M.P.H.

BOEING 377
STRATOCRUISER

FROM THE STRATOCRUISER TO AEROBATICS

Boeing 377 Stratocruiser

The Boeing 377, known as the Stratocruiser, arrived on the scene of the PAA international carriers (1949), as well as for long distance U.S. domestic carriers, as the "ultimate" in luxurious flying. Pressurized, it could fly up to 25,000 feet. As a first class passenger aircraft, it provided very comfortable seats, plenty of room, meals served course by course with all the frills. There was a downstairs lounge, reached by a stairway. There one could be served refreshments, while seated comfortably with an excellent view through the windows. This was an excellent place to visit while your bed, or berth, was being prepared for you to sleep while crossing the ocean or jungle, perhaps to Rio de Janeiro. The cockpit had more than ample room with a navigator's table, large views for the pilot, and even reclining chairs.

The Super Stratocruiser joined Pan Am service in 1954, embodying some major technical improvement. Propeller revolutions-per-minute were reduced, without affecting the 3500-horse-power output of each of the P&W engines.

Chapter Fourteen

The double decked Boeing 377, known as the Stratocruiser, arrived on the scene of international carriers in 1949. As a first class passenger aircraft, it provided very comfortable seats, private staterooms, sleeperette service and a downstairs lounge. In the lounge, passengers could be served refreshments while their beds or berths were being prepared for sleeping as the aircraft crossed the jungle or ocean enroute to Rio.

As sector chief pilot of the Latin American Division, I was checked out to fly the B-377 in 1950. Checking out required our flying the Dehmel trainer, which was the aviation industry's first four engine ground simulator for flight crews. Designed by Dr. Richard Dehmel, the simulator reproduced all of the flight characteristics encountered while flying the B-377.

The trainer had an exact replica of the entire cockpit for the pilots and flight engineers. From a control station behind the captain, the instructor could introduce all types of problems for the flight crew to handle. Fires, electrical

Dr. Richard Dehmel

problems, engine failures, hydraulic failures, etc., could be compounded to give the crew more problems to handle in one training session than the pilot would encounter in a lifetime. Complete with sound, motion, and instrument problems, this trainng device represented a technological leap which saved the aviation industry millions of dollars. More importantly, many lives were saved through utilization of Dr. Dehmel's trainer.

After familiarization flights to Europe, I was given the responsibility for flying the first Stratocruiser flight to South America, introducing the new *El Presidente and Publishers Flight* service from New York to Buenos Aires. This first flight was conducted as the eighth of a series of Publishers Flights which were first organized in 1934 to acquaint the nation's leading publishers with conditions in overseas countries, and expose them to the latest advances in commercial aviation technology.

With 36 publishers, editors, and governmental officials aboard as guests of Pan American President, Juan T. Trippe, the El Presidente configuration exemplified the ideal airline luxury image. Others on this special round trip, of nearly 13,000 miles, were leaders of both the U.S. Senate and House of Representatives, officials of Pan American Airways, our Board of Directors, and ten of our foremost master pilot captains to be qualified over the route.

The flight was a preview of the extra fare sleeper service to be flown on a schedule of two round trips each week, providing service to Buenos Aires in twenty-six hours and ten minutes, a time schedule which shaved off eleven and one half hours of the current schedule. This double-decker clipper also made possible a nineteen and one half hour one stop flight to Rio.

Each passenger was to have a berth or a sleeperette, a six foot long adjustable seat which allowed the passenger to recline fully for a night's rest. The two types of sleeping arrangements cost $10.00 for the upper berths, and $20.00 for the lower accommodations. Among the amenities were complimentary champagne, breakfast in bed, and a vial of Lanvin Arpege perfume for female passengers. Dinner was a seven course affair with the extra space between the seats allowing the use of dining tables with linen table cloths and silver table service.

The special high performance fuel for the aircraft, introduced by Shell Oil Company, was taken directly from storage tanks along a four inch underground line right up to the tarmac where the hydrant's passed the fuel through several filters via four hoses to the Stratocruiser. Since the enormous aircraft required many extra services on the ground such as electrical power, baggage carts, and food service trucks, there was not enough room for three large fuel trucks on the scene to utilize the more general type of refueling process.

The fueling dollies, two three wheeled units holding the filters, took up very little room, and permitted a fueling speed of 270 gallons per minute to be attained to meet the fuel requirements of 5,000 U.S. gallons, at a total refueling time of only one hour.

With the introduction of the Boeing 377. the real impact of modern aircraft design was realized. The Stratocruiser provided pressurization of the latest automatic controlled type, and humidity control. However, controlling the amount of moisture in the cabin was so intricate and complex that no one seemed capable of making it work properly. The system was so poor during descent from high altitudes that it would rain inside of the cockpit and cabin. Water accumulated everywhere and formed drops of water which eventually dropped on everything and everybody. This mechanism to provide water sufficient to make the air comfortable was so heavy it was finally discarded.

The pressurization worked beautifully. In fact, on a subsequent flight from Rio to New York, a rather overweight female passenger of mine, who was responding to a call of nature, made her way into one of the forward toilets just as we began our descent to land in New York. Later estimates indicated that she seated herself on the toilet just as we received clearance to descend from 25,000 feet to 3,000 feet to approach our destination airport in New York.

The normal descent rate expected by air traffic control-

BOEING 377 STRATOCRUISER

lers is 3,000 feet per minute for all pressurized aircraft, however, the captain may elect to descend at a greater rate to avoid flying in clouds ahead of him. The pressurization system could be adjusted in such a manner that the cabin rate would, at the most, be 500 feet per minute. Our flight engineers set their panel system for the cabin to have a pressure altitude of 3,000 feet, but to reach that at a much slower rate than that of the airplane. The cabin rate of descent, pressurizing the cabin air, was set for only 500 feet per minute to avoid the heavy clouds ahead. But, what of the lady seated on the toilet?

In a few minutes, while descending, the air began to feel bumpy, and I put on the seat belt sign. Of course, in the toilet the sign read: RETURN TO YOUR SEAT. The woman could not move from the toilet seat. She was stuck! She could not get up because the increasing cabin air pressure was holding her down on the seat, and the further we descended, the tighter she was held down. The toilet area below her was retaining its high altitude low pressure creating a partial vacuum, and the only way its pressure would be equal to the above cabin pressure was through the open toilet seat which was now sealed closed by the pressure of the lady seated upon it.

In due time, the OCCUPIED sign was noticed by a stewardess who knocked on the door, and advised the occupant to return to her seat. When a strange response followed her request, she opened the door, and discovered the problem. The steward informed the flight engineer who brought the dilemma to me. I realized the difficulty quickly, and put the airplane into a climb, after clearance from air traffic control. As the pressure was being reduced, I sent the flight attendendants down to assist the lady in distress. Embarrassing as it was to all concerned, the rescue was safely accomplished as she was "popped" off her seat.

These growing pains were not infrequent in our introduction of sophisticated airliners to the world. The problem of toilet seats was later resolved by quite simply, by drilling holes under the seat covering the toilet, so that, even with large people being accommodated, the pressure would be equalized if one remained seated during rapid descent.

The toilet area was the scene of another incident on a flight from San Juan, Puerto Rico to New York when a young woman went to the aft toilet, seated herself and delivered a baby! She was observed on her way to the toilet by a stewardess who later became concerned with the length of time the passenger was occupying the toilet. When the stewardess knocked on the door there was no reply. After unlocking the door, the stewardess immediately summoned help from the other flight attendants. Nothing could be done! The mother had borne the baby down into the conical shaped funnel, and with its head, shoulders and arms below the funnel, the attendants could not raise the child who was still attached by the umbilical cord to its mother.

The captain was advised, and sent the flight engineer back to assist in the dilemma. Ashen faced and shaken, the flight engineer returned to the cockpit area, and collected his tools while he explained the difficulty to the captain. Back at the toilet, he knelt down in the very restricted area with the mother on the seat holding onto the lower half of the baby as firmly as she could. With his tools, the flight engineer unscrewed the seat from the floor, and placed mother, baby, and the toilet seat down on the floor in the aisle. From that vantage point he and the flight attendants extracted the baby boy through the toilet seat, and mother and son were rescued without any injuries.

In late 1950, I was interviewed by General Harold Harris, then executive vice president of the Atlantic Division of Pan American, for the positions of operations manager or chief pilot. I knew little about General Harris, except that he was the first pilot to save his life by utilizing a parachute. Consequently, I did not hesitate telling him about my working my way through the University of Maryland by jumping out of airplanes, and I was careful to underscore my invention, development and work on the steerable parachute.

With a choice of being considered for both positions, I leaned heavily for the positions of chief pilot. In the interview, I pushed hard on the my ideas for modernization and updating of Pan American operations. Luckily, I was awarded the position of chief pilot on January 1, 1951. I was thrilled and most grateful for the opportunity to be chief pilot of the largest division of the world's most renowned airline, but I had a problem. I had a contract to fly my Schweizer 1-23 sailplane in the Miami Air Show on the 6th and 7th of January, where I had a commitment to put on a demonstration as World Aerobatic Sailplane Champion.

The general agreed to allow me to start the job as chief pilot on my return from the weekend air show in Miami, and I set about to make my arrangements for the event. My own tow plane and tow pilot were up north in New York, and not available for the show, so I had to lease a tow plane, and hire a pilot to tow me for the demonstration.

After flying to Miami, with my wife, Gloria, I leased a sign carrying tow plane, whose pilot had never towed a glider. His airplane was capable of towing a sailplane because of the tail hook assembly it employed for releasing signs after towing them up and down Miami Beach. I met the pilot, discussed glider towing, and arranged for him to meet me on the day before the show for a trial run, so that I could brief him on the pattern of flight I wanted from him on tow.

At the appointed time, we met. I looked over his Stearman and advised him that I wanted, on a trial basis, to take off in a normal fashion with me in tow. He was to climb to 500 feet, circle inside the airport, and then come back over the same runway. On takeoff, at the point along the runway where I would be 100 feet high on the day of the show, I would roll my sailplane on the end of the tow line, and become inverted. He was then to fly inside of the large airport, with me inverted on tow, and stay at 500 feet through one 360 degree turn. I would then fly upright, on tow, climbing to 3,000 feet where I would release myself from the tow line, and put on my aerobatic demonstration of an outside loop, inverted flying, and a spot landing on a newspaper.

The pilot flew this trial flight very well, remaining at 500 feet as I had requested. We circled inside of the airport in front of the stands, and I rolled upright, released the sailplane

...One of Kim's specialties was the inverted aero tow and its was this that proved his undoing at Miami Airport in 1951. He was flying behind an inexperienced pilot, on a hot day, with a full load of water. While rolling into the inverted position, immediately after take-off he dug in a wing tip and crashed. It was quite a while before Kim flew again.

Although he was best known for his aerobatics Kim did do competition flying as well. In 1949 he won first place in the Beechcraft Speed Event with 49.8 m.p.h. and retained this title in Texas the next year. In September of 1949 he won the Mid-Atlantic Soaring Championship at Alexandria, Virginia...

SOARING OCTOBER... 1966

from the tow line, and waved good-bye to him, I located some thermals, climbed up over Miami to about 17,000 feet, played with clouds and birds, returned to the airport, and landed. My tow plane pilot had landed and departed for home by the time of my return to the airport.

The opening the air show the next day brought several changes. The tow pilot arrived. However, he now had a different Stearman aircraft which had less power than the one we used the previous day (a fact which he forgot to advise me). I now filled my wings with 40 gallons of water (which I failed to advise him). The water, of course, was to be released after I dived to make my outside loop dive using the weight of the water to give me the speed I would need to go around in an inverted loop.

From 3,000 feet I would dive inverted over 200 miles per hour at the center of the airport. As I pushed the nose up from the inverted dive, I would pull the dump valve on my wing ranks, and out would spray colored water. The loss of water allowed me to climb inverted up over the top of the loop, dive down the other side with enough speed to do slow rolls and fly by the grandstands inverted.

On the first day of the show, the tow plane was in takeoff position on the runway, the tow line attached to my sailplane, the tow pilot was ready for takeoff, and the ground crew awaiting to raise my wing tip off the ground as the signal for him to apply power and take off. All was normal, except the water in my wings made the sailplane heavy, and the under-powered Stearman was going to take a longer run before becoming airborne.

The air show officials waved a flag in the distance as the signal for our takeoff. My wing tip man raised the wing to a level position, the tow pilot applied full power, the tow line became taut, and we began to move. The tow plane became airborne. I remained close to the ground until it was about 50 feet above me, and then I allowed the sailplane to climb with me in low tow position.

As I passed the 200 foot level, I raised the nose of the sailplane, and began a roll to the left to become inverted. As I became inverted, it was necessary to push the nose of the sailplane up further, due to my being inverted, carrying water in my wings, and the lack of power and forward speed of the tow plane. From his level position at 300 feet, looking in his mirror, the tow pilot saw the high angle of attack I was carrying with the nose of the sailplane held high, and he, instinctively, put the tow plane into a climb to give me what he thought was more and safer altitude.

The effect was that his climbing slowed down his forward speed to the point that I realized that I was about to stall and so was the tow plane. I knew I had to roll out of my inverted position to avoid stalling the tow plane. I thought I could cut loose from the tow line, and fly upright as I had done before. However, with my other experience in a similar jam, I did not have water in my wings, and had more speed for the roll into the upright position.

If I had stayed on the tow line a little longer, completed my half roll and remained on the tow line, I could have recovered and landed with no trouble, because I was receiving lift as well as speed from the tow plane. I did not and the result of my early release from the two line was that I began to sink as I rolled, and did not complete the roll to an upright position. I went into the ground in an inverted position. Fortunately, I did not go into the runway, but into the grass area beside it.

I carried a shoulder harness in the sailplane, but did not wear it because it prevented my moving the control stick far enough forward to do the outside loop. I only wore a single seat belt, and the result of this choice was that I struck the ground upside down, and went head first into the instrument panel.

I woke up at Jackson Memorial Hospital several days later to discover that the spectators and participants in the air show had lifted the inverted sailplane, and I had fallen out.

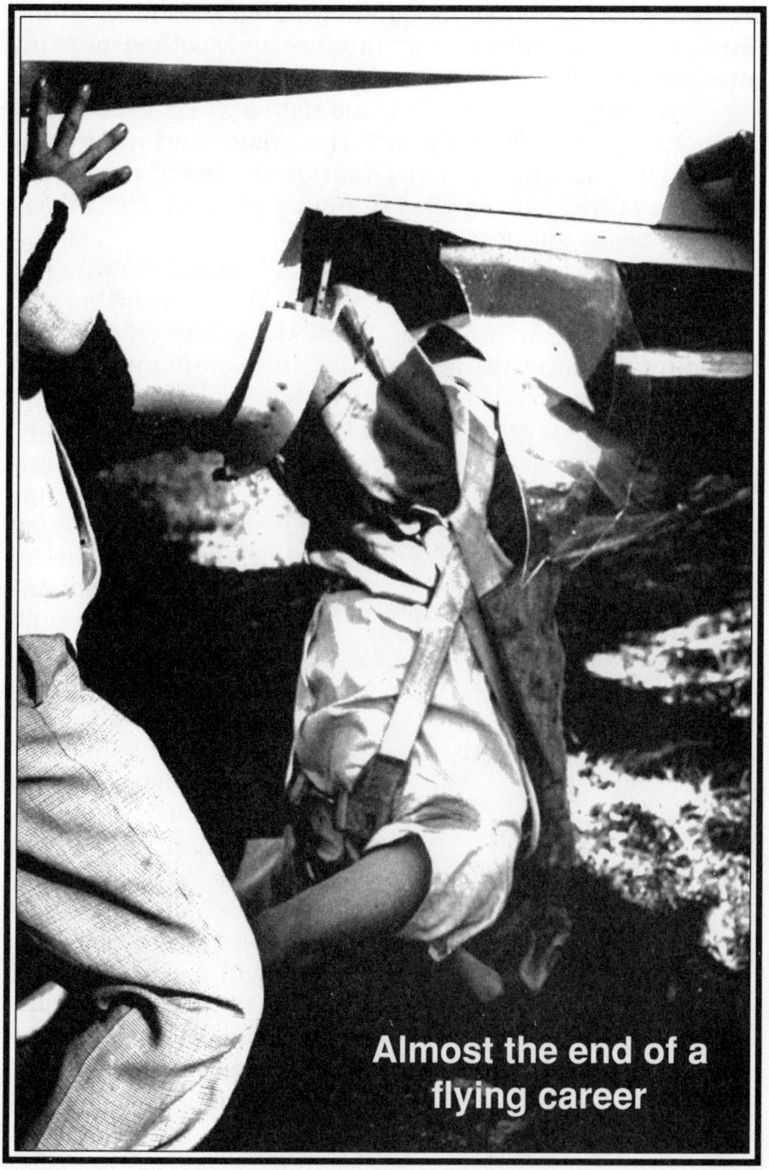

Almost the end of a flying career

My wife, Gloria, who was pregnant with our second daughter, Susan, rode with me in the ambulance and soothed me in my unconscious state.

My nose, jaw, front teeth, and right leg were broken. My right foot was pushed up into the ankle, and my left leg pushed through my hip. I had dual vision, a concussion, and because of internal injuries to my diaphragm, the wildest case of incessant hiccups on record.

Again my wonderful luck held, for I had Gloria with me, and surgical assistance of Dr. Leon Mims, an orthopedic specialist in the Miami area. Many days later, after finally stopping the hiccups, he was able to operate on my right ankle, bolting it together rather than having to fuse it, enabling me to have the mobility I required to handle airplane and automobile brake action, and to walk without a limp.

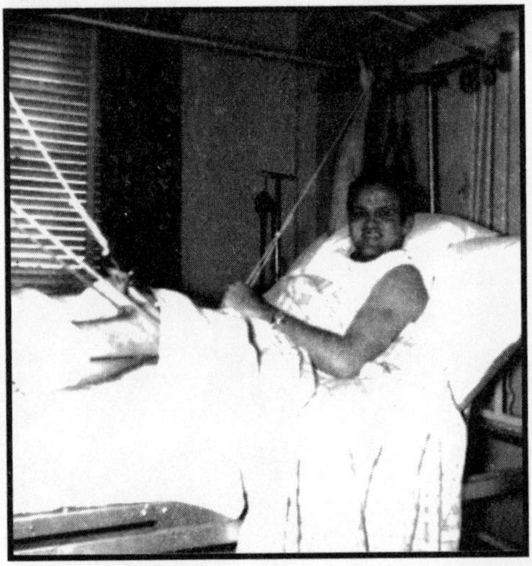

Dr. Mims was able to extract my left leg from its penetration through my pelvic hip joint by pulling the leg back out, and allowing the hip joint to replace itself. Using constant traction weights to hold my leg in a stationary position allowed the joint to heal. This meant that I had to remain on my back, which necessitated tying me down to keep me from moving in order to allow the broken hip to heal. With Gloria at my side, and encouragement from friends and hospital staff, I managed the duration of the healing process. Throughout the process, I kept asking for reassurances from the medical staff that I would be able

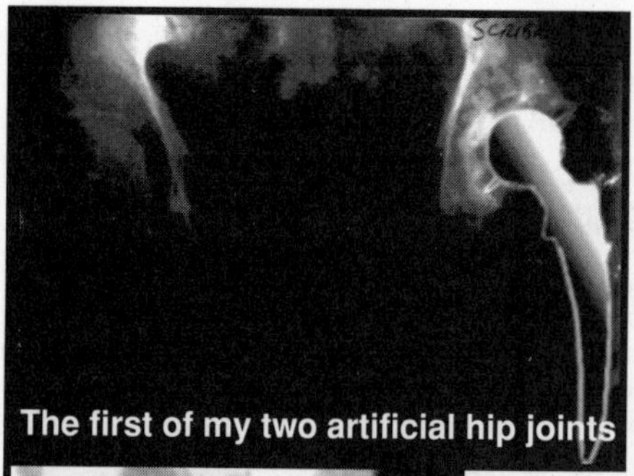

The first of my two artificial hip joints

Second joint placed in 1986

Both joints via Dr. Thurman Gillespie

to fly again. They could not even give me the odds on being able to walk again.

Pan American was wonderful to me, sending wires and an eye specialist who was able to correct my dual vision. Several months later, I was able to return to work in a wheel chair. I was basically physically incapacitated. I could not walk, much less fly an airplane. How could I be chief pilot?

In New York, I went to the Flushing Hospital every day to learn to walk again, using crutches. During this process, the new operations manager, Sam Miller, a former chief pilot, gave me a free hand to study our new pilot's agreement. There was more than sufficient work necessary for the assignment, since I was faced with grievances from the pilots regarding the agreement, and was kept quite busy handling the administrative responsibilities of the job.

Gloria, champion as always, assured that we managed each work day to get to La Guardia. Our living in a small second story apartment with no elevator presented stiff challenges for us to master, with our daily ritual of getting me from bed to the wheel chair, down flights of stairs, into the car, and off to La Guardia.

Into the car we would go, with our two year old daughter,

Colleen. On arriving, it was out of the car, into the wheel chair, up the freight elevator to the top floor, and into my office. With a brown bag lunch placed in my desk drawer, I was set for my work day. My pregnant wife and Colleen would

arrive at the end of the day to repeat the ritual for returning home. My recovery process was a fairly taxing one, and Gloria's exertions, no doubt, led to the premature birth of our second daughter, Susan.

My major assignment with the pilot's agreement required handling formal recorded hearings on pilot grievances. Fortunately, I was very familiar with the agreement because of the extended time I had spent studying it while I was lying flat on my back in the hospital. My attending the negotiations which led to the agreement eased my way, because I knew the true intent of the agreements as they were reached.

This was a real assistance, because once attorneys put an agreed item into fine print, both sides are likely to think the proper interpretation of the written agreement favors them. For instance, the pilots brought a grievance against the company stating Pan American violated the 'best effort' clause in the agreement referring to establishing and maintaining a proper pilot quota to insure against flying pilots more than 80 hours per month.

Economically speaking, I had no recourse except to make every effort to employ sufficient pilots, but no more than were required. Bids had to be posted for more captains, the chain reaction was phenomenal. For example, say a captain was required in San Franciso: the senior copilot bidding and winning the position lives in Miami, and flies only DC-4s. He must transfer to San Francisco, go to ground school on the planes being used, get a rating, have his navigation capability check, be route checked, and finally fly in command. Meanwhile, his first officer position in Miami had to be filled in a similar manner.

This transfer of pilots, training them, and not having enough pilots to fill all vacancies, was compounded by having three divisions in which each division had its own way of flying the same airplane. Each had separate route manuals, different flight training procedures, and separate operations manuals to fly the same type of airplane.

Having transferred back and forth between the Atlantic and Latin American Divisions in all my assignments, no one was more aware of the lack of standardization than I. Too, I was very conscious that the basic policy of President Juan Trippe was to have his three divisions operate unilaterally with no regard or concern for standardization.

He and the other Pan American management hierarchy had no real concern with this basic policy of competition between its divisions until the Airline Pilot's Association came into being, with its system seniority between all three divisions forcing the issues of training each pilot to fly the same plane in a different way with different manuals. It was only through secret visits to the Pan American system headquarters in the Chrysler Building, that I was able to convince the vice president of engineering, Andre Priester, that consideration should be given toward standardization of flight operations between divisions.

The exchange of pilots between the three divisions, resulting from the pilot's contract, permitting system bidding for pilots to upgrade themselves, gave me the ammunition I needed. I was able to graphically show the hundreds of thousands of dollars the duplication of training and time lost were costing the airline.

After evidencing great surprise to my revelations, Andre Priester issued a wire to all three division operations managers requesting that they have their division chief pilots each visit the other divisions, meet with all assistant chief pilots, and standardize flight route and flight operations manuals. If Mr. Priester had issued a directive that one chief

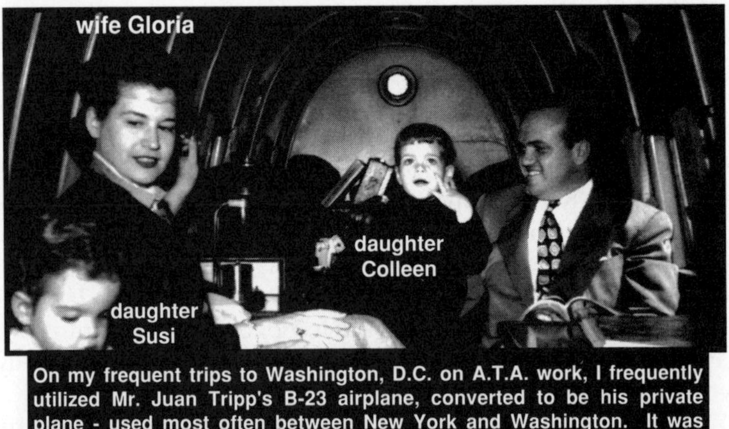

On my frequent trips to Washington, D.C. on A.T.A. work, I frequently utilized Mr. Juan Tripp's B-23 airplane, converted to be his private plane - used most often between New York and Washington. It was flown only by Al Ueltschi, then a Pan Am pilot assigned to this plane. Al eventually initiated the program for training and checking Corporate pilots. His company, Flight Safety, is currently the world's largest commercial pilot training company (nearly $200M/yr. in sales).

pilot be considered chairman and that there was one "best way", the results would have been quite different from what we were able to achieve. With chief pilots and assistant chief pilots having separate and joint meetings and discussions, we all returned to our respective headquarters with only a few small items standardized.

After my return to New York, I went to an appointment with the owner and publisher of Jeppeson Flight Manuals, Mr. E. B. Jeppeson. In a steam bath at the Biltmore Hotel, we talked about his route manual versus Pan American's. Jepp told me Pan American was literally stealing his information and most of his formats from his copyrighted manuals.

Later he came to my home and showed me illustrations, exact duplications. Laughing, he said, "I've been through this before with other airlines. I could pull the rug out from under Pan American on this, but I would rather show you I can do it cheaper and better for Pan American. Your three divisions each "borrowing" Jeppeson data, and each maintaining a printing staff and presses is costing Pan American more than having me print a Pan American logo on up to date pertinent and essential material which has been approved by the CAA.

Eliminating three division departments responsible for Pan American flight manuals was no small undertaking. Again, I visited the Chrysler Building to show how Jeppeson could print better approach charts which were current and maintained revisions for all pilots. The word finally came out to each division to show cause why Pan American should not utilize this service.

Arguments came from the Latin American Division that their pages with larger printing were more readable, and they had certain instrument approaches which were unique, such as Rio. This was resolved by advising them they could and would be expected to send pertinent data to Jeppeson who would see that the manual needs were as specific as need be. Today, and for many years, Pan American has been using Jeppeson Flight Manuals.

Chapter Fifteen

OCEAN FLYING THE DC-3

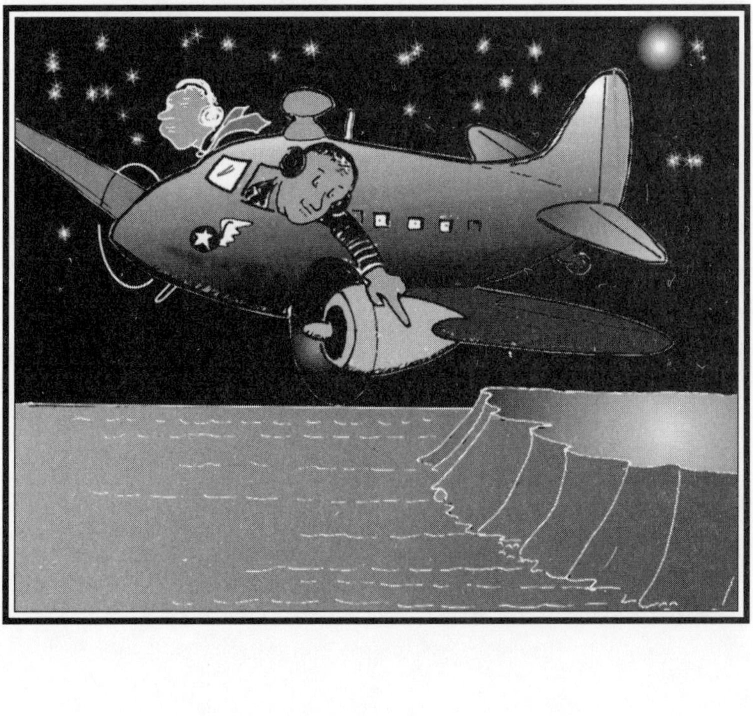

My Accumulated Flight Experience (1933-1949)

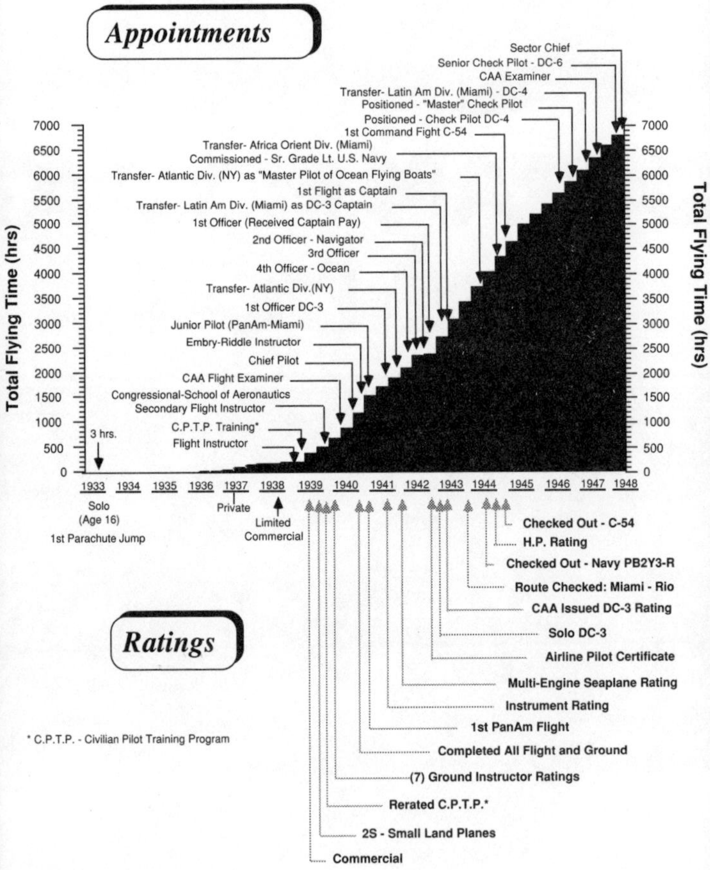

Chapter Fifteen

At a flight operations meeting, in May of 1952, I pointed out that our pilot training practice of using four engine type aircraft was an unnecessarily high expense which could be cut if we used the more economical DC-3 for the job. General Harold Harris, vice president of the Atlantic Division, concurred, and lamented only that we had no DC-3 available. I advised him that we still owned a DC-3 which could be reclaimed from the failed Liberian National Airline.

That DC-3 remained our property because it had never been paid for prior to the failure of the Liberian company. Though the condition of the airplane was uncertain (it had been staked out in the jungle for over a year) I felt strongly that it could be reconditioned and readied for use. I requested permission to send one of our best mechanics to Africa to inspect the airplane, requisition any required parts for repair, and perform work necessary for us to salvage it. I offered to fly it back to New York, and on to Brownsville, Texas for a total overhaul. General Harris agreed to my suggestions, and confirmed that I could bring the DC-3 back, asking no questions on how I would do it.

I found an excellent technician and repairman, briefed him with great care, and sent him off to Roberts Field in Liberia, with the understanding that when he certified the aircraft was ready for flight he would be on the test flight. Placing him on the test flight was my way of insuring his extra care in preparation of the aircraft.

The mechanic found the DC-3 in surprisingly good condition, with the tires flat, and various parts rusted, but the engines had been 'pickled' and protected. The radio equipment was, of course, not up to the current quality and advances, but that was not a real concern, since I planned to fly only in good daylight weather for the legs of the ferry flight back through Germany, England, Iceland, Greenland, and landing in New York. In a short time, I received a wire from the mechanic indicating that the airplane was ready for a test flight.

I selected Lennert (Lenny) E. Thorrell, an experienced DC-3 pilot to accompany me as copilot. Lenny had come as a first officer to us from the American Overseas Airline when it had been absorbed by Pan American. At American Overseas Airline, he had not been allowed to fly on international routes during the war, because, though born in the United States, he had been reared in Germany, and was treated with measures of the German alien status regulations implemented during World War II. This prohibition had limited his ability to accrue seniority as a line pilot, and left him to fly as

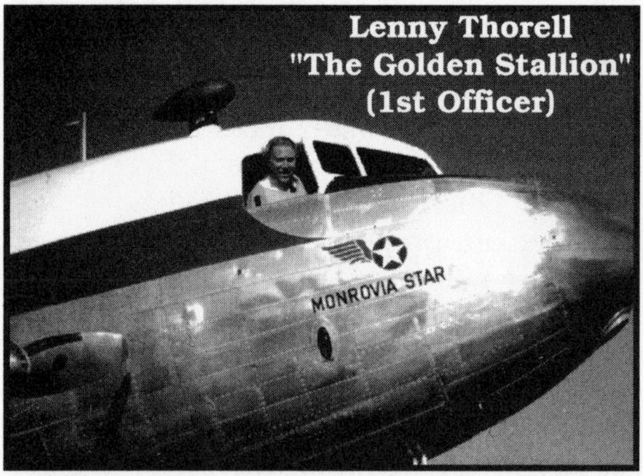

Lenny Thorell
"The Golden Stallion"
(1st Officer)

an instructor with American Overseas .

An accomplished pilot, linguist, noted ladies man, and delightful friend, Lenny provided fun and adventure wherever he went. When he arrived at the airport to join me for our deadhead trip to Lisbon, I noticed that, in addition to his flight case, he carried another container which turned out to be his portable record player, records, and a transformer to convert any type of electrical current. This necessary baggage had the sole purpose of providing music wherever he happened to be.

Upon our arrival at Roberts Field, Liberia, we found the mechanic polishing the propellers. He and the DC-3 were ready. On the next day, following an intensive ground check, we ran a test flight, and found no trouble, except for the poor radios. In this independent operation, we had the advantage of using options of improved accommodations for ourselves along our route. Where there were no Pan American facilities to accommodate our layovers enroute to Frankfurt, I sent wires so vague that no one could understand who was arriving or why, leaving genteel dignitaries of the various layover cities no recourse, but to send a car to meet us. All sorts of excellent assistance resulted.

The first leg of our flight was to Villa Cisneros Airport, north of Liberia on the West African Coast. In response to one of my vague wires, we were greeted at the very isolated airport by the French government administrator of aviation, who took us to his home to enjoy drinks, a splendid supper, and Lenny's records. Casablanca was our next stop, and then on to Morocco.

We wanted a stop at Gibraltar, but the British got stuffy, and refused permission to land, so we flew around the rock, took photos, and continued on to Spain, where we stopped for two days while a rough engine was checked, and spark plugs changed. My memory is foggy on whether or not the engines were rough, or whether the two days were needed for an adequate tour of Barcelona.

After arrival at Frankfurt, Germany, after 21 hours 30 minutes of flying time, the maintenance crew announced that the compasses were in sad shape, had to be swung, and compensation corrections made for the aircraft to be readied for the Atlantic leg of the journey. The process required several weeks to handle these repairs, and the necessary installation of two extra gas tanks, so we deadheaded home as passengers to New York.

When the German Pan American office wired me 3 months later that the DC-3 was ready, I found Lenny unavailable for the flight, and had to locate a copilot. Checking through our master pilots listings, I found Captain Page Smith was vacationing on a big game hunting trip in South Africa. He accepted my offer to save some of his allotted vacation time by meeting me in Germany to copilot the ferry flight back to New York. Our crew was complete when Pat Reynolds (chief navigator of Pan American) agreed to be our navigator.

Pat Reynolds - PAA Chief Navigator Instructor

Captain Page Smith (P. Willy) - Senior Master Pilot

Inspection of the plane in Frankfurt showed all was fine, except that the mechanics had done nothing about the magnetic compass hanging in front of the pilots in the cockpit. We were informed that there was no way at Frankfurt to position the airplane out on a taxiway, apart from interfering electrical disturbances, to properly adjust the compass.

We were advised that there was a compass rose available in Amsterdam, where the compass could be swung properly. It was necessary to adjust the compass because it was so far out of phase we could not make an ocean crossing with it as it was. The weather at Frankfurt was marginal, but we decided that with the relatively short distance to Amsterdam we could manage the weather, get the compass problem solved, and fly onto London, where the weather was forecast to be fine.

On a west takeoff with the DC-3 facing down the center of the runway, the compass was way off. Instead of indicating 270 degrees west, it showed a heading of about 230 degrees. We had an instrument clearance, took off and proceeded toward Amsterdam. Radar surveillance at Amsterdam area control picked us up, gave us a clearance to descend to make a straight in instrument approach on their instrument landing system runway. We completed our check list for landing. Still on instruments, we were approaching the outer marker, descending on the glide path, when everything electrical on the DC-3 failed.

Terror is the best word to describe our reactions at this moment. We were on instruments with no control of our direction of flight, no lights, out of communication, and no way to continue our instrument approach to the runway. Since we were established on the instrument landing system localizer, heading toward the runway, we allowed the plane to continue to descend on the same heading.

We guessed that we should soon see the runway lights. However, still descending, the first thing we saw out of the side windows were buildings at our same level. Enough of this! I applied full power and raised the nose to climb. We did not know what had happened, no radios, only the rate of climb and altimeter operating on the instrument panel. All gyro horizon, and turn, and bank, instruments all dead!

I climbed until we broke out on top of the solid cloud formation at about 4,000 feet. What to do? The seaboard had a frontal weather condition which closed all airports for us in Europe, but England was forecast to be open. In quick discussion, we agreed that the only logical thing for us to do was to dead reckon our way over the English Channel, then descend down almost to the water, continue westward as best we could with our crazy compass, find England, any airport, and land.

With two qualified captains and Pan American's chief navigator aboard, how could we possibly miss distinguishing England from Amsterdam? We took a heading we all agreed to be westerly. After we were certain we were well past the Holland coastline, we began a slow descent through the solid layer of clouds, with the altimeters set on the barometric pressure given to us for the airport at Amsterdam before we had lost all radios.

Descending very carefully, at about 300 feet we sighted water and eased down to stay under the overcast, expecting to encounter England at the point the Thames comes into the channel. The water was rough, white caps breaking gave us the opportunity to sight on them against the propeller hubs to get a drift angle, average them, and apply it to the heading. We felt certain we were flying toward the white cliffs of Dover. With the visibility we now had, we expected to encounter the coastline, then locate Heathrow or Gatwick Airport.

Finally, seeing the coastline to our left, we followed it. We could not understand the rough water we saw, until all of a sudden the coastline made a sharp turn to the left. A glance at our map revealed that the only place we could be was at Calais, France, the opposite side of the channel from where we thought we were. Well, we had plenty of fuel, no problem. We looked at our crazy compass, and visually established a heading from the coastline directly toward the cliffs of Dover

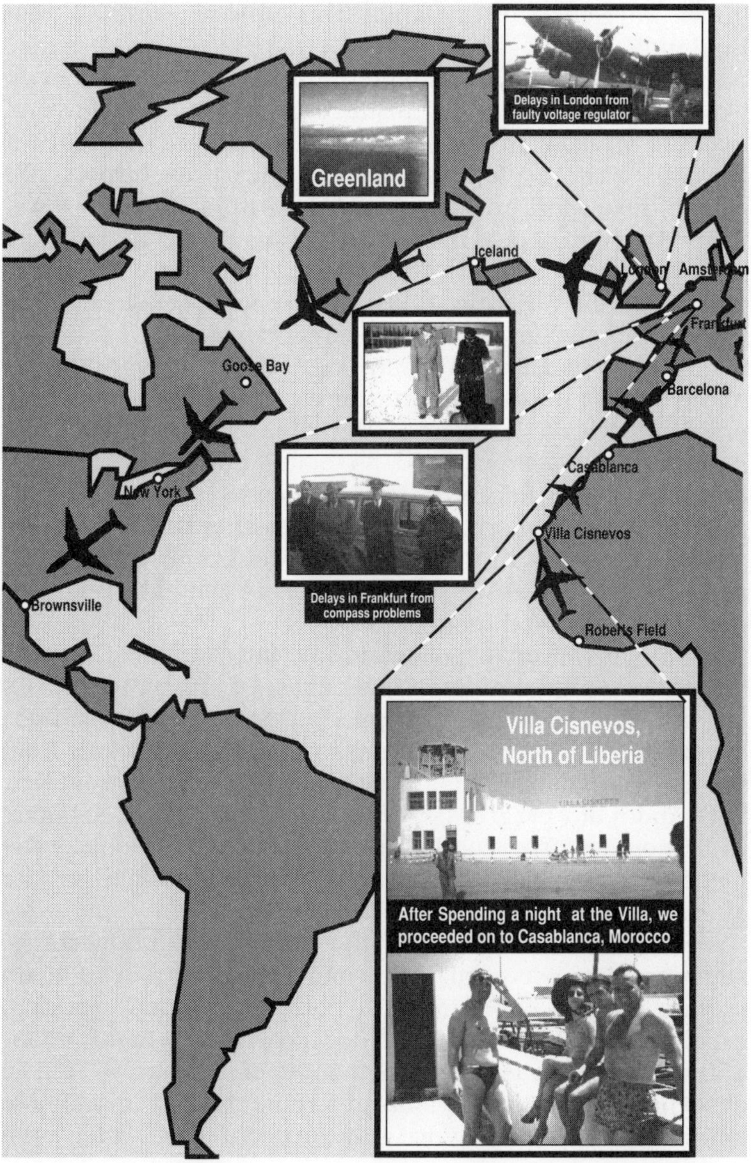
Delays in London from
faulty voltage regulator
Greenland
Iceland
London
Amsterdam
Frankfurt
Goose Bay
Barcelona
New York
Casablanca
Villa Cisnevos
Brownsville
Delays in Frankfurt from
compass problems
Roberts Field
Villa Cisnevos,
North of Liberia
After Spending a night at the Villa, we
proceeded on to Casablanca, Morocco

on the east coast of England. This time we couldn't miss England!

We flew low, and visibility improved as we flew northwest. There in front of us appeared the white cliffs of Dover. Because of airline traffic, we stayed low, climbed up to go over the cliffs, and, in a few minutes, saw Heathrow Airport. We circled the airport, rocking the wings until, finally, the tower flashed a green light at us, indicating we were cleared to land. After landing, we left directions for the maintenance crew to check out the airplane, find out why we lost all electrical power, and give us a call at the crew hotel.

We had had it with that airplane. While sitting at the bar in the hotel, a phone call came for me, informing me that the problem was a failed voltage regulator. In great detail, the malfunction was explained as being due to an internal component part failure. They did not have a replacement part for the voltage regulator, but reported that they could repair the old one in their shop. Without other choices, we agreed, and were assured that the plane would be ready for the flight to Iceland the next day.

All was well on the following day, with our new compass, repaired voltage regulator, and charged up batteries. In Iceland though, we were stopped because of bad weather. Several days of poor weather passed, with strong winds from the west prevailing. Finally, with inquiries coming from New York about our progress, we decided we had better go home. In view of the current and forecast weather conditions for the flight, we all decided it was best to depart Iceland in late afternoon to arrive at Goose Bay after dark.

Enroute, after dark, and flying along at 8,000 feet, the same problem occurred. The voltage regulator failed again leaving us over Labrador with nothing electrical working, except our flashlights. To locate Goose Bay at night, about 150 miles out, was no small maneuver. Again we had to descend and maintain visual reference to find identifiable landmarks to locate Goose Bay Airport. Fortunately, the weather remained clear, we saw airport lights, circled the airport, received the green light, and landed.

In time, the DC-3 made its journey to Brownsville, was overhauled and put into service. As we anticipated, the idea proved solid. We saved considerable money using the DC-3 for training. Pan American used it flying locally out of La Guardia Airport, checking new pilots and captains. However, the lure of the plane combined with human impulsiveness and ego cost a very high price.

In using it for daily trainings, a young mechanic was checked out to taxi it for the training and flight check operations. Every day he taxied the DC-3 alone. Eventually, he could stand it no more, he just knew he could fly it. Instead of taxiing across the active runway 4 to the terminal to turn it over the flight instructor, he turned down the runway, applied full power, took off, went into a steep climb, stalled, crashed into the bay, and was killed.

Chapter Sixteen

TAKE ONE AND...ACTION!

CIVIL AERONAUTICS BOARD
WASHINGTON 25

June 18, 1954

Mr. Harold Gray
Executive Vice-President
Atlantic Division
Pan American World Airways, Inc.

Dear Mr. Gray,

I wish to take the opportunity to express the appreciation of the Bureau of Safety Regulations for Pan American Airways' kind invitation to view the pilot airport qualification film developed by Captain Scribner.

As you are doubtless aware, the Board has been plagued for many years with the question of what standards to apply with respect to route and airport qualification for air carrier operation....<u>The use of training aids such as your airport qualification film shows excellent promise of providing a good answer.</u>

Sincerely Yours,

John M. Chamberlain
Director, Bureau of Safety Regulations

The photograph above was taken at a briefing of pilots by the LaGuardia Airport manager and air traffic controllers prior to movies taken of approaches to all runways.

Courtesy of GE SCSD

In view of the developments in visual aids over the next thirty-five years, Mr. Chamberlain's prediction was quite accurate. Although the introduction of movies to qualify pilots for airport familiarization may have seemed like a radical change at the time, this technique later evolved into the use of computer-generated images displayed in simulators. Shown to the left is an example of scenes displayed on GE's PT-2000 image generator which provides a sufficient degree of realism to qualify pilots transitioning to new aircraft and approaching new airports.

Chapter Sixteen

During the 1950s, one of the most costly training expenses of any airline was that related to qualifying their captains to fly into regular and refueling airports utilized on scheduled passenger routes. This was particularly expensive for an international airline such as Pan American, with its routes extending around the world. Each captain had to be qualified into each airport, accompanied by a check captain. This meant double captain's pay, plus the additional increment which the check captain received. The check captain's non-productive flying hours, about fifty percent, were lost by the airline.

After a captain bid and was awarded the right to fly a larger type of aircraft, it usually meant considerable loss of productivity for the captain and/or copilot involved in the transitional training for the new airplane. On full salary, ground school attendance, simulator training, check out flights, and route checks for captains, flying the newly assigned routes became very expensive. The chain effect of filling a vacancy for a captain was difficult to realize. Each move created another vacancy, which must, in turn, be filled by the bid system for pilots to move up in classification.

As chief pilot, responsible for establishing pilot quotas for scheduled operations, and arranging for transfers and training programs, it became obvious to me that the aviation industry needed a more efficient, practical, and less costly way to qualify captains into airports to which they had never flown. I found the major obstacle was Civil Air Regulations 40.303 and 41.50 (c), which established requirements under which actual approaches in an airplane must be made into regular, provisional, and refueling airports under supervision of a check pilot.

The alternative method I devised to satisfy this basic safety provision of the civil air regulations was use of motion picture training films, each with a sound track describing principal physical characteristics of the airport, its runways, taxiways, obstructions around the airport, and availability of emergency equipment. That no one had attempted this plan before was not surprising to me, for to change a civil air regulation is tantamount to suggestions of changing a Bible text.

My earlier success in obtaining alterations of various regulations led me to believe that the project was a hopeful one, and that I should attempt to produce an airport training film, and sell the concept to the government. My proposal included utilization of the La Guardia Airport, the DC-3 training flights, the airport manager, air traffic controllers, and meteorologists to introduce the token project, with the only major cost lying in production expenses.

There was no way to justify the costs of such a film until the CAA and CAB approved the required change of regulations. However, savings to the aviation industry could be in the millions of dollars, and the new motion picture procedure would be far more effective than the current method. I sought to convince the operations manager that with my writing the script, flying the airplane, directing the film, conducting the interviews, and doing everything else, except shooting the film and processing it, I could produce it for less that Pan American had spent on some of its films for stewardess training.

I offered to take the completed film to Washington, D.C. for government approval, and to submit a proposed change of civil air regulations which would permit the airline industry to qualify their pilots into airports with motion pictures. The questions I was asked were: "How much?" "How do you expect to get it approved?" "Do you realize that we are not in the research and development business?" "How can you justify the quoted cost of $10,000 which you are asking us to invest in an experiment?" The answer to my request was a clear "No."

I could not accept this answer, because I was certain that the plan was feasible, possible, and I meant to do it. In a few days, I put my plans into action at my own expense. In shopping around within Pan American departments which had occasion to contract with motion picture producers to train flight services personnel and produce travel films for us, I found just the person I needed: Harry Coleman. On a handshake agreement, he joined me to handle the filming and processing of the film. The payoff for Harry was a hope for improved relations with Pan American, because he had experienced some difficulty in past contract arrangements.

Harry Coleman

Harry had never taken motion pictures from an airplane, but that was easily remedied. To aid the shooting of the film, we built a device which held the camera protruding from the open right side cockpit window. In our desire to produce a truly unusual film, we had to look for something outstanding and different. I had heard about a new filming process developed by Lowell Thomas at The Explorer's Club in New York, and I thought this might just fit the bill.

The Explorer's Club is a multi-disciplinary association of impressive, scientific and educational achievements and leaders. It is international in scope, although 90% of its members reside in the United States. Its eminent membership has included Robert Peary, Theodore Roosevelt, Herbert Wilkins, William Beebe, Wilhjalmur Stephansson, General Charles Lindbergh, Sir Edmund Hillary, Thor Heyerdahl, seven Nobel laureates, and many of the astronauts.

At its headquarters on East 70th Street in New York, there are lecture and meeting facilities, with many programs open to the public. It holds one of the world's most extensive libraries, containing over 25,000 catalogued volumes devoted to exploration and related sciences, plus a valuable collection of over 5,000 maps, charts, pieces of correspondence, photographs, and memorabilia.

Dr. Lowell Thomas, who died in 1981 at the age of 89, served as honorary president of the august organization. A world renowned commentator, explorer and writer, Dr. Thomas was instrumental in the development of Cinerama. He stimulated action for its experimental development in laboratories established on a tennis court of a large estate on Long Island in New York. In his first film, Dr. Thomas provided his famous voice to accompany the three simultaneous motion picture projections on the wide screen without evidence or lines of demarcation between the three projections.

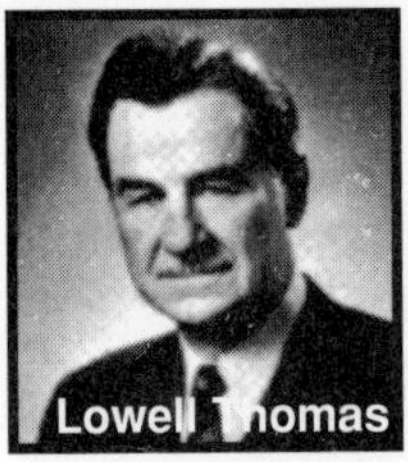
Lowell Thomas

As a guest of Dr. Thomas, I had witnessed this phenomenal development in a pre-release of his first Cinerama film, and I spoke to him about the wide screen function of cinerama for qualifying pilots into airports. He was most enthusiastic about the idea and invited his cohorts who were

by Capt. Kimball J. Scribner

Chief Pilot, Atlantic Division
Pan American World Airways

Airport Qualification via WIDE-SCREEN FILM

FIRST ***photograph of the camera installation used by Pan American World Airways in the preparation of wide-screen color motion pictures for use in qualifying pilots into regular, provisional, refueling and alternate airports. Harry Coleman is shown testing the all seeing eye of the anamorphic lens of the camera prior to take-off at LaGuardia. The New York airport was the first filmed by PAA in its program of adapting the Cinemascope color projection principle to the job of improving pilot airport qualification.***

The Cinemascope principle of wide-screen color projection, which makes possible those big, breathtaking close-ups at the neighborhood theater, is the medium through which the world's scheduled airlines can revolutionize and improve the costly, time-consuming method of qualifying pilots into regular, provisional, refueling and alternate airports.

This new use of 16 mm wide-scope color motion pictures, accompanied by oral breifing on the sound track, has been under development by Pan American World Airways for more than a year. On the basis of our initial success, the Civil Aeronautics Board has been formally requested to modify its regulations ro permit air carriers to adapt the film technique to their airport qualification operations. It is another conspicuous "first" in a long line of notable Pan Am contributions to aviation safety and dependability.

Specifically, PAA applied for modifications or re-interpretation of CAR Part 41.50 (c) to enable airlines to use the film qualification method *in lieu* of the current requirement under which actual approaches must be made into regular, provisional and refueling airports under supervision of a check pilot.

This medium of qualification is not designed to change the way the current methods of insuring and checking a pilot's flying proficiency and ability to make instrument approaches or to be route qualified. Rather, the use of wide-scope color and sound projection is recommended solely to satisfy the "visual reference" requirements of the CAR as far as airport familiarization is concerned and, at the same time, to provide more adequate airport qualification of pilots than is sometimes possible.

CLOSE-UP ***of 16 mm Cinekodak Special camera with Bell & Howell lens in position***

Cinerama enthusiasts to visit our base at La Guardia. In depth review proved the use of Cinerama filming techniques prohibitively expensive, and I had no recourse, but to let the plan drop.

However, Bell and Howell had just developed a 16mm special camera with their new anamorphic lens, which would permit taking wide screen color movies from an airplane using a single camera. Just what I needed. After a few phone calls to executives of the company, we agreed for a loan of their new lens for the project. Having the lens available was one thing, but I still faced a real problem, I had not sold the concept to the Pan American operations department. I was a new Atlantic Division chief pilot, and to expect a sizeable sum of money to come from a newly appointed operations manager for this experiment was foolhardy. I still had the final phase of the project, its implementation, to work out.

Approaching to land at LaGuardia

I carefully selected four experts on La Guardia Airport who had operational information related to flying into and out of the airport. I interviewed them, and the chief meteorologist of the CAA, the chief air traffic controller, the chief tower operator and the airport manager. With Harry behind

Sam Pryor

the camera, shooting film in good weather, and much cooperation from all areas of Pan American personnel, we wrapped up the filming.

I took the completed footage home with me, and at night, in my basement, counted the picture frames to determine how much time there was available for me to write the script to be recorded on the film sound track. I then had the challenge of fitting the film I wanted into the time available, using titles, selected music, and voice over for the most dramatic effect. With the wide screen color film with sound track completed, and with a production bill of several thousand dollars in my pocket, what was I going to do with the film now?

I approached Sam Pryor, vice president of Pan American in New York, and a direct advisor to President Juan Trippe. Mr. Pryor had been instrumental in establishing contacts at Washington levels for our company, and if anyone could pave the way for me to introduce the film to the CAB, CAA, the Air Transport Association, and political associations and parties, it would be he.

I showed him the film in a small, borrowed theatre at the Chrysler building. At the end of it he gave me a list of 134 congressmen and senators, members of the CAB, and the administrator of the CAA, and asked me to write each of them inviting them to the National Press Club in D.C. for cocktails and dinner to see the premier showing of my film. He then commented, "No one from Pan American will attend, only you." I added, "And my wife Gloria." "Of course," he replied. Gloria was needed not just as company for me; her charm, intelligence and social skills were just what was needed for the smooth flow of such an evening.

I drafted a letter of invitation, which Mr. Pryor approved, and mailed it to my prospective audience. There was a terrific response to the invitations, with four of five members of the CAB, CAA administrator, Fred Lee, and about 75 senators and congressmen agreeing to attend.

On the evening of my premier showing of the film, after an excellent dinner, the film was introduced, screened, and garnered a standing ovation. I responded quickly, giving a copy of the proposed change of civil air regulations. They read and agreed to the proposal that night. Soon, thereafter, I made a formal presentation with a request for change of the civil air regulations. After review by the industry, a showing of my film to the Airline Pilots Association, and the chief pilots of all airlines, the process was approved.

Mr. Sam Pryor is due tremendous credit for this improvement in the procedural qualification of pilots into airports, and the resulting multi-million dollar savings for Pan American Airways, and the industry at large, His direct

Briefing of pilots by Laguardia Airport manager and air traffic controllers prior to movies of runway approaches.

action taken in recommending and approving the unique presentation to the highest levels in our government assured my being able to make a success of this project.

This alteration of civil air regulations has meant a savings of millions of dollars, and was broad enough in its scope to permit color film slides, taken from various positions around an airport, and along the glide path to instrument approach runways, accompanied by clear voice, recorded instructions, to satisfy FAA qualifications requirements.

Today, a captain can come to his departure airport early enough to observe, listen to the approach procedures involved, and study specific area characteristics, noise abatement procedures, emergency equipment locations, et al. Then, he takes a reasonable written examination, signs himself off, and is now better qualified than if he had flown into that airport with a check pilot at night in rain, and landed without seeing the obstruction, or having been exposed to the truly important aspects of an airport.

Chapter Seventeen

RACKING, HACKING & DROPPING GARBAGE

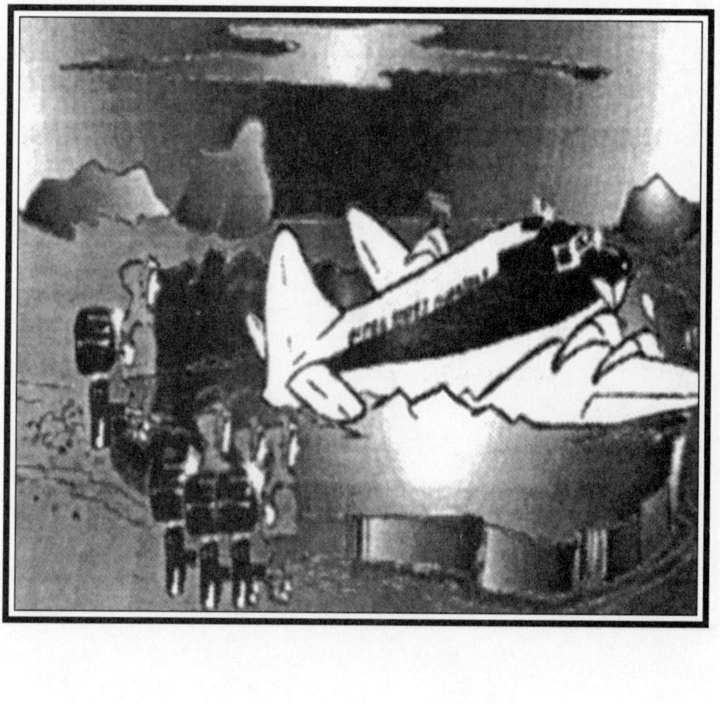

the
story
of
AIRCOACH
The Greatest Innovation in Commercial
Aviation Since Airmail
TRANSPORT
AIRCOACH

Chapter Seventeen

As a result of the success of the project to permit motion pictures to be used to qualify pilots into airports. I encountered a dilemma. I had to submit an expense report to the operations manager, John Shannon, for about four thousand dollars to cover the actual production costs for which I had personally obligated myself to Harry Coleman Productions. Secondly, though there was much recognition for this innovative enterprise, and tremendous savings experienced, I had deliberately bypassed a directive not to produce the film. How could I invite the operations manager to see the completed film? How could I advise him that I had shown the film to Sam Pryor, vice president of PanAmerican, and a panel of senators, congressmen, CAA and CAB officials without having invited him?

I simply submitted the expense report without explanation. I was paid without comment. With seven years of work as chief pilot under my belt, and with my great desire to fly the new B-707 jet transport about to be delivered to Pan American, I elected to submit a letter of resignation from the chief pilot's position in November, 1954, with a plan to

Pan American was the first operator of any jetliner: the 707-120.

regular line flying in January, 1955. John Shannon gave me an excellent farewell dinner, and the Pan American pilots, flight engineers, dispatchers, et al, my treasured Rolex.

Prior to resignation and resumption of regular line flying duties. I was invited to be a member of an Air Transport Associatlon committee concerned with the lntroduction of jet transports to the traffic patterns of flight around busy airports. The ATA, Alr Force, and, other govern-ment agency sections wanted to plan for the introduction of the fast flying jet transports. They were concerned with the areas of penetration of the jet transport from high level altitudes, a radical change from the propeller driven aircraft with their low level approaches.

Since I had not been even close to a jet airplane of any kind, I felt that I did not have any ideas to contribute to the project. When I related this to the Air Force general who was coordlnatlng the interests of the military he replied, "Well, well fix that." He immediately made arrangements for me to go to the Moody Air Force base in Georgia for a jet flight training in a special Air Force instrument pilot course which had been established for senior officers.

Pan American authorized a month's leave, with the provision that I use my vacation time for the course, and I was off on a new adventure. At the Moody Air Force Base, I was met by an officer who drove me to my quarters, some excellent officers' digs. I was issued flying clothes, upon which there was no indication of rank. My fellow classmates, I believe, must have thought me the Secretary of War or some other

I was elected Chairman of the
Air Transport Association's
Chief Pilots Committee.

civilian of elevated status.

After completion of the five day jet ground school academic classes and examinations, I was assigned to Air Force Major Albert K. Hansen, Jr. as his student to fly a T-38A for the mandatory ten hours of flying work. My only problem was his language. The major said. "After takeoff, rack it to the left, drop your garbage and watch your speed, then hack it." I was agog, not knowing what he meant. Sensing my dilemma, he laughed and explained what he meant with use of gestures. Rack it, or hack it, meant steep turns, and drop the garbage meant to extend flaps and gear.

When I told him I was an airline captain, a total change in his demeanor occurred. He explained that he was leaving the military service soon, and would love to fly for Pan American. Though he had passed his written examinations for an airline transport license, he was unable to afford, or find a way to take the flight test. I suggested he locate a twin engine aircraft available at the base, explaining that I was a CAA flight examiner, and would be happy to administer his flight test, but that all sorts of presentations were truly needed.

As a result of being Chairman of the Chief Pilot's Committee of the A.T.A., I was invited by the Air Force to become familiar with their jet planes and I agreed to take their Senior Oficer Jet Instrument course in Valdesta, Georgia. While attending, I gave my instructor, a Major, flight tests in a B-25 for an Airline Transport Rating. He passed with no problems.

Delightedly, he informed me that he could get a B-25 any time. I had never been in a B-25, but that did not matter, I was not going to fly it, he was. He knew all of the various procedures and types of maneuvers he had to do for me including evacuation of crew and passengers from a DC-6, emergency procedures, engine failures, single engine approach under the hood, and orientations of various kinds which he had practiced in the simulator at the base. As expected, Major Hansen passed his flight test for an Airline Transport Rating with flying colors.

On completion of the required paperwork. he could not do enough to assist me, giving me the front seat check out in the T-38A, and allowing me to perform all of the acrobatics I wanted. What a superb experience: high speed, fast rolls and inverted flight, a total of ten hours in the "T-Bird" and one hour in the B-25 with him. Not a bad exchange rate.

On return to regular line flying, I found that I had time between flights to establish ways and means of producing visual training aids for any airline to use. My focusing only on emergency procedures made this project possible without a conflict of interest with my work at Pan American. Each airline had a make believe shift course to provide their crews with limited training to satisfy the civil air regulations. In these films, ground instructors demonstrated the use of life jackets, rafts, and described the emergency provisions contrained in the survival equipment.

None of the airlines had a professionally prepared presentation including demonstrations of how to put a life jacket on a child, or how best to put a life jacket on one's own body. With the safety instructions offering less intensive instructions than was truly required, all sorts of presentation-tions were crying to be produced.

Under the aegis of my own new company, Aeronautical Visual Training Aids Corporation, I set about producing a slide show, with sound accompaniment, on emergency evacuations of passengers and crew from a DC-6 for Pan American.I had no contract with the airline to produce such a film, so, at my own expense, I had photographs shot at the Flushing YMCA swimming pool showing how best to put a life jacket on while in the water, how to inflate a raft in the water, and all the other major emergency procedures needed. When it was completed, I was allowed to show it to a relatively large group of Pan American pilots, flight engineers and instructors.

I then presented the production to the new chief pilot, Chili Vaughn, for his consideration. When he asked what I intended to charge for the film presentation, I replied that I would accept the same fee that Pan American was paying other companies for this type of film instruction. His response was, "It looks like a buyer's market. Since you had no contract to prepare this training aid, we will pay you for the cost of materials only." "No thanks." I retorted, "I'Il sell it to the other airlines by changing the titles and eliminating any reference to Pan American."

In a short time, I received a letter implying that I was involving myself in an occupation which represented a conflict of interest with my employment at Pan American. A quick visit and explanation to the Atlantic Division Manager of Pan American, Captain Horace Block, solved the issue. He saw no conflict of interest in my preparation of training aids to assist in saving lives.

This occasion led me to decide it was time to establish my own corporation. I selected the name Professional Aviation Associates, or PAA, with myself as president (I always wondered what it would be like to be President of PAA.), and good friends Captain Jess Tranter and Gill Robb Wilson, as vice president, and chairman of the board, respectively. Even with our private enterprise of professional Aviation Associates, Gill Robb Wilson, Jess Tranter, and I all reflected a strong feeling of loyalty to Pan American. In discussing our plans to train flight crews, we had a number of ideas for improving passenger relationships, comfort and enjoyment.

We wanted to show them a preflight film which would teach them about airplanes, giving them confidence in the crew, and enhancing the flight experience. We wanted a communication system installed aboard the airplanes which would allow the individual passenger to tune in or out on flight information, and select audio entertainment and music as he chose. We got nowhere with our suggestions to Pan American, so we turned back to our private enterprise to work on advanced systems.

When the airline did install a communication system to some of the planes, there was no planned program to provide select entertainment for its passengers. When I was moping about the missed opportunity to my friend Tip Tippett, he told me that Sid Luft, husband of Judy Garland, was seeking just that sort of closed circuit system to be available to offer select and unique programs via ear phones.

Sid Luft and I met in New York to discuss the prospect of this programming. Handing me a check for $500.00, he asked to have an experimental program put on a Pan American flight from New York to Bermuda. With the cooperation of a Pan American vice president of sales promo-tion, I managed to arrange the installation of a system for that route. Despite a terrific response from the passengers to the appealing programs, the company vice president declared. "We do not need to entertain our passengers, what we need is more seats." Only a short time later, TWA came out with in-flight motion pictures and Pan American, of course, had to follow and provide the same. Being right is not as much fun as getting to do things right the first time.

Our most useful and productive activities in our private firm were those with United States Overseas Airlines, a company owned and operated by my good friend and former roommate, Dr. Ralph Cox. U.S.O.A. owned DC-4s and DC-6s, so the training film presentation was applicable to either airplane, and his need for manuals, and other areas of our expertise were mutually beneficial. Dr. Cox, an accredited

dentist, became a Navy pilot during his term in the military. On his departure from the service, he joined American Overseas Airlines as a pilot operating out of New York, where he and I shared a luxurious apartment with two other commercial airline pilots. When American Overseas Airlines was taken over by Pan American, Ralph did not opt to become an employee pilot of Pan American, choosing instead to start his own United States Overseas Airlines.

U.S.O.A. was one of the first non scheduled airlines flying out of New York to Miami. In the early 1950s these non skeds revolutionized air transportation with their cut rate charter flights for commercial travelers. They operated free of the restrictions of the airline industry, and promoted a healthy competition to the industry monopoly of fares and flight schedules. However, they became too successful. Major airlines were feeling the impact of the reduced fare rates offered, so they brought extreme pressure to bear through instigating unnecessarily detailed CAA examinations of all aspects of flight operations of all non scheduled airlines.

Paper work became mind boggling, restrictions and limitations were tightened, and the type of flying they operated was subject to daily surveillance. Though U.S.O.A. was without a single accident. and making money, they needed help to assure that the airline was following proper procedures.

They did not have a simulator for the airline which would satisfy the requirements for the DC-4 and DC-6. That problem was handled when our private company made it possible for a simulator to be quickly changed from a DC-4 to a DC-6 by movement of the forward instrument compartment, and corrections applied to the basic flight characteristics of the simulator controlling electrical equipment.

With all of their DC-6 equipment coming from surplus sales, there was a lack of proper DC-6 operating manuals which had to be approved by the CAA. I made a careful review of its operating manuals, compared them with the many varied types used by other airlines. and then condensed and revised their manuals for CAA approval.

U.S.O.A. was very successful in their various military contracts, operating all over the world. This was achieved in spite of tremendous odds. A federal board denied new aircraft purchases to the non-scheduled airlines, based on wartime allocations, despite the fact that communist countries were allowed to purchase such aircraft.

Dr. Cox's claim to fame for his airline was the fact that from U.S.O.A.'s civilian and military charter flights, over two billion miles had been flown without a flight fatality or passenger injury. Calling his airline the "Woolworth's of the airline business, the common folks airline without the fancy frills and expensive jets", he proved the need for options to travelers and cargo freight customers.

On their operations into New York, they were confined to Teterboro, New Jersey. Finally, some forced their way into Newark, and then on to La Guardia, but they were always confined to the back alley areas of such airports. Denied the use of the public address systems, their passengers, who were searching to find the supplemental airline counter to check in for a flight, must have thought back to the days of trying to find a speakeasy.

Operating from its home base in Wildwood, New Jersey, U.S.O.A. performed many missions in the national and public interest, actively participating in the Berlin and Korean airlifts, providing personnel and aircraft in 1951 to combat a locust plague in Iran, and carried priority cargo under contract with private firms for construction of Air Force bases. It took an active part in furnishing emergency transportation to Hungarian refugees in 1955, and carried emergency cargo to British Honduras in 1961 for the relief of

COMPARISON OF TRAVEL COST — COAST TO COAST

TRAVELING BY....	TIME	FARE AND TAX	FOOD & SERVICE TIPS	VALUE OF TIME at $10 per day	TOTAL
 AIR COACH	12 to 14 Hours	$99.00 14.85 $113.85	Tipping not permitted	$5.00	$118.85
 BUS	4 Days	$49.80 7.47 $57.27	$24.00	$40.00	$121.27
 RAIL COACH	3 Days	$88.81 13.32 $102.13	$18.00	$30.00	$150.13
 PREMIUM-FARE AIR LINES	11 to 12 Hours	$157.85 23.68 $181.53	Tipping not permitted	$5.00	$186.53
 PULLMAN	3 Days	$140.70 21.10 $161.80	$18.00	$30.00	$209.80

One of the most significant single development in commercial aviation during the first 50 years of powered flight was the establishment of low cost air-coach (non-scheduled) service, hailed by most aviation historians as the greatest innovation in commercial aviation since airmail. Dr. Ralph Cox was one of those that capitalized on the booming trend before its demise promulgated by industry infighting and government interventions.

Prior to World War II, air travel was a high cost, luxury mode of transportation, which approximately 90 percent of our population could not afford. it was inevitable, then, that one day a low-cost, less luxurious mode of air travel would be established to meet a strong public demand for economical air transportation at a price the average American could afford to pay.

An unusual combination of events and conditions which marked the end of World War II were almost perfect for the starting of low-cost passenger air travel. The war had been fought primarily in the air. Most of the Air Force veterans had learned to fly and maintain planes and had seen the possibilities of air transport. The Air Force has a surplus of excellent air craft on its hands and it stood to lose a great deal of money unless some use could be found for the planes. The government saw in the large number of air-minded veterans a vast market for this equipment. The War Assets Administration offered the surplus planes to veterans at very attractive prices, explaining how the planes could be fitted with seats and used as passenger-carrying aircraft. Many of these veterans saw a ready market for low-cost air service in the large number of civilians who had worked so hard at home during the war but now wanted to travel, by air if air travel could be brought within their means. Consequently, what is commonly referred to as air-coach was born.

hurricane victims.

When non skeds were allowed to provide military charters, traffic increased by the regular route carriers by over 5,000 per cent. When the regular route carriers were seeking additional subsidy, and alleging that the air traffic market had peaked, the supplementals were confronted with growth beyond their wildest dreams. Today, it is evident that these supplemental airlines were the catalyst which made the air transport industry blossom forth into gigantic billion dollar airlines.

The major carriers and the CAB often contended that non skeds skimmed the cream off the air travel market. Yet, these supplemental carriers were limited to ten trips monthly between major points, while the certificated carriers operated twenty to thirty flights daily in the same markets. The real skimming came only as a result of market forces, and the travelers seeking out low cost air travel. In only a few years, the demise of these airlines was fraught with much more sinister motivations than market competition.

Dr. Cox asserts that his company and other non-skeds were, by conspiracy, forced out of business in the 1960s by the C.IA The C.I.A. acquired Southern Air in the early 1960s, diverted two hundred fifty million dollars of military air transport contracts to that airline, and forced the independent non skeds into bankruptcy. The C.I.A. will not discuss the matter, but the government's role in the nonscheduled airlines' failures came to light in government documents obtained through the Freedom of Information Act.

In 1976-77, the airlines put out of business gave testimony before the Senate Small Business Committee, providing documents which showed that business was diverted to Southern Air and five other carriers alleged to know about the C.I.A. connection. Led by Dr. Cox, the defunct airline owners have filed suit in several courts claiming damages of 540 million dollars, written formal letters of complaint to the C.I.A., and petitioned the Civil Aeronautics Board.

Their claims have all been rejected. While they still feel victimized at the hands of an element of their federal government, they have given up the battle. "It costs too damned much to fight the government," says Ralph Cox. "They can put 200 attorneys against you and tie you up for 10 years; we just don't have those resources."

Ralph Cox is known for his innovative and adventuresome spirit. Among his most interesting exploits is his extraordinary arctic salvage of a DC-4 freighter belonging to U.S.O.A. which made a crash landing on the pressure ridged surface of an icefloe in Hudson Bay on May 10,1955. The aircraft was so badly damaged, and in such a critical position, with the ice already showing signs of breaking up under the influence of an abnormally warm spring, that Lloyd's of London considered the plane both irreparable and unsalvageable, and paid the airline half a million dollars in insurance.

Two and a half years later, that same DC-4, still incorporating more than 75% of its original structure, went into service again after being the subject of one of the most

DC-4 N90407 on icefloe
30 miles from Churchill
- on Hudson Bay
Right main gear struck
ice ridge 8' 10" high

remarkable aircraft salvage operations ever undertaken. In 1955, DC-4 N90407 was one of many aircraft taking part in the great airlift which made possible the construction of the Distant Early Warning (DEW) Radar Line in arctic Canada. On May 10, it was returning to Churchill from a supply mission, and ran Into severe headwinds which reached up to 150 miles per hour. The aircraft was guzzling fuel at such a rate in the pressure of the headwinds that the captain had to make an emergency landing.

The captain, acting under extreme pressures and split second decision making, skillfully piloted the plane through turbulent conditions to a landing onto an icefloe one thousand feet below the point of descent. The plane incurred damage when a cross ridge on the icefloe claimed the starboard landing gear. The aircraft slithered to a standstill on its port undercarriage, starboard propellers, and engine nacelles.

From the looks of its settled landing, insurance claims personnel decided to write off the plane as unsalvageable. Ralph Cox would not. After flying in from Europe within five days of the incident, and exploring the possibilities for salvage, he developed a plan to secure the aircraft, preserving the icefloe upon which it rested, until he could use the two good remaining engines of the DC-4 to propel the floe shoreward.

If the surface of the floe could be insulated from the warming rays of the sun, it was reckoned that the ice cold waters of the Hudson Bay would keep N90407's ice platform intact until long after the rest of the bay ice had disappeared. There was a little known precedent for this unusual scheme. The basic idea for a floating ice platform was one of the many highly-imaginative proposals of Sir Winston Churchill who, in one of his famous personal Minutes, proposed, and urged the prompt examination of the idea of using mobile artificial icebergs as staging points for aircraft in the wide expanses of the north Atlantic. Carved from the mass of raw material available in the Arctic, it was suggested that these floating ice islands could be reinforced, provided with propelling machinery, living quarters, defense and all the paraphernalia of a mobile seadrome.

Experiments in connection with this scheme were actually made in Canada, and a small scale ice island was produced in one of the northern lakes, using that well known by-product of Canada's lumber industry "sawdust" as a toughener and insulator. Canada's sub-zero weather did the rest. It was not a very expensive experiment, and when other means of extending the range of aircraft were developed, the project was dropped and soon forgotten by all except the few directly concerned with the Canadian experiments. It was their recollection of the remarkable binding and insulating properties of sawdust that suggested a possible means of saving N90407. If the icefloe could be covered with a layer of

sawdust, and then with an additional loose covering of hay or straw as an additional insulator, it was believed that the wet sawdust would be frozen into the surface of the floe to provide perfect protection and an ideal working platform.

The possibilities of this highly original scheme appealed to Ralph Cox. His marooned DC-4, destined by the experts to end up at the bottom of Hudson Bay, could ill be spared. With the insurance money paid up, there seemed little to lose and everything to gain by trying to save the stricken aircraft. So Cox paid Lloyd's $5,000 for the salvage rights, and took up the challenge. A sister DC-4 was brought in to airlift material, stores, food, etc., and a helicopter was chartered to provide an air link between shore and the icefloe. Eskimos and a dog team were hired for work on the floe; engineers and mechanics were flown in; and a headquarters office was set up in Churchill to direct operations.

Dropping sacked sawdust and hay

Sacked sawdust and bundles of hay were bought and transported by rail from The Pas, 500 miles away, to Churchill airport. Inflatable rubber pontoons, from a surplus military pontoon bridge, were acquired in the United States, flown up to Churchill, and dropped on the floe to be packed under and around the wings and fuselage of N90407 so that if the worst happened, the aircraft would not sink. A quantity of plastic preservative paint such as that used by the U.S. Navy to mothball its equipment was flown in to protect the airframe inside and out from the effects of salt water.

In the meantime, a sawdust airlift had gone into operation out of Churchill. The floe was "bombed" with the sacked sawdust, the sacks bursting on impact to help to spread their contents. Then followed the bundles of hay which had to be distributed by the skilled Eskimos and the dog team. And all this time the ice in the Bay was slowly softening and disintegrating around the reinforced ice platform. There were many anxious moments for Ralph Cox and his team. Although the floe was standing up splendidly, ominous cracks were beginning to appear around its edges, and it was feared that if some part did break off the balance of the platform might be upset and the whole thing might capsize. The inevitable fogs of this time of the year cut communication for days at a time, while the surrounding ice was thinning out and winds and currents were beginning to push the floe around.

An attempt to navigate the ice platform with the aid of N90407's two good engines was a complete failure, so half a dozen boats powered by outboard motors were hired. More than once the platform was pushed and edged to within a mile or so of the shore, only to be defeated by wind or current. By this time, the end of June, Hudson Bay was virtually clear of ice. The platform was still perfectly sound, but how much longer it could last was problematical.

Actually, it did not survive much more than 48 hours. On July 2, while being towed towards Churchill harbor it

Towing and lifting the DC-4 after ice melt

suddenly ran into a layer of comparatively warm, fresh water from the Churchill River, and the platform simply melted away, leaving N90407 afloat on its pontoons. Two days later the aircraft was towed and pushed alongside the dock, where cranes hoisted it on to dry land, its first contact with mother earth for practically two months.

Once ashore, N90407 was dismantled and loaded on to a train of five flat cars. From Churchill the train took a month to reach Winnipeg, and a further month had elapsed before it arrived at May County Airport, Wildwood, New Jersey, where the offices and repair and maintenance facilities of

United States Overseas Airlines were situated. Here a detailed inspection showed that the repairs needed were beyond the capabilities of the Wildwood shops, and for a long time the dismembered N90407 lay forlornly in the open while the company debated whether it was worth going to much further expense to have the aircraft made airworthy.

Military contract operations by U.S.O.A.

Finally, it was decided to complete the job, and once again N90407 set off by rail, this time for Brownsville, Texas, and the overhaul base of Pan American World Airways. This journey added another 25 days of railroad time to the leg.

At Brownsville a new center fuselage section, a new starboard wing spar and four new engines were fitted, and the whole airframe was given a complete overhaul, repainted in United States Overseas Airlines' colors and looking as good as new N90407. After having spent two months on an icefloe, clocking over 2,000 railroad hours, and having been off the active roster for two and a half years, the aircraft went back into service again.

The overall cost of this extraordinary salvage operation, including railroad transportation and repairs, exceeded by several thousands of dollars the half million insurance valuation. Ironically, in the two and a half years N90407 was out of service, the value of used DC-4's had fallen from around $650,000 to $700,000 to something much nearer $500,000, so many wags said that it would seem that Lloyd's of London knew what it was doing when it met its obligations back in 1955, and left the salvage to others. Ralph Cox doesn't see it that way.

Chapter Eighteen

JUMP STARTING A DC-3

My Brother and I in Villa Cisneros enroute to Liberia

Chapter Eighteen

With final formal approval of the CAA and CAB for airport qualification of pilots by visual means, all airlines were faced with the problem of obtaining training films for their pilots. The only film available at Pan American was the prototype color film about La Guardia Airport which I had produced. Coincidental to this formal approval, an unusual opportunity presented itself for Pan American to produce the needed airport films at minimal cost.

Color motion pictures of all airports along the east coast of the United States, Canada, Iceland, Ireland, Scotland, England, France, Spain, Portugal, and west coastal Africa down to Roberts Field in Liberia, could be made on a single journey from a DC-3 while it was being ferried to its new owner, Liberian National Airline.

This opportunity came as a result of Liberian President Tubman's offer to Pan American to purchase a DC-3 for his newly formed, government owned airline. The sale agreement was made, and I was approached by Pan American to consider flying the DC-3 to Africa from its base in Brownsville, Texas. Recognizing at once the opportunity for filming, I agreed to ferry the plane, with the provision of my having unlimited rights to utilize the DC-3 enroute for taking motion pictures.

Immediately, I received permission from the Liberian government to use their airplane for the filming; there was a quick confirmation of my request to the Canadian government to take pictures of their airports, and the U.S. Air Force bases, enroute, gladly offered their cooperation. I enlisted my brother Bourdon, and his excellent photographic equipment for the camera work. The Explorers Club agreed to provide the needed film along with an Explorers flag, because the project was considered an exploratory one. Their only request was their choice of the films to be printed at their expense.

Imagine my surprise when I learned that the new chief pilot, Captain Chili Vaughn, had advised our operations manager that I was not interested in flying the plane to Africa. I responded quickly on learning of his statement, and advised him that I would ferry the DC-3 in order to obtain the motion pictures enroute. With Lenny Thorell as first officer, and Frank Donohoe as navigator for the flight, we arrived early at the Brownsville Airport, where the plane was being readied for the ferry to Africa.

Only two days later, we test flew it, and prepared for our departure on the third day. At my motel, I received a telephone call from Captain Vaughn, wherein he advised me that he was denying me the right or the authority to take my brother on the ferry flight, and that I was not to take any motion pictures from the DC-3, because it might jeopardize the delivery of the aircraft to Africa.

I was astounded. With all the various endorsements and agreements obtained, a projected savings of considerable amounts of money for the airline, and the certainty of saving months of time for the filming, why not? I reviewed all these reasons with the new chief pilot, but he advised me that he was issuing a directive to me, and that he was assuming that since I could not take the motion pictures that I would not then ferry the airplane to Africa. I told him his rationale was beyond belief to me, that I was going over his head to discuss the matter with John Shannon, operations manager.

I located John Shannon at his country club playing golf, and indicated to personnel there that my call was of such urgency that he must be called from the links to the telephone. He was so angry at me for disturbing him at his club that he refused to discuss the matter. He reminded me that Chili Vaughn was now the new chief pilot, that the decision was fully within his authority, then he hung up on me.

I flew the ferry to Africa anyway. To offset the disappointment for my brother, who had arranged time off from his work as a scientist at the Bureau of Standards, I bought him a full fare trip on Pan American to London, where I planned to pick him up in the DC-3. Since the Liberians assumed ownership of the plane in London, and I had clearance from them for his coming with me, he was to fly down to Roberts Field with us, and from there I had a ticket for him to return to New York with my first officer and me.

After our arrival with the DC-3 at Robert's Field, we found there was a grand program set up for the inauguration of the new Liberian National Airline, spotlighting the airplane, to be held a short distance away at the James Spriggs Payne Airfield in Monrovia. When we landed at Monrovia, we saw thousands of people at the airfield, a big tent and many soldiers. As we taxied, we could see the hangar. Because there were no paved runways or taxiways, we parked the plane just in front of the area established for the president and his entourage.

The ceremony was delayed due to a sudden torrential rain shower which came without warning, and drove us all into the hangar and tent. President Tubman arrived to great acclaim from those assembled and, when the rain stopped, signalled for the ceremony to begin. In a hushed atmosphere, the postmaster general introduced the president, the captain of the new DC-3 introduced me to President Tubman, and I presented a copy of the aircraft registration to officially transfer the title of the airplane to the Liberian National Airline via President Tubman. The sun shone brightly now, and all of us became aware of the heat as they progressed with an elaborate ceremony, including an officiating bishop and a full choir. At the end of the ceremonies we prepared for the scheduled local inaugural flight. With the suffocating heat, and no air conditioning available for the DC-3 cabin, the president was the last to go on board.

Having turned over the airplane to the new captain, I was happily nestled under the cooler air beneath the awning of the tent. The captain began turning over the right engine to build up pressure before turning on the ignition, finally, he turned on the ignition for that engine. A loud bang resulted, smoke poured out from around the cowling, the engine stopped. It was overloaded with fuel and had stalled.

Knowing it should have been allowed to clear out with the ignition off, and throttle wide open to start the other engine, I felt I should go aboard, and, if possible, lend a hand. As I climbed the stairway at the open doorway, there stood the president. I felt terribly embarrassed, and stopped to explain the situation to him. I chatted with him, hoping at any moment now that the captain would have the other engine started to supply a continuing charge to the plane's battery.

The president was smoking a cigar which rested in a holder, and he held it out past me to tap off accumulated ashes. As he tapped the holder, the cigar fell out, and dropped to the ground into the mud at the doorway. I felt the least I could do was pick up the cigar, and flip it out the doorway of the DC-3. I had it between my fingers to flip when the president reached over, took it from me, replaced it into his holder, and continued to smoke it.

My real concern lay with the battery, which I had noticed was now turning the engine more and more slowly as the captain attempted to start the same engine. Then, the battery went dead. Everyone was asked to exit the aircraft, leaving us to see if we could start the engine. I got a negative

reply when I asked if there were any batteries at the airport, so I asked to be supplied with heavy rope to try to start the other engine propeller by having the men pull the propeller through on the rope.

Using the long heavy rope with a loop on the end of it, for it to slide off after the blade was pulled around, the local men were briefed to run along and pull the prop through. After several such movements, with about ten men pulling the prop, a compression point was reached, and the ignition switch was turned on. I gave the signal for the sweating rope pullers to run extra fast. Bingo! With a loud bang and smoke, the engine started. Now, all went well, I stayed on the ground, the president and his entourage flew off with the new captain for a fine inaugural jaunt. Bourdon, my crew and I made the best of the trip by having a terrific time.

Following my return to New York, I found that the chief pilot had taken no action to start a library of airport films. With the arrival of our new vice-president, Captain Harold Gray, it was not long before Captain Vaughn was called to account for his failure to produce a series of airport qualification films such as those being produced by the other Pan American divisions.

Harold E. Gray

In a short time, I received an incredible request from our new chief pilot, Captain Vaughn. He advised me that his brother, an official with Kodak, was providing Pan American and its DC-3 with elaborate camera equipment and personnel to take motion pictures of Newark Airport. He alluded to the portable camera mount which I had designed to hold the 16mm camera out of the window of the aircraft to shoot motion pictures for my film of La Guardia Airport, and asked if he might use the mount I had built. But that wasn't enough. He needed my instructions on how to mount it properly.

I felt I had no choice. In order for the airline to utilize this necessary process as quickly as possible, I must assist. While I could have ignored his request, my loyalty to Pan American, and my need to complete the process necessitated my helping with the project. After a very formal beginning with the personnel from Kodak, I began asking questions. Did they have any aviation experience? Had one of them taken motion pictures from an airplane? Could they write the script to accompany the film? The answers were all no. I knew what was coming. Captain Vaughn asked, "Since you are here, would you mind flying the DC-3 for them to use in taking the motion pictures? After a moment, I said I would. "Can you direct the filming?" I answered, "Okay." I then agreed to write the script, and do the voice production.

The Liberian Crew takes
over their modified DC-3

Chapter Nineteen

FLYING THE JET STREAM

CHARLES LINDBERGH

Chapter Nineteen

Brigadier General Charles A. Lindbergh served as a member of the board of directors, and functioned as an operational consultant to Pan American Airways. Among many other achievements and activities, he established a committee to review and make recommendations to the board regarding the types of airline transport the airline should consider purchasing.

Charles Lindbergh

General Lindbergh made frequent flights with Pan American throughout the world. Traveling incognito, not advising the crew of his presence, and frequently flying in the tourist section, he observed a host of activity and operations without interference from fawning or curious crew members and passengers. When the captain was advised he was aboard, he was invited to the cockpit, offering an opportunity for both him and staff to discuss flight characteristics, reliability, comfort for passengers, and other essential information to establish a means of comparing Douglas, Boeing, and Lockheed aircraft.

General Lindbergh was also instrumental in establishing the capacity of the P-38 to sustain long range flying capability. He personally made many experimental flights in active war zones. The long range P-38 served in every theater in a variety of capacities against the Japanese and was credited with shooting down more Japanese aircraft than any other type

In Paris, the general met with me to speak of his concern about an extensive advertising campaign being pursued by our prime competitor, Trans World Airlines, with their advertising claim that "TWA Flies the Jet Stream". I had seen this advertising claim, and shared the general's concern that it was misleading with its suggestion that only TWA knew how to take advantage of flying in the strong west to east jet stream winds to reduce flight time over the Atlantic.

Of course, all airlines had the same capability of selecting the most favorable west-east route to assure that at least a portion of the flight was aided by a jet stream of up to 150 miles per hour. It was the function of the weather bureau's information services to determine the 'least time' track to fly. It was the captain's duty to submit a flight plan request for his planned route to be in line with the jet stream, if possible.

However, once their selected flight plan was approved, it was a commitment, and the flight plan must be carefully adhered to by the flight crew. It was possible to alter the flight plan routing to stay in the jet stream, but it required considerable coordination between the ocean air traffic controllers on both sides of the Atlantic.

Such a complete analysis of all traffic involved had to be reviewed to avoid any conflict in traffic movements. I shared with General Lindbergh my own plan to utilize more effectively the forecast of jet stream winds which, at best, might be six hours old. My research had convinced me that there was one prime factor of identifying characteristics which might make it possible for an aircraft to prolong its stay in the jet stream. That characteristic was temperature. When a jet stream was encountered enroute, and its wind velocity reported, temperature was always reported. The same jet stream reported from various positions along its path had the same temperature.

The general shared my enthusiasm, and with his encouragement, plans were swiftly put into motion to establish an experimental ocean crossing flight from New York to Paris to prove the hypothesis: that an aircraft utilizing a super sensitive outside air temperature instrument, with the capacity to measure the ambient air temperature to within one tenth of one degree, could enable a flight to remain in the jet stream.

We realized that the jet stream over the North Atlantic would be narrow, that its path would wander about high and low pressure areas as it made its way eastward. Ocean crossing flight traffic usually followed "least time" tracks which seldom ventured too far away from the great circle or "least distance" flight tracks. Some aircraft, flying away from the shortest distance route, trying to fly in a jet stream far off the direct course, would often be required to spend more time and fuel in reaching their destination.

Once a jet stream was encountered, and its direction and speed was favorable to the desired flight plan, the temperature of the air would be the key to the plane's remaining in it. The air temperature could be measured, and every effort made to maintain this exact temperature by keeping the airplane in that same air temperature which identified the jet stream. If the outside air temperature began to rise, the flight would be going toward the south of the jet stream, if it reduced, the airplane would be going north of the stream.

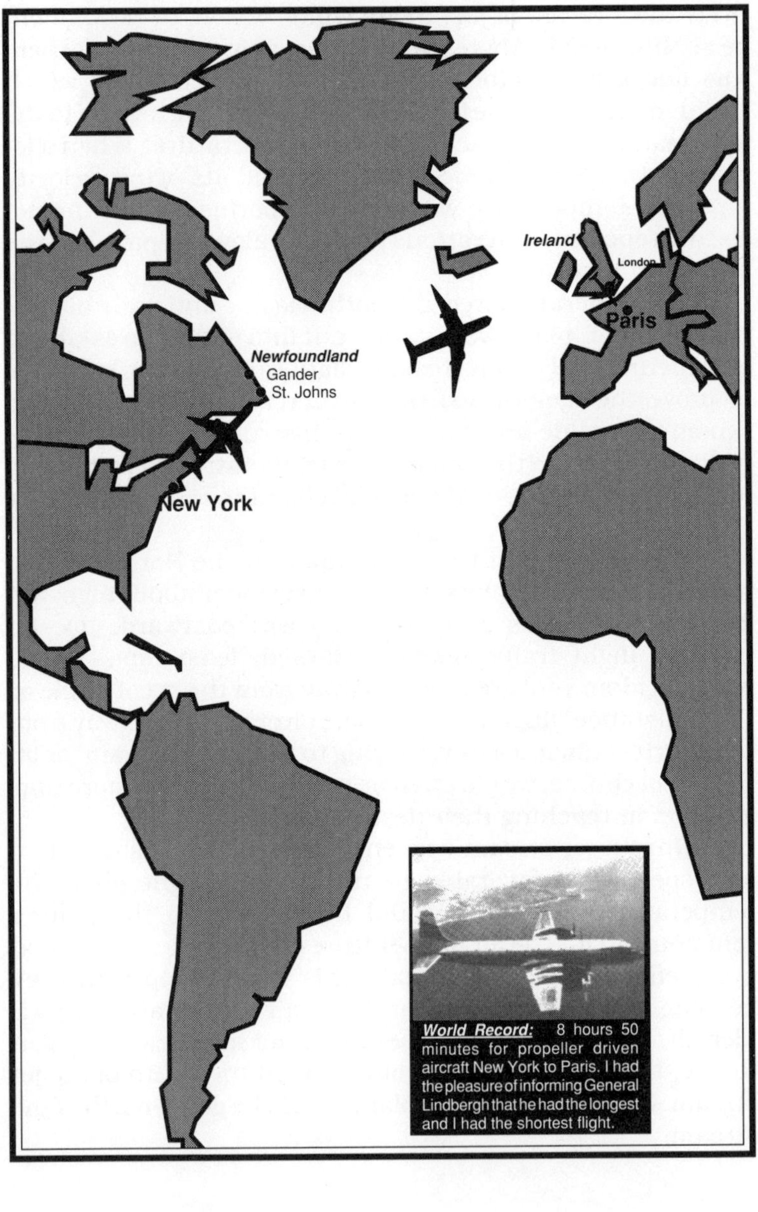

World Record: 8 hours 50 minutes for propeller driven aircraft New York to Paris. I had the pleasure of informing General Lindbergh that he had the longest and I had the shortest flight.

By keeping the flight in the air temperature identified as being that of the high tail wind jet stream, the ground speed could be outstanding, but there was the problem of changing headings and tracks which would intersect the flight path of other aircraft. Actually, a captain would then be zig-zagging across the Atlantic, contrary to the initially approved flight plan route.

For our proposed experimental flight we had a super sensitive outside air temperature instrument gauge in readiness for swift installation in a DC-7 aircraft. We were ready for the non stop New York to Paris flight, waiting for a favorable jet stream forecast. Extensive coordination was arranged with the U.S., Canadian, over ocean, and European air traffic controllers. Alertness was necessary for the flight crew to handle constant navigation heading changes, changes of estimated next position points, arrival times, ground speed, and variable routes.

On January 30, 1957, word came from a dispatcher friend, Bill Prudden, that, "Tonight's your big night for the Paris flight." The jet stream was forecast very high with winds up to 150 miles per hour, prevailing south of all normal 'least distance' tracks both east and westbound, giving us freedom to change course as we chased the jet stream.

In accordance with our pilot's agreement, I exchanged a later flight for which I was slated, in order to fly the experimental flight. The sensitive air temperature instrument was quickly installed, and off we went to break the world's record for a non stop flight from New York to Paris. I had a long briefing with my crew, including a separate session with the flight services staff so that they could give informed answers to the questions of the passengers. I informed the passengers of the process and purpose of the special research we would be handling in the flight time for their journey, reminding them that we would be following the jet stream, no matter what its path.

Prior to departure, we received word that the majority of

Although the DC-7's was technically sophisticated for its time, the aircraft had a relatively short service life. With their pressurized cabins, four 18 cylinders, and geared turbo-super charged engines, they were in high demand for non-stop USA coast-to-coast passenger and, in the particular case of the DC-7C, the Transatalntic market as well.

The turbo-super charged engines turned out to be a major shortcoming. Failures from the utilization of high blowers for high altitude reduced the aircraft to DC-6 performance and resulting in DC-7s having to fly at low altitudes.

Despite these limitations, however, I elected to utilize the DC-7C on my record breaking flight from New York to Paris in the jet stream (with my fingers crossed). Fortunately, we had no "high blower" problems.

The DC-7's transcontinental speed advantage disappeared with the entry of jets. Some were converted to freighters, but even those retired relatively quickly because of the higher operating costs in comparison to similarly converted DC-6s. Of the 338 DC-7s built between 1953 and 1958, over half had been retired from scheduled airline service by 1963.

all ocean flights, east and west, were flight planned over the 'least distance', or great circle routes, between New York and Europe, overheading Ireland. This gave us flexibility in our anticipated necessary route changes to be able to stay with the jet stream. All air traffic controllers were put on alert to aid us.

After takeoff from La Guardia, with an almost direct flight toward St. Johns, Newfoundland, we found ourselves, at times, making ground speed of over 150 miles per hour above our true air speed. We made note of the outside indicated air temperature, recorded it, and began the game of keeping with that same temperature.

Over the Atlantic, on a southeast track over which the jet stream was forecast to flow, the navigator projected our flight path to be traveled in the next half hour, and we transmitted the information to the ocean air traffic control. Based on the ground speed we were making, due to the great push of the jet stream, the air traffic controllers on duty were given the latitude and longitude of the next position. The next position would not only be our position, it would also be the center line of movement of the high speed jet stream.

The Canadian controllers received our position reports, including direction and velocity of the wind. Of course, there was no drift, because we were in the stream, flying with it. This message was relayed to Ireland, England and France. We were kept quite busy concentrating upon maintenance of the same outside air temperature, altering our headings carefully, keeping a close watch on our progress, and re-positioning ourselves when we changed our flight path. Ordinarily, such changes would put overseas air control into a fit, not on this flight.

We kept in contact with Gander, then Shannon, as we made our way across the Atlantic in the jet stream, studying our weather map of the forecast jet stream, and making corrections on it. We found determining our projection of the stream path ahead of us to be very effective in reducing the number of heading changes required to remain in it. Approaching Ireland, we discussed our progress with the Shannon controllers, who, by land phone, made contact with London control center for clearance for us to fly off airways to remain in the jet stream as it made its way toward France.

On approach to the coastline of France, Paris radar control picked us up, giving us clearance to descend at our discretion, and land straight in at Orly Airport without circling or being radar vectored into line with the other airlines to land in normal sequence. Our landing time, officially recorded by the tower at Orly, revealed we had broken all records of flight time for that route. The time was 8 hours and 50 minutes from takeoff to landing, and was, incidentally my 339th crossing of the Atlantic. This record time for propeller driven airplanes remains unbroken, though the later jet transports changed forever the way we look at flight time records.

Our conventional airliner's establishment of a world record reveals some interesting facts. It broke the previous record by 28 minutes, was approximately the 60,863 trip flown between New York and Paris, and was a distance flown of 3,294 nautical miles at an altitude of 24,000 feet. The average ground speed was 370 knots, average tail wind component 75 knots, and the strongest wind encountered was 150 knots. Fuel on board at takeoff was 36,000 pounds, the burn off was 29,000 pounds. It was an absolutely terrific experience, with the 39 passengers sharing and enjoying every minute of it.

Chapter Twenty

MASTERING THE DUTCH ROLL

THE WASHINGTON POST OCTOBER 26, 1958

Pan Am puts first 707 on Atlantic Route

Pan American World Airlines began regular transatlantic jet airliner service today when a Boeing 707 flew from New York International Airport to Paris. Pan American will also start jet service to Rome in two days, in what is regarded as the beginning of mass travel by jet liner. Pan Am is the second airline to open regular transatlantic jet service. British Overseas Airways began New York-to-London service on October 4, the day after noise rules that had prevented use of jet aircraft at New York airports were changed. The jet flight takes seven hours, about a third less than the fastest propeller plane (DC-7C) flown by Captain Kim Scribner from New York to Paris on January 30, 1957.

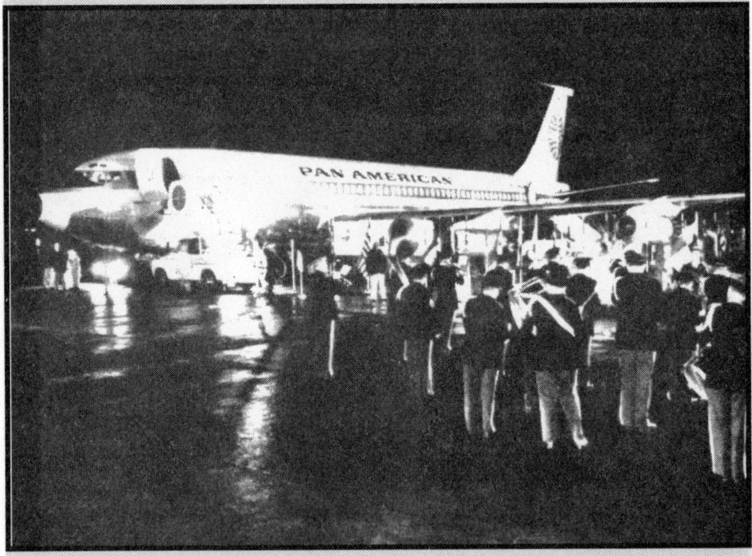

An upbeat marching band sends the 707 off on its inaugural N.Y. - Paris flight.

Chapter Twenty

When Pan American received its first Boeing 707 aircraft, there was no Air Line Pilots Association contract established for pilot pay to fly this wonderful new bird. The result was that all administrative pilots, check pilots, senior check pilots, assistant chief pilots, sector, and division chief pilots were directed to fly the B-707. Those non-management pilots who were A.L.P.A. members had to await a contract and clearance to fly the new jet transports.

To be fair to the administrative pilots, what choice did they have? They had worked very hard to be established in their positions. The difference in pay to them, between their high salaries, and that to be expected when the pilots' contract set jet pay provisions, was incidental compared to their being first to fly the jet transport. They justified their flying the new jets by introducing the world into the jet age while their subordinate cohorts were refusing to fly jets without contract provisions. Meanwhile, Pan American could realize the significant advantage of being the first airline to fly the jet transport.

While the pilots' negotiations droned on, the initial

flying of the Boeing 707-100 series was continuing. Eventually, a jet flying contract was established to govern flying pay and working conditions, and all the eligible pilots joined the training program to fly the new jet aircraft.

The new jets had the capacity to fly non stop from New York to Europe, though on some return flights, against the prevailing head winds, the operation became marginal. The consumption of fuel was very difficult to monitor enroute, because the only way fuel was determined to have been consumed was by averaging the rate of consumption per engine, computing the total hourly rate of consumption, adding it to the amount already determined to have been consumed, and then subtracting that total from the amount of fuel put on the airplane prior to its departure.

There were no fuel gauges to indicate fuel remaining on the jet, no way to measure how much fuel was burned during the taxi, no way to know how much burned while waiting for takeoff clearance, or how much was used in the climb to cruising altitude. With all operating crew members attempting to compute fuel burned, none could agree, making holding times at airports a critical and stressful matter.

Another disconcerting factor was an unstable flight characteristic known as the 'Dutch Roll'. In flight, at its normal cruising altitude, in quiet air, the airplane had an almost constant left-right movement, even with the auto pilot engaged. In some cases the slight roll of the wings became so definite that the pilot would be compelled to disengage the automatic pilot, and attempt to reduce the roll by manually flying the airplane, applying various cross flight control pressures, and changing speeds. Many months passed before vortex generators, or deflectors, were applied to various surfaces on the Boeing to reduce the roll.

During the flight training periods, the instructor would introduce a 'Dutch Roll', and turn over the controls to the trainee, who was to apply specific control movements properly. If he did not apply the correct control movements, the

Delivery in 1958 of the first Boeing 707 Clippers gave Pan Am the country's first commercial jet transports...as well as a big jump on the Jet Age.

Almost overnight, a large number of longstanding performance records were shattered. For instance, cruising speed shot up to 575m.p.h. operating altitude to somewhere between 25,000 and 35,000 feet. Range to over 5000 miles. Passenger capacity to over 140.

One of the innovations introduced on the 707-121 (the first jet Clipper of the Pan Am fleet of 44 turbine powered transports) was two main entrance and exit doors for rapid loading and unloading of passengers.

Introduced in 1959, the Boeing 707-321 had non-stop capability between New York (or Washington) and any Western European capital.

Fitted with fan engines, the Boeing 707-321B was introduced in 1962 and could fly non-stop from California to Europe. While measuring the same length as the 321, the 321B had a wing span of 145 feet, 9 inches. The vertical stabilizer stood 42 feeet, 5.5 inches from the ground. The aircraft had a fuel capacity of 23, 812 gallons.

roll could be exaggerated. On one training flight conducted by a chief pilot during a night layover period in England, the check pilot put the 707 into a very positive 'Dutch Roll', then turned it over to the trainee captain, who, without hesitation, applied strong aileron and rudder action in the wrong direction. The result was that an outboard engine was thrown off the airplane, landing somewhere in the country side.

When the 707 simulator became available, this difficulty was reduced by the introduction of the roll in training to develop proper recovery technique. In time, alterations were made to the wing root flair cowling which gave the B-707 normal straight forward flight characteristics.

Following the resolution of the pilot's contract for the jet flights, I had the wonderful experience of checking out in the new aircraft. I had started ground school training in August of 1959, and between my Douglas DC-7 flights to Europe, I attended jet ground school. I flew in November as an observer on the 707 from New York to Paris and return, then deadheaded to Miami for flight training. Six days later, I had my first forty minute training flight with our renowned Dutch Redfield as my instructor. There were no jets in Miami following that first flight, so I came back to New York to get my training.

It was not until the second week of December that I was given my second training flight, a twenty minute session, making a total of one hour of flight training. Since the scheduling of free jet time in New York was so cramped, I was sent out to San Francisco to get my third flight training period of one hour. By December, I had six hours and 55 minutes flight training in 30 days. Along with my fellow captains, I devoted my time in concentrated study of all of the B-707 systems, and on January 5, 1960, I received my Boeing 707-100/200/300 series rating.

As the first airline to fly the Boeing 707 jet transport, Pan American was exposed to proving the capability of the jet

1958...Juan T. Trippe joins Mrs. Dwight D. eisonhower as she christens the jet Clipper America to open the Jet Age for commercial transportation.

The 'Jet Age' came to the airlines with the order and purchase by Pan American of a series of Boeing 707s. The first one was delivered on August, 1958. The same captains who had flown all or most of the airplanes shown up to this point were faced with not just another type of airplane, but an entirely new concept of flying, which raised a number of concerns and questions.

The dispatch, flight planning and selection of alternates, plus the fuel to be carried, meant that a lot of preplanning had to be undertaken. Before the 707s were delivered, basic knowledge of its performance was known. The knowledge of these factors allowed us to make "papermate" or theoretical flights between New York and London. Actual wires were sent to London dispatch center and the theoretical flight was plotted and observed as it supposedly made its way over the ocean. In this manner, experience was gained on these make believe flights to the point where enough background of "jet operation" was on hand to handle the real jet flights without trouble.

The first series of Boeing 707s were limited with respect to their fuel range or capacity to endure long flights. The later series of 707s were equipped with 'fan engines' which increased the range of operation by about twenty percent. This new type fan jet enabled the flight to save on fuel, and brought the cost of flying the airplane down considerably. This positive circle of events brought the jet age to everyone. With this continued improvement in the safety of flying and the reduction of flying costs, the airline business looked forward to greater developments and improvements than was ever thought possible in the past.

The Douglas DC-8 followed the Boeing 707 on Feb. 1960 and has taken a comparable place in the jet age. It has, generally speaking, the same operational capabilities as the 707. The engines were the same and the overall appearance, dimensions and passenger accommodations are similar to the point that only technical differences in systems such as hydraulic, electrical, reversing, etc., exist. The DC-8 has proven itself to be a great contributor through its performance and safety record.

transport day after day. Initially, the four Pratt and Whitney jet engines were operationally marginal in the areas of power thrust for takeoff, and their management of flight over the ocean in great distances. Many factors were to be considered by a captain in establishing plans to fly these airplanes on a flight of any appreciable distance. Fuel required, runway conditions, wind direction and velocity, barometric pressure, temperature, and visibility, all or singularly, could limit the critical bottom line of allowable gross weight for takeoff.

Temperature accountability is the most significant

variable factor which affects the thrust or power delivered by the jet engine. It is so critical that the hot ground temperature at airports in latitudes such as New Delhi resulted in the scheduling of takeoffs to be made only at night to avoid the temperatures created by the sun in daylight.

In 1960, I flew 833 hours on the Boeing 707. The various European flights, some to Bangkok, involved some interesting experiences, all of them routine until April Fool's Day. On that day, on a flight from New York to Bangkok, I encountered a strange weather situation as we were approaching to land in Istanbul. Approaching to land, in a storm with strong winds and heavy rain, I turned on the windshield wipers on both the windows. Just as we were reaching our final altitude, I looked ahead and down for the approach lights which I had requested turned up to bright, due to the heavy rain. The windows turned red with mud, I could see nothing but red mud. I leveled the plane at our minimum altitude and continued. Out of our side windows we looked down at the airport, its runways and buildings, we could see out the sides, but not out the front windows where it was raining red mud.

I had no recourse, but to apply power to all engines, and climb into our missed approach pattern, up into the storm. We were granted clearance to our alternate airport in Ankara. The strong winds had picked up dust and carried it below the heavy clouds where thermal movements of the rising air took the dust up into the rain clouds, where water particulant matter formed drops of muddy water. This, in turn covered our windshields. As we climbed higher in the rain, the water was clean, washing our windshields for us. However, we could not return to the tower, because red muddy rain continued for Istanbul.

A few months later, on a flight to Paris from New York enroute to Rome, on which my brother's science associate was a passenger, I came aboard the airplane to find the cockpit full of maintenance men who had my instrument panel disassembled, and were in process of changing parts. In the long wait for other necessary replacement parts to arrive, passengers began to board. While the instrument panel was being properly fastened into place, my first officer and I stood behind our seats, eager to get started. I motioned for our check list to be read in order that we might save time, avoiding a departure delay.

As the copilot read off the pre-start check list, I placed various switches into their proper position. As he read: no smoking, seat belts, etc., I responded, "ON" and leaned forward to place the switches into their down position. However, placed next to those switches was a switch marked 'EMERGENCY'. From my standing position, it was not easy to read the words on the switches, and I placed the switch down, since that was the normal position of all the switches next to it.

In that single movement of the emergency switch, I caused the oxygen masks above every seat to drop out of their enclosed position to dangle up and down just in front of each passenger. Luckily, no oxygen was released through the masks, they were of the demand type, releasing oxygen only if the passenger wearing it drew in oxygen as he breathed. As soon as I put that switch down and leaned forward, I could see my mistake. I yanked the switch back. Too late! All the masks were down. We have since enclosed this switch.

To replace all of those masks required experience, so all passengers had to be out of their seats for this operation, going back into the terminal to wait until all of the masks had been properly replaced. As the one responsible for the mistake, I had no choice, but to tell the passengers the truth. When informed later, my brother Bourdon enjoyed my goof tremendously. The passengers were a bit more compassionate, and had only minor fun at my expense.

On another unusual B-707 flight, with Princess Grace of Monaco aboard, a fire warning bell and flashing red lights indicated a fire in number three engine. I was making a takeoff, following a stop in Prestwick, Scotland, on the way to New York, and had not reached the critical speed during the takeoff. I reduced the power on all engines, and pulled the air brake control to raise the spoilers on each wing as I reversed all four engines.

We had no problem bringing the airplane to a stop as we went through the process of preparing to fight the engine fire. Then, the fire warning light went out, indicating a false alarm. All engines were normal, no smoke. We still shut the engine, and taxied back to the terminal. I explained the problem to the passengers, maintenance checked us out thoroughly, and in an hour we were advised that a faulty micro switch was to blame.

We took off, flew direct to New York and broke the world's existing jet flying record for that route, making the flight in 4 hours, 43 minutes, 15 minutes faster that the previous record. We just happened to be able to fly around some low pressure areas, and picked up tail winds, instead of the usual head winds. Princess Grace was her usual poised, serene, enchanting self amid the changes, giving our crew highest compliments.

With the advent of the jet clippers, the world was shrunk by nearly half. New York City became closer to Nassau than by train to Albany, Boston closer to Paris than by train to Philadelphia. There came an increased emphasis on air cargo as shippers took advantage of the nearly five ton cargo capacity then available in each passenger jet.

A most pleasant passenger of mine was the enchanting Princess Grace

Pan American introduced the first jet freighters in 1963. Prior to 1958, the airline was carrying less than 100 million ton miles of cargo

With the advent of the jet age, worldwide travel became a reality

per year. In 1961, for the fourth consecutive year, Pan American was still the only carrier to top the 100 million ton mile figure, and by 1967 it had surpassed 600 million ton miles.

With the continued growth of air freight, the airline constructed an eight million dollar fully automated cargo terminal in New York which housed the most advanced freight handling system ever designed. To develop volume air freight, Pan American introduced World Wide Marketing Service, the first international marketing advisory service established by an airline.

Behind the development of Pan American was the philosophy that providing an overseas trip for the average person at an affordable price was a worthy goal. Our airline was in the forefront of commercial airline industry efforts to reduce passenger fares and cargo rates, so that more and more businesses, industries and tourists utilized Pan Americans services.

With my crew on first P.A.A. Boeing 707 New York to Johannesburg (Accra, Ghana...Oct. 2, 1968)

Chapter Twenty One

SKIDDING OFF THE RUNWAY

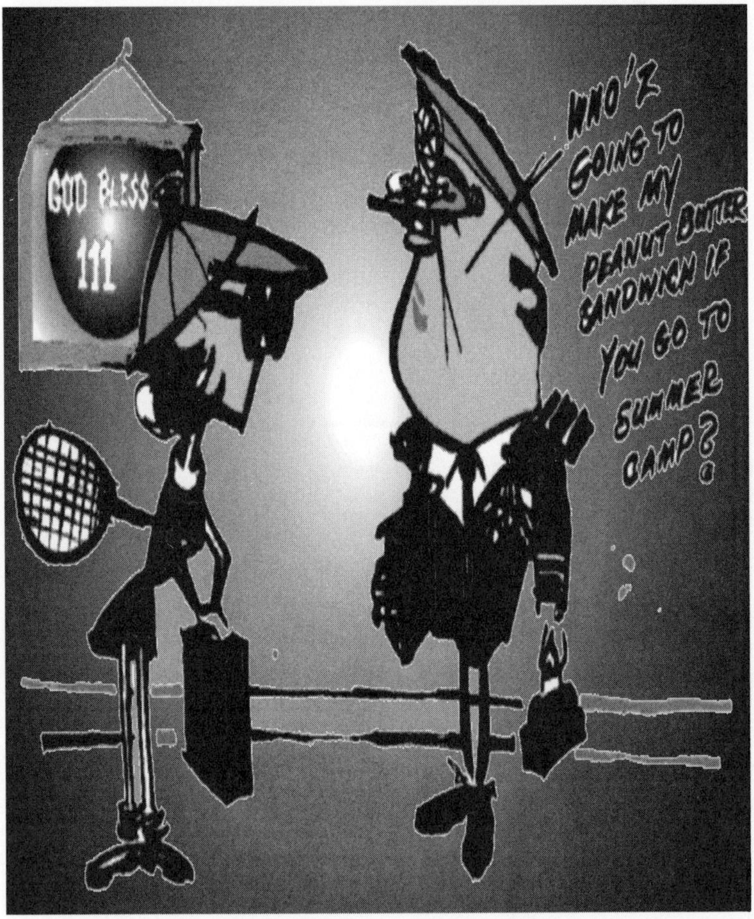
GOD BLESS
111
WHO'Z GOING TO MAKE MY PEANUT BUTTER SANDWICH IF YOU GO TO SUMMER CAMP?

Chapter Twenty-One

On a routine round the world flight in May 1961, I landed at Munich Airport for refueling to continue eastbound for our next stop at Istanbul. In the refueling process, an error was made by the ground maintenance crew who loaded 10,000 pounds excess fuel over that required.

This was no great problem, the airplane was not exceeding the takeoff allowable gross weight, or its maximum allowable landing weight. The problem was that the excess fuel was loaded into the aft tanks on the airplane, affecting the center of gravity of the B-707. On learning of the overload, we checked this item very carefully, and found that the center of gravity was just within the allowable limits for us to preset the horizontal stabilizer in the cockpit. We set the control exactly according the regulations, proceeded with our check lists, and started up the engines.

After receiving clearance, I taxied into position, applied takeoff power, and we started to roll down the runway. At an indicated 90 knots, I released my left hand on the nose wheel control, and placed it on the yoke being held forward by the first officer, Lon Steiner. My right hand held all four throttles in their adjusted forward takeoff position.

After reaching 100 knots, a loud warning horn sounded, serving as a signal to the pilot to abort the takeoff, provided that he has not reached the critical, pre-determined V-1 speed (when takeoff must be continued on three out of four engines, because the plane is moving too fast to be stopped on the runway). With our V-1 speed beyond 120 knots, I knew that I must abort the takeoff.

I closed all four throttles fully back against their stops, and brought back the speed brake control to stop the air lift on the wings, putting about 80% of the airplane's weight on its eighteen wheels. I put all four engines into reverse, but only the number one engine light indicator showed the reverse position, the other three remained in forward position.

I was not too concerned, the runway was long, and I had experienced engines being slow as they went into reverse. On all of those occasions they eventually went into reverse. Usually, an engine balks going into reverse because its throttle is not fully closed.

The first officer, flight engineer, and I kept pulling back on those throttles, not wanting to apply power on the reversed left number one outboard engine, because it would turn the 707 to the left off the runway. I applied all brakes, but the anti-skid function on the brakes kept releasing them to prevent skidding the tires on the wet runway. I placed my hand back on the nose steering wheel, but since we had been loaded tail heavy by the extra fuel, the nose wheel had no traction on the runway, and it slid along depriving me of directional control.

The number one engine, in idle reverse, turned the plane to the left, and when we departed the runway at a slight angle onto the open grass I knew we could stop. Not so! As soon as the left main landing gear wheels encountered the soft grass and earth, the left turn was accentuated, moving us off the runway out of control.

As I applied power to number one engine we began to slow down. In turning farther to the left, number two and three engines reversed. We began slowly to sink into the ground, encountered a hedge, and came to a very smooth gradual stop on the belly of the 707. The passengers were in no panic, they thought we had returned to the terminal.

The normal procedure to be followed in this circumstance is to evacuate all passengers and crew, in case the brakes overheat, and fire might result. Following this emergency procedure, I carefully advised all passengers that we must all exit from the airplane, and told them to avoid rushing as they all slid down the forward left door emergency chute. I then advised the flight service people to open the front left door, and evacuate all passengers via the extended slide.

The cabin door was opened, whereupon the slide fell out onto the ground like a wash cloth. It did not inflate, it was just hanging there. I immediately instructed the purser to open the front right side galley door to use the slide attached there. The door opened but the emergency slide fittings which had been attached to the floor fittings did not fit. They were smashed together.

At this point, I just held up my hand and quietly told the passengers to be seated, to wait for the trucks, buses, and stairway I had ordered to transport them to the terminal. As the passengers gathered up their belongings, the first officer

We defueled the right wing to taxi the plane over the planks

and I read the after landing check list, then the final check list. I then requested the first officer to take his camera and lower himself to the ground to take pictures showing the path of the 707 as it left the runway, ingested and digested the hedge on which we were nested.

With passengers and crew safely at the terminal, I wired Pan American Airways in New York to explain the incident. The big problem remained, how to get that 707 back onto the runway? The United States Army came to the rescue, using two huge tanks from the nearby Army base. They hooked chains to the main gear, laid planks out in the tracks made by the plane as it sank to its belly, and backed up pulling the plane from its sunken position.

After washing the airplane down, the maintenance crew found no damage had been inflicted. They changed number three engine which had digested the hedge, and all was OK. With the 707 out away from the buildings, they ran up the engines and put them all into reverse as I had attempted to do on takeoff. All four engines moved their respective cowling, and the four reversing systems worked perfectly on all engines.

They telephoned me at my hotel early the next morning to advise me that there was nothing wrong with the reversing of all the engines. I expected just such a report and asked to speak with the maintenance chief. In his report on the aircraft, he also advised me that they had found tapes over the air inlet valves on both ends of the evacuation chute which had prevented the chute from inflating. I requested him to take the aircraft out far away from the terminal, run the engines up to takeoff power, leave the power on for twenty seconds, close the throttles, pull back the speed brake, reverse all engines, and then phone a report to me.

After the test, he reported that when all the engines had been put through the test none of the engines reversed, including the new engine which had been installed during the night. This revealed that after takeoff power had been applied for twenty seconds, followed by the reversing of the engines, there was not sufficient time for the equalizing of temperature in the metal joint linkage of the cowling fittings. All those joints near the hot engines had expanded, and the operating links in the actuating series of metal parts were cold. This difference in expansion between the metal parts had caused the joints to tighten up and lock, preventing their proper movement.

All we had to do, following an aborted takeoff, was to open up the clearances in the cowling reverse to allow for this difference of metal temperatures, and the cowling would reverse as it does following a normal landing. This further clarified why, on some landings, engines would be slower than others going into reverse.

A three engine landing is no problem, especially in a jet transport. However, to encounter a series of conditions, any of which could be considered extreme enough to create an emergency situation, is most unusual. On just such an occasion in July of that year, I flew a Boeing 707 military charter flight from McGuire Air Force Base in New Jersey to Frankfurt. The weather was forecast operational, but minimal, for our arrival. The alternate airport at Munich was the same. Enroute, we kept an eye on the weather at London, Paris, and other airports in Germany.

Upon our overheading London, we were advised that the

Frankfurt airport was closed by a frontal passage which involved heavy rains, strong cross winds, and a low ceiling, but was forecast to open soon after our arrival. We continued, reduced our speed, and remained high to conserve fuel. When we reached Frankfurt, the airport was still closed. In front of us was a Lufthansa jet in the holding pattern at 10,000 feet waiting to land as soon as minimum required weather was reported.

Our aircraft was established 1,000 feet above the Lufthansa jet, in line to land. After about twenty minutes holding, the main control tower reported landing visibility and ceiling were sufficient, and cleared the Lufthansa jet to descend for an instrument approach landing. They then reported the glide path function of the instrument landing system was inoperative, directing that an approach to runway 27 left was available without the glide path.

That frontal system was moving faster into Germany than had been anticipated by the meteorologists. Approach control was reporting strong cross winds on the east-west runway. As the first officer monitored other airports within an hour's flight time, he kept shaking his head as he called out the airports, indicating they were below minimum to land. I pulled back the throttles to reduce power and speed to descend. The number four engine throttle would not move back, it remained available to move forward, but would not come back more than halfway. We shut down this engine, knowing there was a fuel control malfunction.

To add to this the Lufthansa pilot reported that, though the glide slope was still out, he was going to make an approach aided by radar control. I had no choice other than to follow him. The rain was heavy, the turbulence very high, and on our final approach we were holding an average of around 20 degrees drift to hold us on the localizer beam to take us right down to runway 25R.

Next we heard a report given by Lufthansa over the outer marker, and the tower gave clearance to land. We continued our approach. Then came the next report, Lufthansa had missed its approach. The tower gave him a vector heading to fly away from the airport and assigned an altitude to hold. When I asked the Lufthansa captain why he had missed the approach, he replied, "Too heavy cross winds and rain."

My first officer and I knew that our only option was to land. I briefed him and the flight engineer to look out the left window for the runway, not ahead of us. Since I was holding that extreme drift angle of twenty degrees, I could not take off that drift angle when the runway was sighted, but had to hold it all the way down to the runway, taking it off as the airplane touched down.

Though our plan was to reverse all three remaining engines after landing, I did not want to reverse the number one engine, because it would tend to turn the airplane into the wind. On a very wet runway we did not need that. I requested the tower to turn up the runway lights to their maximum brightness. From the outer marker, with gear down and flaps extended, we began a normal 300 feet per minute rate of descent. Radio reception was very poor, yet we all spotted the runway at the same time in the heavy rain.

As I raised the nose to flair the plane and land, I moved the left rudder pedal in to straighten the plane to avoid landing sideways. If I took the drift angle out too soon, we would drift away from our line of direction toward the down wind side of the runway. We touched down in a solid manner, and stayed down, no bounce. With only the inboards in reverse on the long runway, we came to a stop in a hurry with no problems.

This flight represented a typical situation of making a long seven and one half hour flight into European areas where weather was marginal. The natural conservative instinct of the crew calls for extra stored fuel to be put on the plane. However, if every flight carried extra fuel back and forth across the ocean when the weather was forecast to be marginal, the cost burden would be prohibitive. The only sensible way to operate long distance flying, with reference to fuel to be carried, is to have safety of flight be the primary consideration. Minimum fuel requirements have been established so that, with proper and careful weather observations being monitored during a flight, deviations to flight plans can be made to utilize alternates, or landing for additional fuel.

At Pan American we had few incidents which reflected poor judgment on the part of captains. One pilot over flew clear conditions in Shannon, Ireland, and landed in London almost out of fuel and in bad weather, resulting in his being demoted to fly as first officer for a period of time, followed by his being rechecked on the route.

In the case of our landing in Frankfurt and not in London, we were induced to continue our flight due to weather forecasts which trapped us. Needless to say, extra fuel could always have been found on just about any flight. The flight engineer always had a little extra on board for any reason he might dream, but it did not show on the work sheets which determined the maximum allowable gross weight to be carried on that flight. This was especially true on the initial Boeing 707-100 series which did not have an accurate method of measuring fuel on board.

Even with all the crew figuring usage of fuel throughout the flight, we never had the same final fuel remaining figures. There was a real difficulty of measuring fuel remaining in the many fuel tanks due to the different pitch angle that varied with every mode of flight. Even while parked, the angle of the airplane has to be carefully measured against leveling devices for both the fuselage and wings. This was eventually corrected with the installation of 'fuel remaining' totalizers for the jet aircraft.

Chapter Twenty Two

LIFE IN THE JET AGE

Boeing 727

In 1959, Boeing decided to enter the short/medium range jet airliner field with the three-engined 727. The aircraft featured a rear-engine layout with a T-tail, one engine being placed in the rear of the fuselage and the other two on pylons beside it, leaving a completely free, uncluttered wing. The first 727 flew in February 1963 and it has subsequently proved most successful, being developed into cargo and cargo/passenger versions, some models with a longer fuselage. Cruising at 596 mph, the basic 727-100 had a range of 3,430 miles with a 25,000 pay load and a service ceiling of 36,000 ft.

The 727-100 introduced in 1965 had a considerably longer fuselage seating up to 189 passengers.

727 Cockpit

Chapter Twenty-Two

Extremities in weather conditions, technical difficulties, and the growing pains of technological advancements of the airline industry were, by no means, the only adventures I experienced. The real drama of flying was always provided by the unusual people, places, delays, and occurrences.

A stowaway on a B-707 is an unusual happening, especially one in a wheel well where the landing gear retracts. On an occasion in 1961, a young man climbed up into the inboard left wheel well of a 707 I was flying from Amsterdam to London. The flight time of only 45 minutes, with an air time of about 20 minutes for this route, aided his journey, but how he could place himself in the wheel well without being crushed by the retraction of the big four wheel gear remains a mystery. Following our landing in London, he was spotted by the ground crew waiting to service the aircraft. Though quite shaken and cold, he was uninjured.

As novels and movies suggest, we were not immune to the world of international intrigue. In September 1961, Dr. Robert A. Soblen, a convicted Soviet spy was to be deported from London to New York, traveling on my flight. During

June that year, Dr. Soblen, a Lithuanian born psychiatrist, had been convicted of espionage, jumped bail in New York, and fled to Israel using the passport of his dead brother. When the Israelis discovered his presence they expelled him, ordering his return to the United States. On the return flight from Israel, he used a steak knife he confiscated on the plane to slash himself, and was landed in London for treatment.

At the request of the British Home Office, he was to be accompanied on our flight to New York by our Pan American physician, Dr. D. J. Curren, and two U.S. marshals to prevent his making further attempts at suicide. He was to be put on as a first class passenger, not screened from the rest of the passengers, and served, in addition to his breakfast, an order of commitment to begin serving the life sentence handed down by Judge William B. Herlande in the American trial for espionage.

As the plans were revealed to me they seemed satisfactory, except that there had been several threats on the spy's life following his arrival in London. To deal with the specter of those threats, it was agreed that police were to carefully escort him in an armed van, bringing him directly aboard the airplane to avoid his being a target for anyone in the terminal crowd or from a person who might shoot him from an isolated position among the Heathrow Airport buildings.

At my request, all bags were checked as the passengers began to arrive, with each passenger and his baggage being viewed together. However, one passenger whose baggage was put aboard the plane changed his mind and cancelled out. As soon as I discovered this I ordered his bags removed. I had visions of a bomb in one of those bags going off enroute to New York.

Meanwhile, the London police located the passenger who decided at the last minute to opt out of the flight, leaving his baggage aboard. He had returned to the same hotel from which he had checked out that morning. When confronted, his story just didn't wash with the police, or with me. He claimed that at the last minute he had remembered that he put $10,000 in a case in a dresser drawer in his hotel room, forgotten to remove it, and had returned to retrieve it.

An extraordinarily thorough police search of the hotel room, employees, and the hotel at large rendered no evidence of the alleged ten thousand dollars. The search of his bags proved fruitless, only clothing and personal items were found. After all of the waiting and work, a Pan American employee came running with a message that Dr. Soblen had outwitted us all, he had some way obtained poison, and committed suicide enroute to the airport. After such a melodramatic preface the scheduled flight to New York was routine.

Flying a Boeing 707 into Bangkok from Karachi in 1964 was not routine. On our arrival, just before sunrise, we made a landing to the west and made a turn off the runway onto a high speed taxiway. At the end of the taxiway, leading onto the large extended apron area, we could see several U. S. Air Force fighter aircraft parked far out on the apron allowing a minimum area to taxi the 707 in front of them to reach the terminal buildings.

As I reached the apron, my landing lights showed the fighters so very close that I was concerned that my left wing tip would strike a plane as I made the 150 degree turn to head east. There were no taxi ramp lights on, and my landing lights were directional, showing only the area directly in front of my plane.

There were large green lights to indicate the edge of the apron, or so we thought. I asked my first officer if he could see the green edge lights, he answered that he could. I told him to taxi the plane from his side of the cockpit in order to allow the right side outboard main landing gear wheels to come close to the next green boundary light, yet keep us on the pavement.

With intense care, he took over the nose wheel steering wheel available to him on his right side. All wing lights were

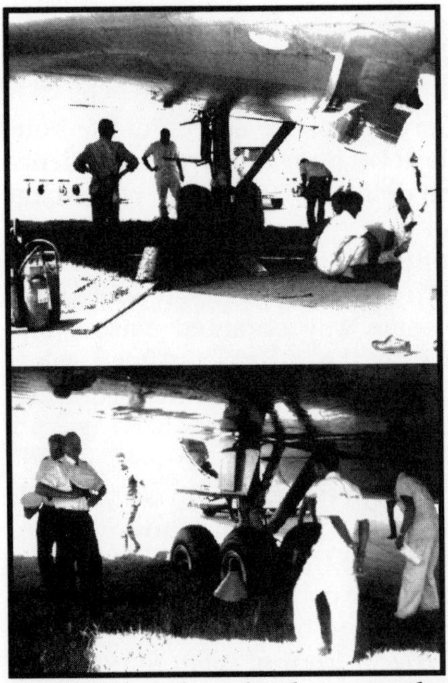

on as I concentrated with the flight engineer to see that we were going to clear the parked fighters. All went well until we all felt the airplane tilt down on the right side. We knew at once that the right main gear truck, with its four wheels, was off the paved apron onto the grass area, and that the airplane was sinking down on its right side into the grass.

I had the option of taking over the plane, moving the throttles way ahead, turning my nose wheel control to the left, moving the plane back up on the runway. Suppose it just went deeper into the grass? Suppose the plane came out violently, and caused me to encounter the fighters before I could stop?

I just closed all the throttles. We came to a full stop. There was no emergency, it did not require an evacuation of the passengers down the exit chutes, so I called Pan American operations to bring out vehicles to the plane to unload the passengers in a normal manner. The cooperative passengers showed no anxiety, and moved easily in their exit.

At sunrise we had the aircraft defueled on its right side, planks placed on the track made by the right gear, and pulled the 707 back up onto the apron. Our problem had been that, in the darkness, the copilot could not see where the apron ended and the grass began. He assumed, as did I, that the green light was on the edge of the apron, but not so, it was

several feet away from the apron cement area in the grass, and had enticed us over onto the soft grass area in the darkness.

We were delayed five hours getting the aircraft back into service for its journey on to Hong Kong. In my report I recommended that they put the green boundary lights as they should be placed, on the boundary of the apron, not out in the grass. They responded accordingly.

Delays, sometimes rather extensive ones, often resulted from internal difficulties. The Pan American pilot strike over Boeing 707 pay is a primary example. In April of 1965, when the strike occurred, I happened to be in Tehran on a round the world 707 flight. There were no Pan American following flights into Tehran as a result of the strike, so my crew and I were forced to remain in the Hilton Tehran Hotel.

What a place to be trapped: beautiful suite, swimming pool, great food, excellent music, hot and cold running waiters, many stewardesses to chaperon, our signing for everything compliments of Pan American, and no idea how

The rough life of a Pan Am Captain at the start of the Jet Age

long the strike would continue. Pan American was obligated to care for us, but the Airline Pilot's Association was responsible to fly us out of Tehran back to New York, since they initiated the strike. With the strike called, Pan American asserted its right to charge APLA for all expenses related to our stay.

After our second day there, I determined that the APLA Headquarters should be alerted to our predicament. I advised them by wire that it would take $5,000 to bring us home by an airline other than Pan American. The strange part of this was the lack of communication, they did not reply at all.

In a burst of resourcefulness, I took it upon myself to become acquainted with the Alitalia airline executives based in Tehran. After many martinis in my suite, they saw no reason why they could not allow my flight crew to deadhead on Alitalia Airlines back to New York on a standby basis. I sent a wire to the APLA chairman in New York that we were returning via Alitalia. I did not inform him that we were returning free of charge. Upon our arrival in New York the fun began.

The local chapter demanded the $5,000 which they advised me they had sent to us in Tehran. I did not reply to the messages I received, I just waited. Finally a phone call came from APLA headquarters to my home on Long Island. "Where is that $5,000 we sent you?" "What $5,000? We never received it." I then requested they submit proof of having sent the money. The reply was, "We understand you flew back on Alitalia, how did you purchase the tickets?" "Martinis, I replied." I never discovered whether the money had been forwarded.

Chapter Twenty Three

EXPLORING THE CAT

THE CLIPPER **AUGUST 1, 1968**

By MORT YOUNG

For a year, a Pan American World Airways captain has been flying into what every other pilot does his best to avoid - clear air turbulence.

Captain Kimball J. Scribner's attempts to find CAT are almost as difficult as others' attempts to fly around it for, as the name implies, CAT is invisible.

The 51-year old pilot has flown a specially equipped glider into the windy maelstroms of New Hampshire's Presidential Mountains to prove his theories and also has worked closely, beginning in February, 1968, with the national Center for Atmospheric Research. NCAR, a scientific arm of 24 universities, is located in the foot hills of the Colorado Rockies near Boulder.

Chapter Twenty-Three

In 1965, my close friend and fellow pilot, Colonel Cloyce "Tip" Tippett, brought to my attention a Swedish company's

aircraft arresting system which used a net to envelop an aircraft at the end of a runway. The application of the system was viable in the event of an aborted takeoff or an emergency landing of an airplane which could run off the end of the runway, if the pilot were unable to draw the aircraft to a stop. The concept for this device evolved from the aircraft arresting system used by the U.S. Navy, whereby fixed wing airplanes could be brought to a fast and safe stop. Of course, such a device could prove a vital resource to further ensure safety for commercial passenger carriers.

In the Navy's system all planes had a tail hook assembly which would catch raised arresting lines erected across the landing strip of the carrier ship. After picking up a line, the plane was permitted a limited distance to be brought to a stop. If the first line were missed, each following line applied more restrictive pressure to bear until the last raised barrier was encountered, giving almost maximum resistance, halting the airplane abruptly if the pilot was unable to stop the aircraft.

Commercial aircraft could not be equipped with tail hook units such as the Navy fighter planes, but a net could be raised in front of an airplane, completely enveloping it and its turning propellers or jet engines, allowing it to be brought to a measured stop with no damage to the aircraft.

The Swedish company which had designed the device had sent an attorney as its representative to the United States to market the project. The inherent difficulty in that plan was that an attorney, without extensive technical expertise, could not satisfactorily handle the technological questions or demonstrate the concept effectively. With no working interrelationships with military and aviation interests in this country, he failed to provoke interest and support needed for the project. Tip was approached to further the project, and he, in turn, called me in to work with him to take over the sales promotion of the arresting net project.

Fortunately, the parent company had a considerable amount of movie film which had been shot of tests, utilizing large U. S. surplus military aircraft at an experimental research base in New Jersey. With those films available to me, I wrote a script, dubbed my own voice, and ended up with a decent film presentation which answered the basic questions about application use of the nets. We then showed the film to diverse groups of commercial airline pilots, and top brass of the Air Force, and Navy at the Pentagon.

Search for a company to take over the manufacturing rights and maintenance of the system led us to Lockheed, in California. Tip made a presentation to that company, because, with his having been a former CAA and I.C.A.O. head, he knew the channels through which specifications of this nature would be created, discussed, altered and finally approved.

There were no competitors, and the specifications were prepared in such a detailed manner that it would discourage most manufacturers from attempting to meet them. After several meetings, a final agreement with Lockheed was then considered.

In a sudden and abrupt move, Lockheed changed its corporate structures, resulting in such a radical change in operations and company priorities that Tip and I decided to discontinue spending any more time, money and energy on the project. With no other company on the horizon with whom to negotiate, we had to let the project go. What a shame to have to do so when one considers how many lives could have been saved by such an innovative and basically simple project.

As it has been throughout my life, none of the energy, time, and money expended in pursuit of the project was wasted. It led me into connections which allowed my engagement in experimental research on clear air turbulence, a project which remains one of the most fascinating, engaging, productive and delightful ventures of my career.

On November 9, 1965, I gave a lecture on the potential usages of the aircraft arresting device to The Explorers Club in New York City. As the audience settled in for my presentation, George Wallace called out to me, "Are you not the Kim Scribner who flew into the ground upside down in Miami?" We laughed, shook hands, and recalled our first meeting when we were introduced by our mutual friend, Harry Doehla, in Fitchburg, Massachusetts.

George Wallace, no relation to the Alabama governor, was the former owner of the Fitchburg Paper Company, and during World War II had produced a special paper for gas coupons required to buy gasoline. My

AVIATION:

Exploring the CAT

Rear Seat: George R. Wallace, President of Explorers Research Corp. **Front Seat:** Captain Kim Scribner, Director of Aviation Research

Making Aviation Still Safer

by Kimball J. Scribner✻

You're flying in cloudless weather, when suddenly your plane plummets 2,000 ft. - why? the Author pilots a research sailplane to explore the nature of clear-air turbulence.

12 / MARCH, 1971

father, a chemist and head of the paper section of the Bureau of Standards, had developed the unique specifications for U.S. currency which was so strong, with its silk content, that it was impossible for counterfeiters to reproduce it. Under the same specifications, he had made a gas ration coupon paper available to George Wallace's company for production of the wartime gasoline coupons.

After reminiscing with George for a few moments, I began my lecture and lead in to show the film I had produced demonstrating the arresting mechanism. At 5:28 p.m. all the lights went out in the New York City area! That night was the occasion of the famous New York City blackout. Candles were brought into the room, and in front of the audience, I began by saying "Ladies and gentlemen, you are all here to see my film, so here it is." I held it up high above my head in its container and proceeded to do my best to present the potential of the project in the candle lit lecture hall. Following the presentation, George Wallace invited me to lunch the next day at the 21 Club to discuss ideas and projects in which we had shared interests.

At that lunch, we discussed The Explorers Club and his desire to rejuvenate the club through establishment of an active research and development program. I suggested a study of clear air turbulence as a possibility for just such a project. CAT, apparently a term coined by pilots who encountered extreme turbulence in clear air, had troubled jet transport, both civilian and military, since the beginning of high altitude flights. It was the suspected cause of several fatal airline accidents involving military and civilian aircraft.

As a safety factor, CAT research and experiment was of paramount importance. The development of a medium of advance detection of clear air turbulence would give pilots sufficient time to take corrective action necessary to avoid the area of CAT, or, at least, take precautions insuring that passengers and all crew members were seated, with safety belts fastened, and appropriate speed reduction made to

flight operations

JULY 1977

CAT detection and avoidance

...The pilot whose sailplane flights measured Mt. Washington and Rocky Mountain turbulence tells how instrumentation and techniques will reduce or minimize the CAT hazard. Most promising is an infrared detector of CAT temperature discontinuity. other systems to help pilots include a radar which can track a bumblebee at 10 miles and laser optics to measure the velocity of turbulent air...

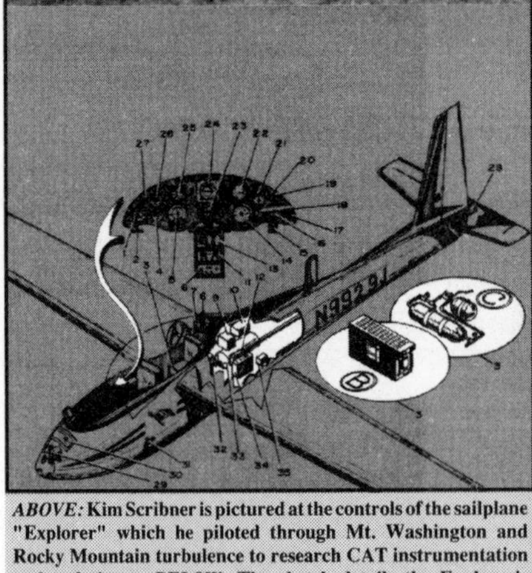

1. ALTIMETER
2. IR WINDOW PROTECTIVE SLIDE
3. (a) 2nd SEAT
   (b) LOW FREQUENCY ELECTROSTATIC FIELD SYSTEM
   (c) AEROSAL UNIT
4. ROSEMOUNT IND
5. VOR
6. B E I COMM
7. IN-FLIGHT CAMERA
8. PRISM SPLIT FIELD
9. RECORDER (CEC)
10. BATTERY
11. MARK 24 VOR/COMM
12. AFCRL ELEC UNIT
13. DISTANCE MEASURING EQUIPMENT
14. P Z L VARIOMETER
15. MAG COMPASS
16. GYRO COMPASS
17. MAG COMPASS CARD
18. CLOCK
20. SYSTEM SHUTDOWN
21. TRANSPONDER
22. RATE OF CLIMB
23. TURN & BANK
24. ARTIFICIAL HORIZON
25. AIRSPEED
26. INFRA RED TEMP IND
27. AEROSOL ON/OFF
28. AEROSOL TUBE
30. ANTENNA FOR 38
31. TEMP ROSEMOUNT
32. ACCELEROMETERS (GENERAL PRECISION)
33. OXYGEN
34. ELECTRICAL UNIT (BARNES)
35. BAROGRAPH

ABOVE: **Kim Scribner is pictured at the controls of the sailplane "Explorer" which he piloted through Mt. Washington and Rocky Mountain turbulence to research CAT instrumentation and techniques.** ***BELOW:*** **The sketch details the Explorer's elaborate instrumentation and equipment as a flying laboratory.**

reduce the effect of the turbulence when it was encountered. After review of my ideas, he requested me to develop a project plan to submit to The Explorers Club. Together, we drew up a proposal to utilize a high performance sailplane for the study, and outlined a policy that the club would initiate actions itself, and not simply supply funding and endorsement with the Explorers Club flag and its considerable influence for support.

In February of 1986, I presented a proposal to the club which entailed development of an affiliate non profit corporation within The Explorers Club. The new non profit organization, while remaining under the full control of the originating body, would focus on important research projects aimed at improving safety of flight for the general public, as well as providing for pilot's safety in their pursuit of private flying. This new non profit corporation was to receive office facilities, but would be responsible for generation of its own funding for operations, research, and development plans.

In May of that year, I received notice of approval of the proposal by the board of directors, and was named chairman of the Aviation and Research Committee. The newly formed Explorers Research Corporation had an august board of directors and officers which included, honorary chairman, Lowell Thomas, adventurer, author, and radio broadcaster, George R. Wallace, director of The Explorers Club, Edward C. Sweeney, president of the National Aeronautical Association, and Ward Randol, executive director of The Explorers Club.

Under our agreement for the clear air turbulence study, research and experimentation was to be accomplished in a high performance sailplane designed and built to my specifications to function as a flying laboratory. A sailplane was chosen as the flying instrument rather than a powered plane, because the weight of a sailplane remains constant compared to the varying weights of a powered plane which reduces weight as fuel is consumed.

Flying at much slower speeds than a powered plane, a

At Jefferson County Airport, near Boulder, George Wallace looks on as I strap myself into the sailplane's cockpit ready for a flight across the 13,000-foot Continental Divide. George Wallace financed the study of Clear Air Turbulence.

Following take-off (*bottom left),* the Explorer sweeps ahead of the tow plane to plunge into a bank of heavy clouds during the New Hampshire flights in an attempt to pit the infra-red temperature detector against violent up- and down drafts.

sailplane could remain within the air mass whose movements were being measured by circling in a more reduced radius of turn than that of the airplane, whose turning radius would take it out of the particular medium of air current. Additionally, the sailplane became a part of the air mass it was measuring, and did not just penetrate through it.

On the date of the approval of my proposal, I was driving George Wallace down to his apartment in Manhattan when he signalled for me to pull over to the curb. When we stopped, he pulled out his checkbook and asked, "Will $10,000 get the engineering design started on a sailplane?" "And how," I replied. I immediately phoned my friend Paul Schweizer of the Schweizer Sailplane Company in Elmira, New York, and outlined my basic requirements.

Paul Schweizer

Paul and his brothers were enthusiastic about the design, and ready to start work on what ended up as the most instrumented, and specifically designed flying laboratory of its kind in the world. The three place, all metal sailplane was modified to carry one or two people, provided ample area and weight carrying capacity to permit carriage of a flying laboratory of instruments, and capable of enduring gust load factors in turbulence in excess of 9 Gs.

Of course, we named this splendid bird The Explorer. Under my design specifications, The Explorer was outfitted with the most elaborate and scientific instrumentation system ever assembled in a sailplane, carrying the same instruments as a jet transport.

Cooperation was received from the Federal Aviation Administration, National Aeronautical and Space Administration, and the Environmental Sciences Administration. A non profit contract with the Air Force Cambridge Research Laboratories in Bedford, Massachusetts, made available a

Barnes infrared air temperature detector to enhance the research.

The sailplane was equipped with distance measuring equipment, a stabilizing flux gate magnetic compass, an air speed pressure transducer, an altitude (static pressure) transducer, a magnetic tape recording system, a voice recorder, and a battery system. For altitudes above 50,000 feet, in addition to an oxygen supply system, an auxiliary power unit was installed to supply heat for the pilot's flying suit capable of counteracting temperatures below minus 100 degrees centigrade. In addition, the power unit could supply the energy necessary to maintain air pressurization for the pilot, provide electricity for radio and flight instruments, and supply heat for deicing the windshield and essential control surfaces.

The data recording system recorder and cartridges were mounted in an insulated electrically heated enclosure where the temperature was automatically maintained above zero degrees. Provision were made to record the file number on the tape being used to insure taped identification. The data clock was normally reset at the start of a flight, continuing to accumulate until the mission was complete.

Two essential systems, the altimeter and the air speed indicator, were each provided with single element aneroids to provide and meet specifications of an altitude of a 40,000 foot range. The altimeter provided resolution of 10 feet, accuracy of 50 feet, and response time of less than one second. For air speed, the specifications were for a range of 2-300 knots, a resolution of 0.1 knots, accuracy $\pm$38, and a response time of less than one second.

With consideration for battery unpredictability in the ranges of temperature to be encountered, it was necessary to insulate the battery completely. With the addition of two sonotone batteries, we provided a total capacity of six to seven hours of operation.

The batteries were routed through a power distribution

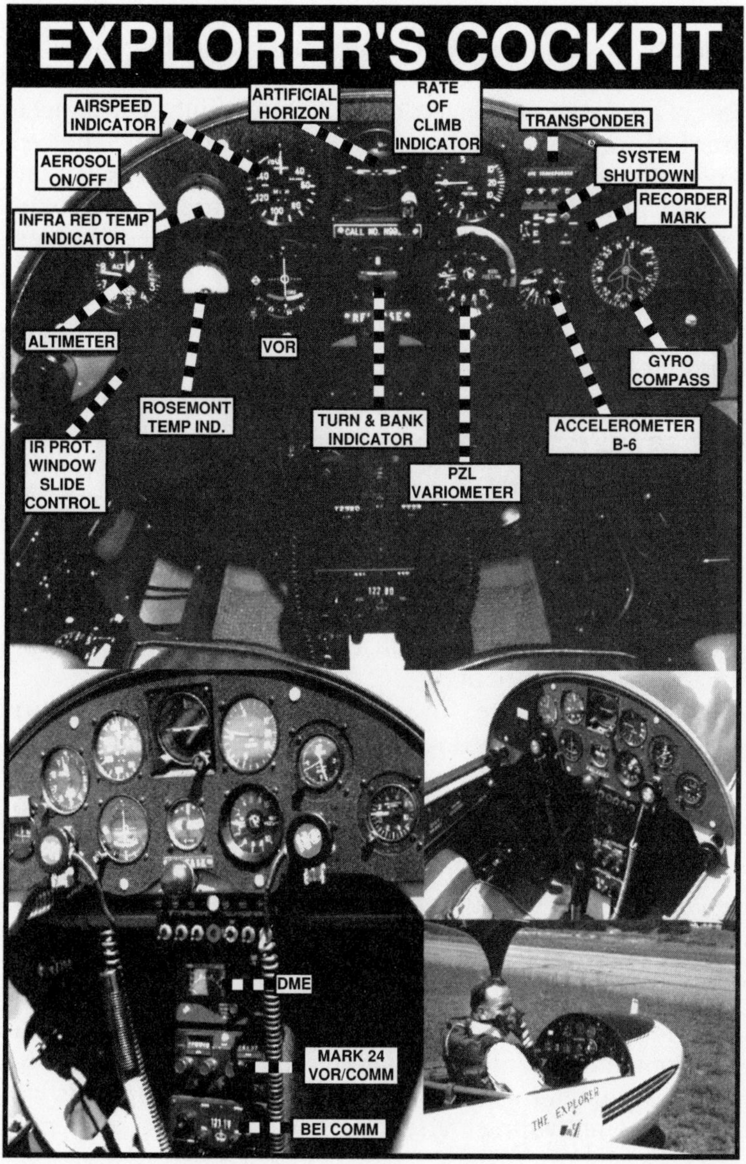
EXPLORER'S COCKPIT
AIRSPEED INDICATOR
ARTIFICIAL HORIZON
RATE OF CLIMB INDICATOR
TRANSPONDER
AEROSOL ON/OFF
SYSTEM SHUTDOWN
RECORDER MARK
INFRA RED TEMP INDICATOR
ALTIMETER
VOR
GYRO COMPASS
ROSEMONT TEMP IND.
TURN & BANK INDICATOR
ACCELEROMETER B-6
IR PROT. WINDOW SLIDE CONTROL
PZL VARIOMETER
DME
MARK 24 VOR/COMM
BEI COMM
THE EXPLORER

panel, so that any one of the batteries could operate the primary avionics load. In this manner, I could control the usage of the electric power, and only use it when I required use of any particular electrically operated unit. The panel in front of me allowed for a selection of units to be utilized. Following a flight mission, external power was applied and inserted into the system to recharge the batteries overnight. All batteries were fused with fast acting magnetic current breakers.

The Explorer's all metal fuselage was constructed and sealed to permit it to float in the event of a necessary water landing. A dual canopy was installed to reduce frost forming on the canopy. The oxygen system, capable of up to 8 hours of supply, was designed to permit exhaling by way of a tube extending through the side of the fuselage, preventing moisture from the pilot's breath from condensing to form crystals inside the dual canopy.

We added a pressurized container of chlorosulphuric acid to be released by a valve controlled by the pilot, passing through an extended small metal tube behind the tail of the sailplane surface. Upon contact with air, the chlorosulphuric acid turned into an expanding white stream, leaving a very noticeable smoke screen which identified the clear air turbulence as it was encountered by the sailplane. The trailing white smoke could then be photographed from the tow plane of The Explorer.

Motion pictures were produced on the study of CAT, not only for their historic and scientific purposes, but for the development of audio visual materials to be used in educational systems. In these materials a primary emphasis was placed on motivating high school and college level audiences to prepare for and enter the aero sciences as a meaningful career. A copy of these audio-visual materials was given to the Soaring Museum at Harris Hill, Elmira, New York.

It is generally understood by the flying public that, by utilization of airborne radar, the pilot is able to greatly reduce exposure of his aircraft and passengers to turbulence associated with cloud formation by nature of his 'seeing eye' which has the capacity of detecting cloud formations, their relative density, and the relative rough turbulence to be encountered. However, clear air turbulence presents unseeable, undetectable properties which made available airborne radar almost useless for this purpose.

Our sailplane was designed for the purposes of providing data regarding the vertical air mass movements associated with clear air turbulence as encountered by jet transports. We were to further the study of 'standing wave' or clear air masses, which rise vertically to heights above 80,000 feet, and their association with the jet streams.

In our research, we made a commitment to coordinate the interests of the Air Force, Weather Bureau, Federal Aviation Agency, and the Air Transport Association in the advancement of modern instrumentation and technology: to identify clear air vertical movements ahead of the aircraft, determine the feasibility of using the various instruments as tools or effective means of identifying clear air turbulence, and provide continued and accurate recordings of all data gathered.

Initially, The Explorer was test flown in the vicinity of Harris Hill, Elmira, New York, where its instrumentation and trial flights were concluded. Following this period of indoctrination, the sailplane was towed to the Mount Washington area in Vermont where it encountered the high lift and turbulence associated with air which rises vertical in the mountain wave. Here, over a period of many months, experimental flights were made into clear air turbulence encountered at various altitudes, providing the environment

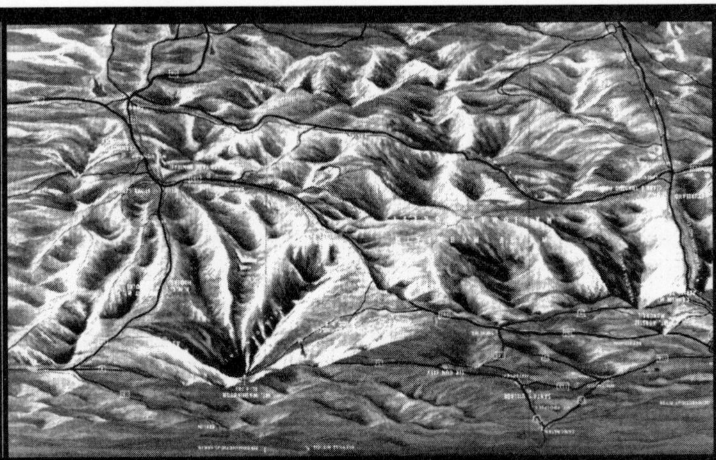

- **<u>Mount Washington</u> 6,288 feet above sea level where the strongest winds (over 200 miles per hour) have been measured. This area provided the *Clear Air Turbulence* required for our testing the turbulence with the equipment installed in the sailplane.**

required for the study of means of using various systems and instrumentation to detect CAT. Then we towed the sailplane across the country to the Rocky Mountain area on the Continental Divide at Boulder, Colorado.

Flights were made to study the effectiveness of infrared temperature detection as a medium through which temperature discontinuity in line of flight would effectively detect the existence of clear air turbulence. All data was recorded by the sailplane's automatic recording mechanism, and correlated by actual photographs, taken simultaneously, of the horizon at the time each temperature reading was made. The Barnes infrared temperature unit and the sailplane's own air temperature probe provided the necessary data from which meaningful results were obtained.

By choosing the precise wave length at which to observe the atmosphere, it was possible to determine an average temperature of the air mass out in front of the sailplane to a pre-determined distance. By changing the wave length slightly it was possible to alter this distance over which the temperature integration occurred. By making observations at two or more wave lengths and comparing these to the local, or ambient, temperature, ranging information was made available.

The prototype infrared unit installed in The Explorer provided the research work with an operational instrument to give warning of turbulence existing in the line of flight ahead. The sailplane was confronted with the basic problem of aircraft pitch at the time the temperatures were taken ahead of the sailplane, causing the sight line to be non-horizontal. Generally, the sailplane did not always fly through the same air which had been measured by the forward sensing unit.

To compensate for this pitch, a data camera recorded the position of the nose and tail of the plane relative to the horizon at the exact time the temperatures were taken. The correlation between temperatures taken in the immediate

I utilized our Pan Am DC-3 to prove the utlization of the Distance Measuring Equipment (D.M.E.) with a variety of observers on board to see how distances could be measured in flight to or from a VOR station equipped to be used in this manner. With charts on hand inflight, we simply oberheaded a VOR station and watched the D.M.E. indicator read out the distance as we flew away or toward the stations. Evaluation of the accuracy was quite simple. All transport and many private planes still utilize the D.M.E.

area and ahead of the sailplane, in conjunction with photos taken reflecting its pitch, followed by flights into the turbulence, resulted in meaningful data necessary to provide a promising clear air turbulence detector.

The ultimate evaluation of the Barnes infrared temperature detection device was conducted by Pan American, Trans World and Eastern Airlines, with the cooperation of Barnes Engineering and Boeing Aircraft Company, to determine if the system was able to consistently detect clear air turbulence at a range great enough to allow flight crews to prepare for or avoid such turbulence.

We were convinced by our research that the solution for reducing the exposures of aircraft and passengers to the uncertainties and dangers of CAT lay in airborne instrumentation which would detect the turbulence. The Explorer's utilization of the prototype infrared temperature detecting device was the key to the success of the project.

The detection techniques employed in the Barnes infrared detector were based upon detection of temperature discontinuities, remotely, at a range of 20 to 40 miles. The method depended upon the thermal radiation emitted by the gasses composing the atmosphere. Fortunately, carbon dioxide is uniformly distributed throughout the atmosphere at the same temperature as the air in which it is mixed. It also had a thermal emission range in a narrow spectral region centered around 15 micron in the infrared, and provided a convenient measure of air temperature. The infrared detector had the capacity of measuring signals emitted from the atmosphere relating temperature in two wave length regions, one at a distance ahead of the aircraft, and the other at the aircraft's position in the air. The difference signal increased as the discontinuity was approached.

Our two and one half years of intensive research were rewarding and exhilarating for all of us who had a hand in the project. The wonderfully cooperative sharing of many areas of resources were exemplary of what can be accomplished in

Dr. Joachim Kuettner (*right*) listens to NCAR meteorologists outline the problem and the next day's chances of turbulence over the Continental Divide. In the background are (*left to right*) glider pilot Bob Anderson, George Wallace, and Dick Fitzpatrick, a Barkley & Dexter engineer who nursemaided the Explorer from the project's inception.

Mr. James Moran
Vice President -
Explorers Research Corp.

an atmosphere of joint ventures as opposed to competitive secrecy. The Explorers Club was rightfully proud of the project which was underwritten by a one hundred thousand dollar contribution of George Wallace, and the exceptional work of James M. Moran.

As the ongoing research of CAT was assumed by commercial, military and other government resource projects, The Explorers Club made a gift of the Explorer sailplane to the National Center for Atmospheric Research for their continued study of atmospherics in the region of the Continental Divide. The gift was made with the commitment of continuation of assistance in technological and engineering aspects of ongoing study, using the sailplane as a flying laboratory. I was honored with the job of consulting on the ongoing project, and I aided by flying the sailplane on research missions.

Dr. Joachim P. Kuettner

In August, 1968, I was invited by Dr. Joachim P. Kuettner, Chairman of the Organisation Scientifique et Technique Internationale Du Vol A Voile (OSTIV) to present a paper at the congress of OSTIV in Poland on the subject of clear air turbulence and mountain wave research. I was tremendously flattered by the opportunity, and no less excited that the congress of OSTIV was occurring simultaneously with the World Gliding Championships being held in Poland.

Chapter Twenty Four

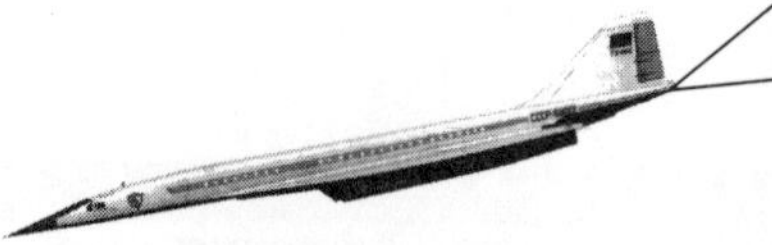

ON TO PHU-CAT AND THE TU-144

WHO'S THE PILOT ?
CAPTAIN EDDIE BUMSTEAD, THE DAREDEVIL
WHAT WAS HIS BEST STUNT ?
DOING THREE ROLL-OVERS
ONLY THREE ROLL-OVERS ?
THAT DOESN'T SOUND LIKE MUCH
IT DOES WHEN YOU'RE THE CAPTAIN OF A 707
YOUNG DRAKE 7-31

Chapter Twenty-Four

In February 1968, during the Vietnam War, Pan American Airways obtained a special military cargo charter flight from Dover, Delaware to Phu-Cat in Vietnam. This type of flight into an active war zone was made available to crew on a voluntary basis only. So, anticipating an unusual experience, I bid on the military charter flight and was awarded it, along with a flight crew who, like me, had never been to Vietnam.

My crew and I were deadheaded to Dover on February 26, and were briefed there by a U. S. Air Force major. When we asked to see our airplane for pre-flight examination, we were advised, for the first time, that the plane, a Pan American 707-C cargo, was parked at an isolated area of the airport, because it was loaded with a specific type of live ammunition as cargo. No one would verify just what type of live ammunition it was we were to fly to Vietnam.

The flight plan required us to fly the cargo to San Francisco, land, park away from all civilian aircraft and terminal buildings, stay overnight, and then head to Hawaii, where we were to land under the same procedures. From Hawaii we were to fly to Guam, land, and then go on the final lap to deliver our cargo to Vietnam.

We were introduced to our briefing Air Force officer who launched into spreading out some charts on a table and preparing us for the flight. The 707 jet was self contained relative to navigation equipment, so we did not require a navigator. With loran, radio and other aids we could handle the navigation from the two forward pilot seats. The flight plan called for our landing on a makeshift landing strip at Phu-Cat, a forward military base, and I had a few questions:

Question:	"Are there any radio aids available at the airport for us to make an instrument approach and landing?"
Answer:	"Not exactly. There is a low powered radio facility there. Here it is on your map."
Question:	"What kind of runway is there?"
Answer:	"It is a Marston strip, made with corrugated metal strung along the ground to afford you braking action."
Question:	"How about its length?"
Answer:	"Unknown, I figure it's about 7,000 feet. That gives you 200 feet over your usual minimum runway length."
Question:	"How about height above sea level?"
Answer:	"Unknown."
Question:	"What is the height of the mountains in the area?"
Answer:	"Unknown."
Question:	"Do you have an approach instrument landing pattern for us?"
Answer:	"Negative. You will be required to

	draft one."
Question:	"What time is breakfast?"
Answer:	"Anytime."

The Air Force officer did tell us that the firing would be 'light'. I asked, "Firing at whom?" "At you," he replied. We ate while studying our materials, then inspected the aircraft, determined all operations figures for fuel, alternate airports, and maximum allowable gross weight for our landing at Phu-Cat. As we waved good-bye, I realized that we were off on the most unusual flight of my career.

On our approach to Phu-Cat, we used military frequencies, giving our position reports, and clearing ourselves as we approached the coastline of Vietnam. We descended, staying away from clouds, and following the coast. In due time, the radio beacon at Phu-Cat started to come in, and we identified it. The landing strip was inland from the coast, and, with great care, we waited until the bearings showed we could turn left 90 degrees, and make a straight in approach to the strip to land.

We estimated the strip to be about 15 miles from the coast line. In clear visibility, we noticed hills around us, and the country side looked very green. We had it made until my first officer called out, "Look over to the right ahead of us! The military planes must be out to practice dive bombing." I advised him rather quickly, " They are not practicing, they are bombing for purpose."

Smoke was rising off to our right of center. We spotted the landing strip and realized that the bombing was several miles on the other side of the strip. At about 1,000 feet over the terrain I called for flaps and gear down. We began to slow down, check lists were read, landing speed determined, and we continued toward landing.

The Marston strip made a good target to look at, except it appeared very, very short in length. There were no obstructions, so I aimed at the strip, and landed just over the start of it with full flaps. Carefully, I raised the spoilers and reversed all engines with the brakes on full. A major concern about using aircraft brakes on a metal Marston strip such as this, was the necessity of avoiding having the strip curl up ahead of one. We came to a stop just before the end of the strip, and a 'follow me' jeep came racing out and pulled up in front of us. On the top of a platform behind the jeep driver sat a soldier who was manning a big mounted machine gun. We followed this jeep as directed to a point for unloading.

We got off the 707, walked into a makeshift building, had a Coke, and waited for the unloading. We, of course, asked about the bombing. With big smiles we were advised, "Routine". After unloading, the airplane was refueled and we prepared for our return flight. All around the area there were jeeps with machine guns patrolling the operations. Nearest us there were C-47's and DC-3s with open windows showing mounted guns. No doubt, some of our ammunition was headed for them. After a very brief visit, we took off, made a sharp turn away from the diving planes and smoke, and headed for the coast, climbing away to return to Guam and then home.

Under a new bilateral agreement between Russia and the United States, I flew the first American scheduled passenger flight from New York to Moscow on July 23, 1968. In the accord for this important break through in international aviation, the Russian airline, Aeroflot, was approved to fly into New York from Moscow. My two captains, R. A. Hovden, Bob Hinds, and I were instructed in our briefing for the flight that in Russia we could use English over the radio, but we must use the metric system in making reference to our altitudes.

The flight required a non-stop run from New York to Copenhagen, to overnight, then on to Moscow's Sheremetyevo Airport. In Copenhagen, we were advised that our flight plan time to Moscow was forecast to be about two hours and fifty minutes. After takeoff, on course, at about half way across the ocean, we were cleared to contact Russian air traffic control on a specific frequency. First officer Hinds made the first contact saying, "Russian air control, this is Pan American Airways flight forty-four, do you read us?" A female voice replied in heavily accented English, "Roger, Pan American, what is your position?" Captain Hinds initiated the return call by saying, "Russian control this is Pan American Clipper forty-four," then he read off our current position giving latitude, longitude, the time, altitude in meters, and the estimate for our next required position report. Finally, he requested the controller to advise us if she received our message.

The Russian woman replied, "Repeat all after Pan American." His position report was quite long, involving a series of numbers relating in altitude, longitude and latitude. After a deep breath the first officer began to convey his lengthy message. During this exchange we were flying 500 miles per hour toward the coast line of Russia, with no clearance to enter their country.

As soon as Captain Hinds began his reply saying, "This is Pan American Clipper," I stopped him and explained, "I think I know our problem, she does not know what Clipper means. She is asking about the one word after Pan American which you are saying." I spoke to her over the radio informing her, "Sorry, we used the word Clipper, we will not use it any more." The urgency of clarification did not allow me time to explain that in Europe, North and South America, Clipper was used in Pan American World Airways as a short cut, or that B.O.A.C used Speed Bird in the same manner. Fortunately, we received clearance to continue to Russia and on to Moscow. However, each time we were handed to another controller we had to remind each other not to use the word Clipper.

The Russian woman speaking English to us was a translator who relayed directives to us from the actual air traffic controller. When headings for us to fly were given to her in Russian for translation into English to us, we had a very difficult time due to the delay of translation. All over the rest of the world the aviation language is English; not in Russia.

After landing we were directed to the parking area, and a stairway was pushed up against the airplane for passengers to disembark. As soon as the passengers cleared the aircraft, Russian photographers poured onto the airplane with flash bulbs popping. They took photos of everything in the galleys, opening ovens and photographing everything in sight and inside cupboards.

Into the cockpit they barged, taking pictures of the instruments, their relative positions, they even photographed how the seats worked. During all this they did not speak a word to us. Finally, either they ran out of film, or they decided they had enough, and disembarked in silence, without a backward glance.

We spent only a couple of hours at the airport, buying caviar and vodka, and eating their borscht for lunch, as the airplane was refueled for the return flight. I spoke to the station manager at Copenhagen about the difficulty with the word Clipper, and he assured me that the interpreters would be briefed in time for the next flight into Russia.

One of the problems we encountered on the initial, and later flights, was the utilization of their instrument landing system. They transmitted a carrier radio wave on the established frequency, but it was not interrupted periodically with any identification signal. We simply established the frequency as indicated, watched the flags on the instrument disappear, and assumed we were receiving radio signals from that airport instrument landing system. However, their radar controllers, via the translators, followed our flights on the instrument landing system telling us when we were off the localizer or glide path.

This continuing service to Moscow from New York was

never financially sound, because no Russian ever flew on Pan American flights, only on their own Aeroflot airline. In moves for effective profit margin management, this was one of the first routes which Pan American cut from its scheduled passenger flights.

Use of English as the universal language was smooth going for American and English pilots, but how about an Italian air traffic controller speaking to a French or Italian pilot in English? When communicating initially with the Italian air traffic controller, and identifying one's flight, giving position and altitude, the Italian reply was always, "Standa bya, I calla you back."

On one occasion, a Pan American pilot reported that an Alitalia aircraft was descending toward a holding point, Civitavecchia, north of Rome. He was cleared to hold in a pattern at 5,000 feet. Almost simultaneously, an air France plane was descending, and the Air France pilot called the Italian controller speaking English, requesting clearance to descend and land. The controller quickly replied saying, "Aira France youra cleared to Civitavecchia, descend to holda at fiva thousanda feeta." After a brief pause, the French pilot said, "We are cleared to Civitavecchia to hold at 5,000 feet, the same altitude and estimated time of arrival as Alitalia?" Whereupon, the Italian controller fired back, "Standa bya, I calla youa back." After several seconds the controller came back and hurriedly said, "Thatsa righta! Watcha outa!"

On December 31, 1968, Russia flew its first TU-144 prototype supersonic transport (SST). The first Concordes,

built in England, flew two months later. The TU-144 was shown for the public for the first time on May 21, 1970. I was quite eager to view this innovation in airline transportation

Tupolev TU-144

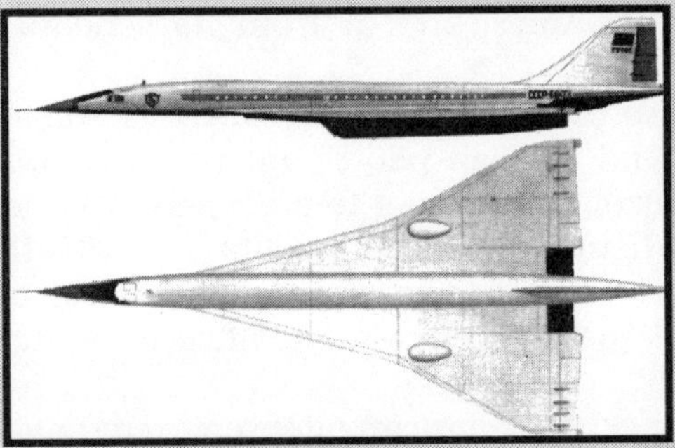

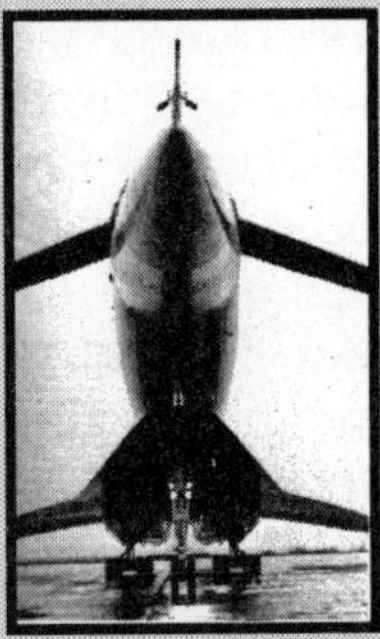

The Tupolev TU-144 was the first supersonic airliner in the world to fly and enter service. First knowledge of this Russian supersonic airliner came in 1965.

The TU-144 displayed a number of similarities with the Concorde but was slightly larger than the Concorde and designed to cruise at higher speeds (Mach 2.2 or 2.3)

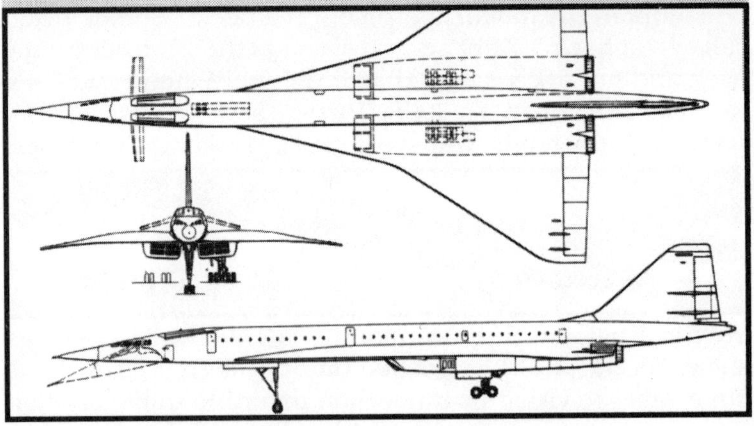

from the time I first heard of it, and was disappointed that my being able to do so was blocked by the Russian obsession with security and secrecy .

On a routine scheduled flight of a Pan American 707 jet from Copenhagen enroute to Moscow, I sought to remedy my unsatisfied curiosity. Following our landing at the Sheremetyevo Airport, in excellent weather, I was directed, as usual, to follow a small vehicle to our parking space. As we were moving our 707 along a taxiway toward the terminal, we were all amazed to see the Supersonic TU-144 parked next to the area to which we were usually directed for parking.

There was a large select crowd of people all gathered around the SST. They were held back by ropes, waist high, on small poles placed several hundred feet away from the airplane. Armed guards were standing about 50 feet apart around the rope fence. At another position point, stood a separate group, obviously dignitaries, no doubt there for some sort of ceremony related to the TU-144.

After receiving the signal to stop the 707, I shut down the engines and continued to watch the select and isolated group of people who were now all looking up at us. I had a brainstorm. I remembered our first exposure of the 707 to the Russians on our inaugural flight into Moscow six months earlier. I recalled how the photographers had swarmed aboard, without invitation, and set about dissecting the aircraft with their camera work. I figured we might as well attempt the same thing, take over their SST.

After all our passengers had descended the stairway, and we were walking toward the terminal, I gathered the crew together and explained how the Russians had taken over on our initial Moscow flight. I asked them if they would like to have some fun. After a few seconds planning, with their hearty agreement, we assembled at the foot of the stairway of our B-707, stood at attention in a very serious manner, and I inspected everyone. After which, they all fell into line and followed me as I headed toward the SST to "take over".

As advised, they paid no attention to anyone, looked straight ahead, and followed my directions. I knew ropes and guards would be in our way, but if we moved positively, we just might be able to bluff our way up to that airplane, up the stairs, and inside the TU-144. Unsmiling, projecting a full routine attitude, they followed me exactly as I wished.

I led the way toward the TU-144 with the crew line up by twos, marching in step, all looking straight ahead. I had no idea how the Russian guards would handle my instructions to lower the ropes, nor how the dignitaries might respond. I simply marched my group up to the carpet which led to the stairway and into the supersonic transport. As we approached, I pointed at the guard, and, in a stern manner, I pointed to the rope. He, it seemed, thought all of this was part of the ceremony, and immediately lowered the rope to the ground, allowing us to pass.

Two guards were standing at attention at the foot of the stairs. I motioned them back. Without a moment's delay, they stepped back, and we marched in single file up the stairs to take over the TU-144. Upon reaching the doorway, I tried to open it. It was locked. Not a sound came from the hundreds of people standing around and below us, until there were motions from one of the Russian dignitaries who pointed first to the guards and then toward us, indicating that we were to be stopped.

A swarm of guards filled the stairs. Needless to say, I was the first to be directed down the steps and toward the important looking assembly of people. I muttered to my crew, "Shake hands with everyone in sight." I began shaking hands with men whose uniforms appeared to indicate their rank as generals, then moved to the apparent civilian dignitaries. Eventually, one spoke English to me. In a moment following my brief explanation of what we were trying to do, and his translation of what I said to the group surrounding us, they all began to laugh.

I was then introduced to the designer of the TU-144, as

well as the other dignitaries who were there for their first time inspection of this huge, fantastic supersonic jet. Then a man, who seemed to function as their public relations person, took from his briefcase a photo of the SST, and, with a grand gesture, had their test pilot hand it to me. At once, I took out

my ball point pen, and handed back the photo to collect their autographs. With many more handshakes all around and more laughter, I took my autographed TU-144 photo and crew, and went into the terminal cleared customs and immigration, enjoyed some borscht, bought some vodka, signed necessary documents, and returned to Copenhagen.

Chapter Twenty Five

YOUR FUTURE AS A PILOT

Chapter Twenty-Five

When Richard Rosen, of Richard Rosen Press, in New York City, requested our vice president of Pan American, General Laurence S. Kuter, to write a book on aviation as a career, General Kuter declined, but recommended me for the opportunity. Under contract to the Rosen Press, I completed my first book *Your Future as a Pilot.*

The purpose of the book was to present the profession to young people in an exciting, informative manner which might encourage them to pursue a career as a civilian pilot. When the book was published and sold well, Dick Rosen offered me the opportunity to have it published in paperback. I was delighted with the plan, and made further agreements on issuing the text under a soft cover.

Dick advised me that he would like to subcontract the publishing of my book to ARCO Publishing, Inc. for the special purpose of reaching black students. I, too, felt concern that our profession needed to draw potential pilots and flight crews from black and other minority populations. I assumed our agreement covering the revisions and updating of the material would be followed to the letter of our new contract. Wrong! When I opened the first of the ten copies I purchased, I was astounded to find that ARCO had placed on the cover a very poor drawing which, I suppose was to represent a captain flying a transport type of aircraft, and several other glaring errors.

The pilot was flying with his hat on, which is never done. World War II style microphones were being worn in a picture published in a 1968 instructional book. The captain's uniform did not have the required four stripes. Finally, the photo on the cover showed the captain using a full control wheel instead of the half wheel which is used in transport type aircraft to provide better vision of the instrument panel.

On turning the first page I was shocked to see a much younger, and, I must say, more handsome man under whose

Captain
Kimball J. Scribner???

photograph was written my name. The real shocker came later on in the book with a photograph of another handsome pilot who was standing in front of a Trans World Airlines sign! Trans World Airlines! Adding insult to injury, the final photograph showed another pilot who was wearing another airline's uniform.

As a long time dedicated career man with Pan American

Airways, I moved swiftly to change these glaring errors. I called Dick Rosen. I called the ARCO people. I hired an attorney. I sent wires and letters. They finally made a change, but they only changed the first photograph with my name on it. When I continued to protest the glaring errors they were presenting, they promised to print another paperback with the exact display of illustrations of my choice, I said, "No, thanks." *Your Future as a Pilot* was updated in 1978 and issued as *Your Future in the Air.* The new edition bore my very carefully designed illustrations, as did another book, *Your Future in Aviation-On the Ground* which was published in 1979.

At a 1968 International Exposition of Flight and General Aviation Conference, I was a speaker and panelist at a symposium on air education and career opportunities, and was seated next to a fellow panelist, Jack Hunt, president of

Jack Hunt

Embry-Riddle Aeronautical Institute. That chance meeting was the beginning of a series of many changes for me and my family. My own experience of having served as an advanced flight instructor in the Embry-Riddle Flying School in Miami in 1940 was an instant connection of common interests between Jack and me. From that first meeting we developed a relationship which drew me into the phenomenal development and expansion of Embry-Riddle.

Jack Hunt was no ordinary man. His life and character manifested themselves in a series of dynamic achievements in aviation history and aeronautical education. In 1942, he served with the United States Army Air Corps, and received officer training for naval aviation. After leaving the Navy in 1946, he flew as chief pilot for Howard Hughes blimp "Outlaw".

He returned to active duty for the Navy in 1951, and received the Naval Reserve Medal. In 1952, Commander Hunt and his 13 crew members set out for an eleven day trans-oceanic flight which set endurance and distance records yet to be beaten. Their airship "Snowbird" traveled over three continents, and remained aloft for 264 hours without refueling. The treacherous 9448 mile journey departed Massachusetts on March 4, 1957, tracked a loop shaped path across the Atlantic and back, and landed in Key West, Florida on March 15th.

The flight was a great success in airship history, and President Eisenhower personally awarded the coveted Harmon International Trophy to Jack Hunt. He was also awarded the Distinguished Flying Cross by Admiral William Halsey. He returned to civilian life in 1958 directing the activities of an aviation consulting and real estate firm in Miami, Florida until his being hired by the Embry-Riddle Aeronautical Institute in 1962. During his term as President of Embry Riddle from 1963 to 1974, his visionary efforts were vital in establishing that center of learning as a primary force in the field of aviation education and training.

Originally, the Embry-Riddle Flying School was created by two midwestern aviators, T. Higbee Embry and J. Paul Riddle at Lunken Airport in Cincinnati, Ohio, in 1926.

Riddle, an Annapolis graduate, barnstormer, air show performer, entrepreneur, and flight instructor met T. Higbee Emery when the latter purchased a ride in one of Riddle's two Jenny biplanes. The rest is, as they say, history. Embry provided the money and business knowledge, and Riddle brought the vision and enthusiasm.

Their first venture as a company offered a flying school, mapping, and surveying on a large scale, courses in aviation to suit any need, air express, and mail delivery. Their first graduation class of 27 students held their commencement exercise in July of 1928. The company remained intact until 1929, when it incorporated and was owned by Aviation Corporation, later known as AVCO Corporation. In 1930, the corporation was taken over by American Airways. Embry moved to California where he lived until his sudden death in 1946. Riddle chose to stay with American Airways until 1932, when he moved to Miami to start new aviation ventures.

In 1939, Riddle joined with John McKay, a prominent attorney, to reopen the Embry-Riddle School of Aviation in Miami. The advent of World War II signalled the urgent need to train specialists for the Army Air Corps and the Royal Air Force of England. The school burgeoned, expanding to train mechanics, navigators, and pilots at its land and seaplane bases in Florida, Tennessee, and Sao Paulo, Brazil. In 1944 McKay and Riddle dissolved the partnership with Riddle taking the Brazilian holdings, and McKay keeping the U.S. operations.

John Paul Riddle

After World War II, with the military air fields phased out, McKay expanded the curriculum and renamed the school Embry-Riddle International School of Aviation with its focus on pilot and technical training for commercial and

Kenneth L. Tallman, *President*

EMBRY-RIDDLE AERONAUTICAL UNIVERSITY

Daytona Beach, Florida Campus

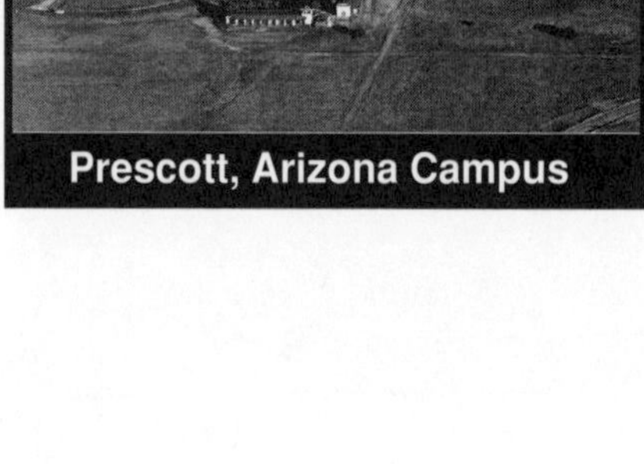

Prescott, Arizona Campus

Embry-Riddle Aeronautical University is the world's largest and oldest, totally aviation-oriented, accredited university. A private, independent, co-educational institution founded in 1926, Embry-Riddle has an enrollment of about 13,000 full-time and part-time students. In addition to its traditional, residential campuses in Daytona Beach, Florida, and Prescott, Arizona, Embry-Riddle serves the continuing education needs of the aviation industry through an extensive network of off-campus centers in the U.S. and Europe and through the sponsorship of programs and seminars covering all facets of aviation. Embry-Riddle offers academic degrees through the Master's level from among its disciplines of engineering, computer science, avionics, aviation maintenance, flight and business administration. Embry-Riddle graduates nearly 2,300 students each year, with approximately 20% receiving degrees in the professional pilot programs.

business aviation. In 1947 they logged their 2 millionth hour of flight.

In 1961, the school was reorganized as an independent nonprofit organization and changed its name to Embry-Riddle Aeronautical Institute.

Jack Hunt assumed the presidency in 1963. Under his guidance, there began plans for expansion and development, and finding a new location offering more room for growth. In April 1965, the Institute moved to its current home at Daytona Beach Regional Airport where there were facilities, and adequate space for the anticipated expansion.

In 1968, the Institute received accreditation from the Southern Association of Colleges and Schools. University status was achieved in 1970. E-RAU is, in fact, the world's only totally aviation oriented university. In addition to the Daytona Beach campus, the university has more than 80 resident centers located world wide, and a western campus located in Prescott, Arizona.

From that first meeting with Jack Hunt I became involved with E-RAU and have been able to observe and participate in its growth, development and many innovations in aviation education. From that initial series of visits to Embry-Riddle, my involvement and commitment led me to relocate to Daytona Beach, and to offer a commitment of time and effort to aid in its outstanding program for development of pilots, technicians and other aviation vocations. My daughters, Susan and Colleen, were among the first women to be enrolled in the pilot training program at Embry-Riddle. In addition to pursuit of my career with Pan American, I was able to serve as a trustee of the University, and was awarded an Honorary Degree, Doctor of Aeronautical Science.

Chapter Twenty Six

THE GREAT RACE

Daily Mail

Announcing the last big adventure before Concorde

The greatest air race ever

Chapter Twenty-Six

In 1969, I embarked on an adventure which would include my entire family. To commemorate the fiftieth anniversary of the first flight across the Atlantic Ocean by two Englishmen, John William Alcock and Arthur Whitten Brown, the London based newspaper, *The Daily Mail,* sponsored an exciting air race over the Atlantic between New York and London. The race, held during eight consecutive days in May of 1969, offered prize money for twenty-one various categories totaling nearly $150,000, and offered enticing challenges for self styled adventurers with imagination.

The Vickers-Vimy biplane flown by Alcock and Brown

The race was unique in that it could be run in either direction over the Atlantic, with the starting or landing points set from the top of the Empire State Building in New York City and/or the Post Office Tower in London. It was open to all comers, be they aircraft owners or ticket holders. Tremendous interest generated from both sides of the Atlantic, attracting 390 competitors from 10 different countries, including military pilots with supersonic aircraft, private pilots with small aircraft, members of royalty, passengers flying a variety of commercial airlines, and representatives from aviation groups such as the Wings Club of New York.

Speed in the air was important, but time saved on the ground was essential. One of the overriding factors to be brought out by the race was that the time spent transporting between the downtown areas of New York, London and their respective airports was excessive and should be reduced. While the original historic race was run from St. Johns, Newfoundland, Canada to Clifden, Ireland, the two metropolitan cities were chosen to underscore the lost time in travel in airport congestion.

Originality and the development of means to reduce ground travel time of the 3,500 mile race were the most important considerations for all of the competitors. All sorts of vehicles were used in the overall race. In addition to the flying craft over the Atlantic, helicopters, motorcycles, taxis, and high powered cars were to be put into action to expedite travel to and from airports.

I discovered the race through my affiliation with the Wings Club, and, at once, saw it as an event not to be missed. I obtained the race rules and applications, and, as I studied the format, realized that with ingenuity, planning, and money to spend, there was no reason why I could not win some of the prize money. By flying a regularly scheduled Pan American route from New York to London, I could obtain the aircraft for the Atlantic crossing. Of course, I could not be a direct contestant, and still fly the Pan American 707. My teenage daughters, Colleen and Susan could though. One daughter could race to London with me from New York, and the other return from London to New York, giving us a shot at winning both ways.

My friend, Colonel Tippett, shared my enthusiasm for the race and suggested that I associate myself with *Sports Illustrated* magazine. Tip felt the magazine might want to participate in the race, and make a feature story of Colleen's and Susan's racing. Through Tip's connections I was able to meet with *Sports Illustrated*'s senior editor, Bob Ottum, and photographer, Jerry Cooke, to discuss my plans. Since no conflict of interest would arise with my daughters racing as independents, there was meat for a great story and a lot of fun available in the project, Bob and Jerry joined the adventure with an agreement that the magazine would pick up special costs involved for land transportation and related race costs, in exchange for an exclusive story.

I carefully planned the project, noting all of the rules and regulations, arranging myself for an appropriate scheduled Pan American New York-London route, and securing early check ins for the flight for the contestants, Susan, Bob and Jerry. Since Colleen was to run the race on the return flight, she flew as a regular passenger for the first race attempt on May 18, 1969, watching the operation so that she might improve her chances for the return to New York.

Sports Illustrated offered their London representative, Bill McDavitt, as coordinator of the project with me. In London he arranged for rental of a helicopter to fly the contestants from Heathrow Airport to the heart of London, rented a barge anchored near the Waterloo Bridge on which to land a helicopter, hired a small boat to take the contestants from the barge to a nearby dock, and reserved three motorcycles with drivers to await the contestants being off-loaded from the dock and race them to the Post Office Tower.

On the afternoon of May 18, I arranged for our Pan American personnel checking the departing passengers to give and collect boarding passes ahead of time from Susan, Bob and Jerry in order for their names to be placed on the passenger manifest. This allowed me to sneak the three of them out a side door fire exit, and into a taxi for a drive to the

Susi Scribner Wins Great Air Race

DID YOU KNOW that in 1969 an alumna of Embry-Riddle set a world's record for traveling from the top of the Empire State Building in New york to the top of the Government Post Office Building in London?

She is Susi Scribner, daughter of Pan Am Capt. Kimball J. Scribner, Chairman of E-RAU's National Advisory Council. Susi's sister, Colleen (now a nurse in E-RAU's Infirmary) entered the race too, traveling in the opposite direction from London to New York, but due to a series of bad breaks, Colleen did not finish in the money. Her experience, too, would make exciting reading, but our story this time centers around Susi and how she was able to beat the pro's at their own game.

AN EXCITED SUSI *shown after she was spirited aboard the Pan Am flight to London. And the race is on!*

HOW IT ALL BEGAN

"No way we can lose this race. No way," said Pan AMerican Airways Captain Kimball J. Scribner as he raised his glass in a final toast to the three members of the newly proclaimed "Sixth Avenue Racing Team" sitting across from him in the plush Manhattan restaurant.

Kim had a very special interest in the team now conspiring together for the last time before the big air race. One of the three - the bouncy, brown-eyed girl smiling back at him now - was his own, 17-year old daughter, Susi.

The other two were Jerry Cooke, bon vivant, world traveling photographer and Bob Ottum, well known writer and adventurer. THEIR reasons for entering the race were obvious. But, why had they chosen young Susi Scribner as their third partner?

Ottum said it this way:

"Susi was selected on the basis of her charm, poise, cuteness, and overall demeanor. Ah, yes, and her daddy who would fly the team to London."

Between the three of them, they hoped to walk away with a lion's share of the $137,400 purse by placing first in each of three different categories.

The daring Transatlantic race, would run for a week. Aside from a few rules, the only thing that mattered was who could make the fastest run from the top of the Empire State Building in New York to the top of the General Post Office Tower in London (or vice versa) during the week. Any mode of transportation was allowed with one exception. Aircraft were not permitted to land on top of either building. This meant miles of heavy city traffic would have to be negotiated on the ground at either end of the run.

"THE GREAT AIR RACE" was dreamed up by the London Daily mail, a gaudy newspaper with a circulation of better than 2 million. Black headlines in ink that comes off on your fingers. Cheesecake, vivid writing - and vivid promotion. The contest was to be international, but everyone knew the London Daily Mail, who stood to get a lot of mileage out of the race, expected an Englishman to win.

AS the time drew near, widely publicized preparations for the

***WINNER'S SMILE** says it all as proud parents, Kim and Gloris Scribner greet Susi back in New York.*

race had taken on all the overtones of a P. T. Barnum extravaganza. For months now, 397 contestants from all over the world and hundreds of "accomplices" had been hatching diabolical schemes to outwit their competitors. It was obvious from the start everyone intended to bend the rules - if not actually break them.

With this in mind, the Sixth Avenue Racing Team and Pilot Kim Scribner went over their master plan one last time.

THE PLAN

The plan was beautiful in its simplicity. Susi's father would be in command of Pan Am's regularly scheduled flight from Kennedy International that night and could help them shave precious minutes off their air time.

Pan Am's infallible computer had promised a jet stream at 27,000 feet that night. With any luck at all, they'd be assigned an altitude that would give them a beautiful tailwind all the way to London.. Then too, he could hold up the flight till the last-minute, then take off immediately once they were on board.

...Towards the end of the race, the Thames River came up under them, then the Waterloo Bridge and beyond that, they could make out their destination - the GPO Tower! AS they sped towards it, they stared at the tower - 36 stories tall, round, with a revolving restaurant at the top.

Looking down, the copter pilot yelled, Where's that barge!"

"There it is! Someone shouted and soon they were settling down shakily onto the deck of a small barge in the Thames River. A waiting motor launch seemed to take forever putt-putting towards the nearest shore. Then, onto the banks of three more motorcycles for the final hair raising ride to the GPO Building.

SUSI'S A WINNER!

Susi was first up in the elevator and punched in for "First Place" in her category - for "unsponsored contestants flying via a regularly scheduled airliner. "

Cooke and Ottum, though close behind her, had entered in different categories and didn't place at all.

By now, the closing hours of the race had brought excitement to a fever pitch on the roof of the GPO Building. Exhuberant spectators, newsmen and photographers from the London Daily Mail were milling about noisily amid endless tangles of television cables and cameras.

Cooke and Ottum caught a brief glimpse of Susi before newsmen closed in on her, asking questions and taking pictures.

*COLLEEN SCRIBNER AND DAD, **Capt. Kim Scribner who flew the team to London. Colleen entered the race too, but met with misfortune and did not place. She helped organize the Daytona Beach Alumni Chapter and became a nurse at Embry-Riddle.***

Empire State Building. Once at the top of roof top area, after identifying themselves as race contestants, they waited for the message from me for the departure time.

At 9:58 p.m. the three contestants officially began the race, setting off on their route to the airport. At 10:00 p.m. I closed the doors of the 707, and signalled the crew that I was ready to depart. We were pushed back, I started all four engines, and received clearance to taxi to the takeoff runway.

The three passengers had been counted as being aboard, though actually they were sitting at the Empire State Building elevator being held open for them by a friend. After

arriving at street level, they scurried to the curb where an ambulance, hired by *Sports Illustrated*, waited. With red lights and sirens blasting, they dashed to a helicopter pad located in lower Manhattan. The ambulance screeched to a halt, and out jumped the contestants, with Jerry madly snapping photographs. As they ran toward the helicopter which was to ferry them to the 707, a police car roared up behind the ambulance. On discerning the mission of the errant ambulance, the police issued a ticket for a $50 fine to *Sports Illustrated.* Meanwhile, I was taxiing the 707 away from the terminal toward the active runway at J. F. K. Airport.

The helicopter approached and landed at the appointed helipad. The three racers jumped out of their whirlybird and into a waiting Pan American car which was equipped with lighted markings, flags, and a radio to speed their journey to the 707 which I was holding for them, and for clearance for takeoff.

As we had practiced on the day before, the drop door beneath the cockpit was utilized for entry of the racers into the aircraft, thus avoiding having to open the regular passenger doors. The drop door permitted entry to the belly (lower 41 section) of the airplane.

All was going famously. I flashed my landing lights in order for the Pan American vehicle driver to locate me among the other aircraft waiting in line for clearance for takeoff. The driver spirited the racers to a quick stop beside my airplane. The engineer descended through the belly compartment onto the ground, assisted the contestants up into the airplane, closed and locked the hatch behind him.

At this point in the race, I could have saved about 15 minutes if I had moved out of position, taxied past three jet transports ahead of me, claiming that I misunderstood the ground controller's instructions, and taken off prematurely, and out of turn. I couldn't do it. It would be unfair, to say the least, since other contestants were on other planes waiting for clearance for takeoff. I was, to put it mildly, chagrined to discover later that a TWA pilot had succumbed to just such a temptation in his race attempt, taking unfair advantage.

Enroute to London, I flew at altitudes where the best speed could be obtained, though not the most economical

with respect to fuel saving. The optimum economical level for flights of this distance eastbound is about 35,000 feet, depending upon wind velocity and direction, as well as air temperature. I flew most of the trip at 27,000 feet where the air density allowed greater air speed and winds were more favorable, utilizing a maximum allowable speed which we called the "jingle bell cruise". The phrase indicates that an airplane is being flown right up to the edge of the maximum allowable indicated air speed, which, if exceeded, causes bells to ring.

Landing at Heathrow Airport was terrific. The controllers were most helpful, allowing us to approach quickly, descend and land straight in. No holding patterns were required. All our coordination efforts began to pay off. Pan American special service representatives were waiting for us as the doors opened. They immediately whisked Susan, Jerry, and Bob through immigrations and customs services, giving their passports and custom forms to a Pan American representative as they all, including the immigration inspector, ran down the ramp into the crowded, busy terminal. Amid the throngs of people in the terminal, shouts were heard from other embarking passengers, "It's those crazy air racers! Watch out, they're Americans!" Out ahead, the Pan American representative had the passports stamped and handed back as the racers flashed by the inspector's smiling face.

Through an appointed doorway, onto the ramp area, the racers forged to a waiting car to carry them to the Heathrow Helipad for their flight into London. Crash helmets were issued to each person as they boarded the waiting helicopter which took them to the rented coal barge, anchored in the

middle of the Thames River. Landing on a small 10 foot, silver painted square hatch top on the barge was smooth, and facilitated with ease. Our racers moved quickly from the barge to the "Gimpy", an old motor launch tied alongside the barge, and motored across the river to the pier.

Atop the pier, at street level, were the waiting leather

clad motorcyclists and bikes. The final leg of the conveyances was fraught with some minor scrapes when, amid heavy traffic, Bob's driver went up the wrong way on a one way street. They faced head on with a truck, slid about and tipped over as they hit the curbing, but swiftly righted themselves and raced through an alley to arrive at the Post Office Tower.

Susan arrived just ahead of Bob. Her driver had skidded to a stop within a few blocks distance of the destination because of a drive chain which fouled up on the sprocket. Unable to drive further, Susan ran down streets (thanks to directions of amazed local citizens), into the elevator and up to the top of Post Office Tower. She clocked out her time for the race at 6 hours, 55 minutes, 48.43 seconds, an average on land, sea and air of 499 miles per hour. Jerry Cooke's motorcycle driver got lost, bringing him in behind Bob Ottum.

Susan won $6,000 for the best time in the Unsponsored Personal Attempt category, one of only five Americans in all who finished in the money. Prizes were awarded a week later in London at a gala event with Prince Phillip, Duke of Edinburgh, participating in the presentation ceremonies.

Susan
Prince Phillip

For the return race with my older daughter Colleen, the fates did not smile so kindly on our efforts. Col-

leen departed the Post Office Tower on a wild motorcycle ride which started out with the cyclist spinning and sliding to a stop on their first turn. As they lifted the cycle to right it on the road a backup cycle came up, and its driver had Colleen jump on with him for her ride to the Heathrow. Once there, I had to deliver the bad news that we had a delay for the flight for a minimum of an hour and a half for maintenance problems.

Once in New York, there was no car to take her to the Empire State Building. After hailing a cab and running furiously, she arrived, checked in and announced, "I think I may have beaten the chimpanzee who entered the race." Sadly, she was wrong about the chimp, even his luck was better than ours this time.

Colleen collected a participant's medal. She and her sister, Susan, were awarded a first class round the world trip from Pan American Airways, and a trip to Africa. The sisters divided the prize money we won, using it to attend Embry Riddle Aeronautical University in the summer of 1970, where they each received their private pilot's licenses, and were among the first women to participate in the university's pilot training programs.

Sports Illustrated published an outstanding story on the race with splendid accompanying photographs. My recent rereading of that piece has led me to ponder about the next similar running of that air race to be held 50 years from that contest. Susan will be 67 years old and Colleen 69. I expect them to carry on the tradition. Of course, my granddaughters, Kimberly and Alissa, may give them a run for their money in 2019.

Chapter Twenty Seven

BUZZING THE COTTON BOWL

AILINE PILOT /February, 1970

Chapter Twenty-Seven

At the end of the 1960's, the steady increase of airline traffic, particularly transatlantic passenger travel, ushered in new considerations and developments for passenger transport. President Juan Trippe, in his usual progressive and bold manner, introduced the Boeing 747, an aircraft which was twice the size of the Boeing 707's, the former flagships of Pan American. This new "ultimate airliner" provided 370 passenger seats, flew at 589 miles per hour, held a statute miles range of 5500, and weighed 15 tons.

In June of 1969, I was awarded a vacant captaincy on the new airliner, due for delivery in six months. My first round of training was ten days at the 747 ground school in New York. Since there was no simulator available for the 747, plans were made to do all of the required flight training in Roswell, New Mexico, an airport with minimum traffic where the weather would be favorable round the clock.

The Atlantic Division chief pilot, Bob Weeks, received his ground school and flight training in Seattle, home of the newly manufactured 747 jumbo jets. The senior captains to be checked out were scheduled to report to Roswell, in order of their seniority, to get their ratings on the airplane.

Pan American accepted the first 747 in Boston, in order to offset the New York state tax. Since it was located in Boston, the public relations people decided to provide free rides to select Boston area citizens. After this choice bit of promotion, the airplane was then to be ferried to Houston, Texas, to exhibit the airplane on New Year's Day, and to pick up more captains to fly out to New Mexico for their flight training.

Bob Weeks phoned me asking if I would like to come up to Boston to fly as copilot to Houston as my introduction to the airplane. I thought this was a perfect idea, and began packing my bag. Since my oldest daughter, Colleen, was then a nurse at Massachusetts General Hospital, I was granted permission for her to ride on one of the demonstration flights in Boston. Actually, she rode the jumbo jet prior to my being able to do so.

Colleen

My first opportunity to go aboard the airplane was a ferry flight with only employees aboard on December 31, 1969. I found the takeoff easy, climbed, and flew to Houston. With cautious directions, Bob allowed me to make the landing in Houston. Bob called out the radio altimeter readings, and, at 30 feet, I brought the nose of the plane to a level off position. The plane actually landed itself, the touch down was fantastic, I could not feel it. I raised the spoilers, put all the engines in reverse, applied a small amount of power for the long runway, then we came to a smooth stop, and began to taxi back.

While we were taxiing toward the terminal, a DC-9 appeared on a parallel taxiway. It kept up with our speed in order to get a good look at us. From our cockpit 34 feet above the ground, the DC-9 looked tiny. We were on the same radio frequency, so Captain Weeks hailed them with, "Hello, little brother." "Hi," came back the reply from the DC-9, "Wanna' drag."

For the flight on New Year's Day, the mayor of Houston

and his guests were invited for a 747 ride. The public relations team came up with the idea that our flight would go up to Dallas, and fly over the Cotton Bowl at half time of the game between Notre Dame and the University of Texas. Of course, the idea was that the television cameras shooting the game could be directed at the 747 as it flew over the football stadium, allowing the millions of Americans watching the game to get their first viewing of our new prize aircraft.

Since I was not due at Roswell for the first group training, Captain Weeks chose me for the flight. Before he left the cockpit to go downstairs to meet with the mayor and his champagne sipping entourage, I spoke to him about our visit to the Cotton Bowl. We agreed that I would fly high over the stadium and return again, but at the same level as the Goodyear blimp, and any other aircraft, taking great care not to come close to them.

Well, our first problem was to find the Cotton Bowl. It was not on our charts, but we knew we could rely on Dallas radar control once we were within their range. I advised Captain Weeks that I would not try to land in the stadium. With a big grin he departed to join the mayor in the 747 lounge.

Without calling upon Dallas radar for directions, one of the pilots aboard called out, "There's the blimp." Off to our left and ahead of us we could see the Goodyear blimp, at about 2,000 feet, circling the Cotton Bowl stadium. We were level with the blimp, settling to remain at that height. One of the Pan American photographers aboard came to me to ask if I could fly over the stadium, and bank up in a turn, in order for him to shoot some shots down into the stadium and playing field. No problem, I put the 747 in a reasonable turn over the area, and he managed to take some fine pictures.

We continued away from the bowl, turned to circle it, still remaining high, as we searched the sky for other aircraft which might be in the area. Realizing all those television cameras would be on us, I made a turn and with flaps extended a bit, and with power reduced, we began a slow descent to be at the same level as the blimp. The blimp was flying around the stadium, not over it, we saw no other aircraft.

The radio altimeter was not turned on. The pressure altimeters were all set for the Dallas barometric pressure, and we could only tell our height above sea level, not above the Cotton Bowl. None of us could tell the height above the ground over which we were flying. We were not at all concerned. We knew we were flying in a safe, careful manner. However, among the spectators viewing the game, there were quite a few Federal Aviation Authority inspectors.

We did not realize at the time that American Airlines was sponsoring the Cotton Bowl game. When they discovered that Pan American was about to reap untold benefits from flying the first 747 on their bill, they refused to allow the cameramen to take any television camera footage as we made that one relatively low pass overhead. An alert newspaper reporter did get an excellent still photograph which ended up on the front page of a Dallas newspaper the next day. As we

flew away and climbed up to return to Houston, no one in the crew or the elegant lounge expressed any comment, or made reference to our low flight.

The FAA had a rather different opinion. They imposed a fine of $1,000.00 on the Captain. Not I. I had no license to fly that airplane, I was not in command. Captain Weeks, who had been with the mayor and his party, was the captain. After landing in Houston, I flew back on the next Eastern Airlines flight to New York.

The FAA officials came aboard the Pan American 747 in Houston, and removed the automatic flight recorder from the airliner. They planned to use that instrument, which records all of the flight information, as their evidence to press the charge that the flight over the Cotton Bowl was too low. The only problem for them was that the flight recorder was not turned on, the flight was not a scheduled passenger flight. They contacted Captain Weeks and stated a fine of $1,000.

At my suggestion, Bob wrote a careful letter to the FAA. mentioning "the flight," not the fact he was not flying the 747.

He indicated very specifically that "the flight" was flown at the same level as the other aircraft in the area, in order to keep them in sight. The response was to modify the fine to $750. I then advised another letter be sent to a higher echelon in the FAA with the same essential explanation. This time he received a further fine reduction down to $500. On hearing of the still exorbitant fine, I advised Bob that he was not writing enough letters. When the final reduction to $250 was received, we both agreed that Pan American could afford to pay this fine back to him in the form of lunch money.

After receiving my 747 rating in February, 1970, I was selected to fly the inaugural Boeing 747 flight 115, New York to Paris, accompanied by Captain Jess Tranter, assistant chief pilot. Since this was an inaugural flight, the FAA assigned their senior operations inspector, Mr. Ray Hirsch, to accompany, and monitor the flight. All of the captains knew Ray Hirsch to be the most demanding of the government aeronautical inspectors. He was tough, and, without hesitation, would "down" a pilot for any infraction of rules or regulations.

I prepared for the flight knowing he would monitor my every move from check in at the flight operations office. On signing in for the flight, I realized immediately that weather was to be a factor for the journey, heavy snowfall was prevailing throughout the European sector of the flight. Selection of an alternate airport, special preparations and computations on fuel, allowable weight, and speeds had to be figured.

The flight to Paris was routine in all respects until we began our approach to the French coastline. We reached the 35,000 foot flight level, and stayed there because Orly Airport, our destination, was closed. Heavy snowfall had reduced the visibility to zero. I had reduced the power of the engines to long range cruise condition several hours prior to reaching France. Since forecasts for the next several hours remained unchanged, we prepared an updated list of all

Boeing 747, the "Jumbo Jet"

Following Boeing's great success with the 707, 727, and 737 jet airliners, the 747 heralds a new class of aircraft described as the "Jumbo Jets". Four 46, 150 pound thrust Pratt & Whitney JT9D&A engines powered this mighty beast. The first 747 flew early in 1969 and orders for 183 had been placed by August 1969. With a wing span of 189 ft. 8 in. and length of 231 ft. 4 in., a variation of layouts enabled anything from 363 to 490 passengers to be carried at a cruising speed of Mach 0.89 for a range of 4,600 miles (with maximum payload). The fuel supply, 7,860 gallons, powers the average car 6 times around the world. Its heating system could warm sixty average-sized houses.

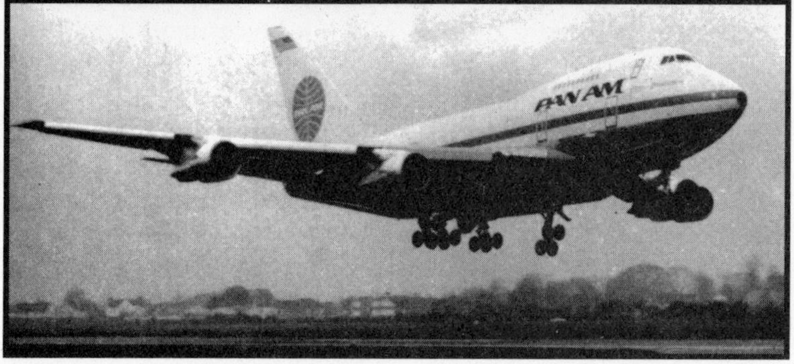

other available airports.

We entered a holding pattern over the Paris area and waited for the snow to abate enough to improve visibility to our minimum of 800 meters.

Finally, the weather changed enough to reach our minimum allowable for instrument approach, we were still very high to conserve fuel. I wanted to expedite the descent, but I was entering into an ice formation condition. I was limited in my speed, I could not reduce all power on the engines, because I needed their generated heat to provide anti-icing for the wing's leading edges. I was, also, too high to utilize the spoilers.

Ray Hirsch sat quietly behind me in the jump seat saying nothing, only watching and listening to the conversations of the copilot and me as we were reading checklists, and receiving radio clearances from Paris traffic control. We were above the twenty two thousand foot level where spoilers were not permitted to be used, because tests had not been made on the 747's stall performance at that altitude. Considering my lack of options, I made the choice to sneak on a bit of spoilers action in order to keep the power up on the engines to give us essential heat. We were in good luck! The weather did not worsen. I was able to implement a low level approach, and effect a quiet landing in the snow.

After the passengers had disembarked, Ray Hirsch came by to shake hands. He commented that the flight was fine, and explained that he would not be returning with us, but would be taking an immediate return flight. Just before leaving the customs area he came over to me, and, with a quick look over his shoulder and around the room, said, "Kim, I saw you put a few degrees of spoilers on above the limit altitude." I paused, smiled, and he smiled broadly back as he waved good-bye.

The publicity over the first arrival of the 747 drew tremendous interest and enthusiasm from the French, causing traffic jams so thick toward the airport that the flight crew was seriously delayed in reaching the terminal for the return flight on the next day. Once aboard the aircraft, we became aware of thousands of smiling French faces awaiting the departure of the aircraft.

On departure, we went through the routine of check lists, door closings, and were advised to release the brakes, so that the aircraft could be pushed back to start the engines. We then entered a series of situations which required quick action. There was not enough heavy ground equipment to push us back with engines running in the wet snow. We were parked in a position so close to the terminal that our radio could not operate properly, because the copilot could not obtain clearance for us to be pushed back. He asked the ground crew to telephone the tower to obtain permission for us to be pushed back, then communicate with them for starting the engines and clearance to taxi to the runway for takeoff.

In preparation for our departure, we had programmed our inertial guidance system right up to the point of placing an essential switch to "navigate" before the airplane was to be moved. However, due to our frantic movements to communicate and obtain permission to be pushed back we failed to flip the switch.

Suddenly, after I released the brakes and we were being pushed back, we realized that we had allowed the plane to be moved without the navigate function being activated. I called quickly to the ground crew to stop the plane, because for the gyros in our inertial guidance system to be realigned properly, the airplane must be still for about twenty minutes after the switch has been activated. Thousands of people were staring at us waiting for the takeoff. What to do? I decided to sit there, and try to give some answer to the ground crew as to why we were holding the plane in place when it should be pushed back a little more to start the engines.

The copilot, flight engineer, and I, had all three made a mistake. Any one of us could and should have put the switch into proper position prior to allowing the plane to be moved. We did what most self respecting Americans do. We moved to save face! We dreamed up some malfunction at the engineer's panel. We swore on our lives never to reveal why we sat there for twenty minutes with all those people looking at us, and I responded with, "Just a few more minutes and we will have our flight engineer's panel operating properly." Time passed, and, with the switch in position, we were off to New York!

With its new Boeing 747's, Pan American was selected to conduct one of the first attempts to demonstrate the utilization of a satellite stationed 28,000 miles above the earth at the equator. Stationary in orbit, the satellite was positioned for responsive radio voice transmission to a large segment of the earth's surface. The Air Transport Association, in conjunction with Air Inc. (a corporate group of airlines), the FAA, and various other government agencies, mounted a unique antenna on a Pan American 747 scheduled to fly a commercial round trip from New York to San Juan, Puerto Rico.

Prior to this innovative development, there existed, on over the ocean flights, the continued problem of maintaining voice communications with ocean flight control stations on land. On flights over land areas, direct communication was established using very high frequencies which gave line of sight direct contact between the airplane and a ground station located within range of the flying plane. The higher a plane flew the greater the line of sight distance.

When a plane flew beyond 200 miles from a land based radio station, a different type of radio transmission was required. The high frequency band of frequencies were used permitting the radio signal to go beyond the line of sight distance. The radio voice was transmitted upward and outward to bounce off a region of ionized gas low in the ionosphere known as the "Heaviside layer". The signal then bounced back beyond the horizon over great distances.

However, the signals were most erratic, due to sun spots, atmospheric conditions, variable air density, humidity, and the time of day, or night, the transmission was made.

Frequently, the reliability was so poor that an aircraft would remain out of communications. In those cases, attempts had to be made between aircraft to pass a message onward to reach a control station on any side of the ocean. Controllers on either side of an ocean used land lines and ocean cables to track and monitor the progress of all ocean flying aircraft.

Ben McLeod, vice president of communications, and Captain Waldo Lynch made all of the provisions for this development test utilizing the satellite for the project identified as Satcom-6. I was asked by Ben McLeod to aid the first inflight voice communication tests, utilizing the satellite on the New York to San Juan route. The plan was made for me to establish the first voice communications from our Pan American 707 to various ground stations located far apart over the United States.

Enroute to San Juan, we flew at various altitudes, and a recording tape was made by Ben McLeod and his engineer of our transmissions made to various radio stations located in Miami, Annapolis, Maryland, and west to California. The results of the test were excellent. It was an historic and thrilling experience to be a part of the implementation of this technological innovation. I got quite a thrill knowing that I made the first phone call ever made from the 707 to the satellite, back to the earth, then by phone lines to various offices around the country.

This communication development made possible our great ease of speaking to and understanding responses of persons in other stations throughout the United States. The tie in with land line phones gave us the same clarity and reliability we would have in any telephone conversation. This test was to bring about the use of stationary satellites not only for voice communications to expedite and safeguard over ocean air traffic control, it led the way toward live television coverage the world over.

In August of 1970, my wife and I moved our family to live in Daytona Beach, Florida. From there I commuted to New York, selecting my flight pattern to fly the maximum allowable time for the first part of one month and the latter part of the next month, which allowed me more free time to pursue personal and avocational projects.I later flew the first 747 into Daytona.

Daytonian Will Pilot first 747 to Land At Regional Airport

Captain Scribner and wife Gloria

If spectators were overwhelmed at the Boeing 747's size at it taxied in Thursday, airport officials and police felt the same about the huge jet that turned out to watch the jumbo jet land. All the Regional Airport's regular parking lot spaces were occupied more than an hour before the big ship set down, forcing hundreds to leave their cars bumper to bumper along the main entrance roadside and down the airport side streets.

Daytona Beach Morning Journal February 27, 1976

...Daddy, why does the 747 have such a high front end?
...Because the crew sits on their wallets!!

747 flying brought many delightful and experiences with a number of interesting passengers and flight events. The passengers, as always, were various and interesting, for they included film and stage stars, athletes, astronauts, pop and rock singers, and those instant celebrities we Americans are so famous for creating. The flight events sometimes came at the most unexpected times from uncontrollable sources.

In early summer of 1970, flying back from San Juan, the 747 I was flying was struck by lightning while we were in a holding pattern in dense clouds over J.F.K. Airport. Of course, we turned up all cockpit lights to full bright to avoid having the lightning flashes blind us. It was difficult at the time to determine if we had been struck by lightning or if we had experienced a discharge (a bolt of lightning, going from our plane to a cloud we were flying through).

Frequently, a plane will build up a potential of electric current. St. Elmo's fire can be seen along the wings, and, if the plane has propellers, there develops a ring of dancing colors around the prop tips. There is then a smell of ozone, one's hair becomes affected, and will stick out. Finally, comes the big bang, and the built up potential is released off of the plane by trailing threaded wire lightning arresters which serve the function of lightning rods.

On this occasion of being struck by lightning, a thorough maintenance check of the aircraft revealed only slight evidence of the strike. We took this as evidence that the 747 was bonded and shielded in an excellent manner to prevent electrical lightning jumping between metal parts of the plane and creating a fire hazard.

On December 30, 1970, flying a 747 from New York to Montego Bay, on the north coast of Jamaica, I was following a route down the east coast of the U. S. to fly over the central part of Cuba. The Cubans had a specific route established passing over Camaguey, Cuba monitored by their radar, which allowed Pan American flights to fly to and from Jamaica without flying around Cuba. We simply requested a radio clearance from Havana control as the flight approached the Cuban area.

After passing abeam Washington, D.C, on the airway taking me toward South Carolina, cruising with the automatic pilot engaged at 35,000 feet, my first officer, Bob Keyes, was giving a position report on our company frequency to Washington D.C. operations office at Dulles Airport. Without

warning, and under normal cruising quiet conditions, Bob's front cockpit window shattered. It did not break through, but, with a loud noise of cracking glass, the outer panel was destroyed. Thousands of cracks formed lines over the surface, and bits of the windshield began to break away.

I immediately pulled the power back on all four engines. I told the flight engineer to monitor our cabin pressure as I took the plane off the auto pilot. I was afraid of an explosive decompression. I called air traffic to explain that I wanted an immediate descent clearance to a low altitude because of the shattered window, and that there was no immediate emergency being declared.

As I eased the nose over, putting the seat belt and no smoking signs on, we received a clearance to descend to 8,000 feet. Without hesitation, I requested a radar vector toward Dulles Airport near Washington, D.C. Without increasing our speed, following the heading we were given to fly, we began a rapid, but smooth descent. More glass chips from the window fell off, but the inner window pane remained intact. I radioed Pan American operations at Dulles to advise them of our situation, and informed the passengers we were returning to D. C., because of some minor mechanical malfunction, for precautionary measures only. We landed without incident, and Pan American personnel began the work of removing the first officer's window panel for replacement.

The fraternity of aviation people is well known. One can hardly review a roster of organizations in the smallest hamlet in the country without coming across some type of "flying fools" who get together under the same banner. As their members will attest, the OX-5 Aviation Pioneers and the International Order of Characters are two of the most interesting and engaging organizations for aviation minded individuals. Each has provided me with delightful, ongoing intellectual stimulation and fun.

The OX-5 organization was founded at Latrobe, Pennsylvania, on August 22, 1956, and was registered and enfranchised in Pennsylvania as the OX-5 Club of America. The name has since been changed to OX-5 Aviation Pioneers, and it currently boasts membership in each of the 50 states and other parts of the world.

Organized exclusively for educational and scientific purposes, the organization compiles and records the history of the development of air transportation. It honors and perpetuates the memory of men and women pioneers in aviation who flew aircraft powered by the OX-5 engine, and persons who owned, were associated with, or participated in the design, construction, repair and maintenance of the OX-5 powered aircraft prior to December 31, 1940. Since I had jumped from and flown various old biplanes with the OX-5 engines in the 1930's, I became a member during the 1940s, and in 1978 was elected to their "Hall of Fame".

The OX-5 Aviation Pioneers support projects and programs designed to increase safety and efficiency in the use of aircraft, and encourage the establishment and operation of aviation museums and the collection of aviation memorabilia, particularly of the 1920-1940 era.

One of the most recent milestones in aviation history was made by my friend and fellow OX-5 member, William H. "Bill" Conrad, owner of Airline Training, Incorporated, in Miami. At the age of 80, on June 19, 1988, Bill made a successful flight test of his sleek, single engine Grumman American "Cheetah", providing the first plane flight powered solely by hydrogen.

Bill Conrad

This remarkable achievement came after 14 years of hard work to prove his theory that we can make inroads toward saving our environment if we convert our land, sea, and air vehicles to run on hydrogen. The project, despite the currently prohibitive price of hydrogen fuel, gives strong evidence that existing jet fuel is not our only fuel resource. Such transport would not only be cleaner and quieter; it would eliminate major pollutants which are endangering our planet.

Bill Conrad was an avid proponent of this alternative, pointing out the fact that hydrogen can be derived from water, and manufactured almost any place on the globe. With such availability, its cost would depend on the process used in its manufacture and the local cost of energy for creation of the fuel. Too, it is the most energetic of any fuel; only about one third as many pounds are required to fly a typical mission.

Hydrogen mixes rapidly and more uniformly with air in the engine fuel injection process, burning more evenly and completely, giving off almost pure, non-polluting vapor. When spilled, its rapid propensity to vaporize and become lighter than air indicates that in a jet crash that the survival chances of the plane's occupants are increased tremendously. Though experts still argue the commercial promise of hydrogen fuel, Bill continues his project, working toward his next goal of building the first hydrogen powered eighteen wheeler. Bill died in 1989. He was a great friend and sponsored my induction into the "Hall of Fame".

James E. Crane

Another favorite aviation oriented organization of mine is the International Order of Characters. Organized by Major James E. Crane, M.D., a flight surgeon with the 13th U.S. Air Force, during the grim early days of World War II in the South Pacific, the I. O. C. was originally created around a nucleus of allied airmen, each of whom was given a special name by Dr. Crane, alias 'The Brain,' on becoming a character.

As a member since 1951, I have carried the name Absolute Ruler, a reference to my position as chief pilot at the time of my induction into the I.O.C.

As the organization grew, it proudly included such members as General James H. Doolittle, William Lear, Colonel Roscoe Turner, Scott Crossfield, Colonel Francis Gabreski, Herbert Fisher, Arthur Godfrey, Tony Le Vier, Walter Schirra, James McDivitt, Pete Knight, Dick Merrill, Igor Sikorsky, Admiral Rosendahl, and many other civilian and military aviation related professionals equally worthy of mention.

Some I.O.C. members included Barry Goldwater *(Top left)*, General Doolittle *(Right)*, and Dick Merrill and Arthur Godfrey *(Bottom)*

It is a non profit college educational foundation which has granted over one hundred thousand dollars in scholarships to the children of deceased and incapacitated pilots. The I.O.C. meets twice a year, with a symposium held in Stamford, Connecticut each spring. The second meeting each year is held at interesting locations around the world, including Germany, England, Japan, Portugal, Greece, Italy, and New Zealand.

Another famous I.O.C. member is Senator Barry Goldwater. Senator Goldwater began his aviation carrer in 1929. He has logged over 15,000 flying hours which includes more than 2,000 hours of military. He entered the military four months prior to Pearl Harbor and served until after VJ day

1945. He is experienced in over 162 type of aricraft, from the great Lakes Trainer to helicopters and jets. The senator received the Air Medal and many other awards, dedicating his life to aviation as a flyer, military officer and a political constituent of air space issues of world importance.

Aviation has proven to be the greatest fraternity in the world for me. Even with language differences, cultural diversities and divisions, the shared challenges, stresses, dangers, and, most of all, the passion for flying transcend almost all the gaps.

Chapter Twenty Eight

GREAT YEARS WITH PAN AM

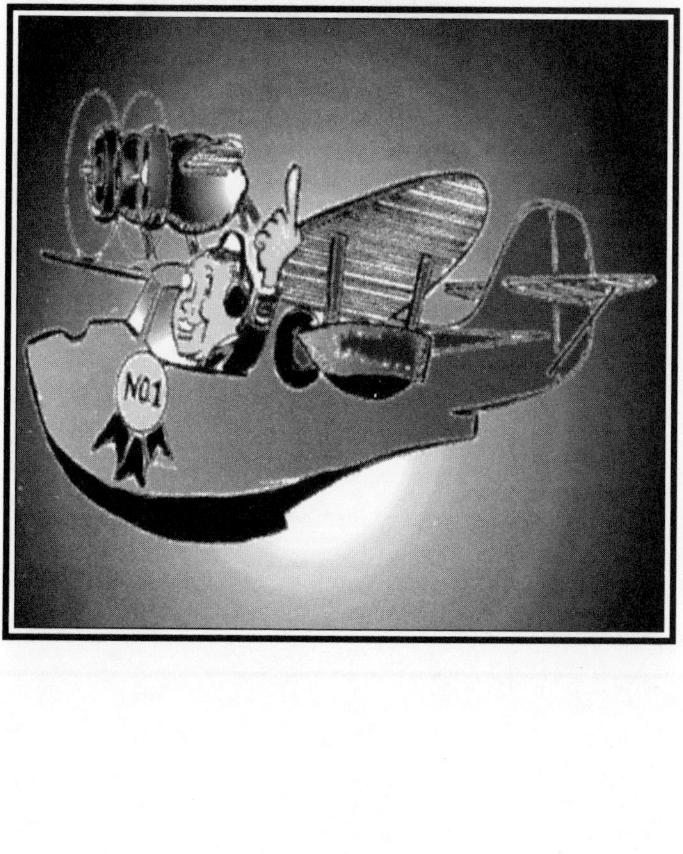

My Accumulated Flight Experience (1948-1977)

Appointments, Assignments & Checkouts

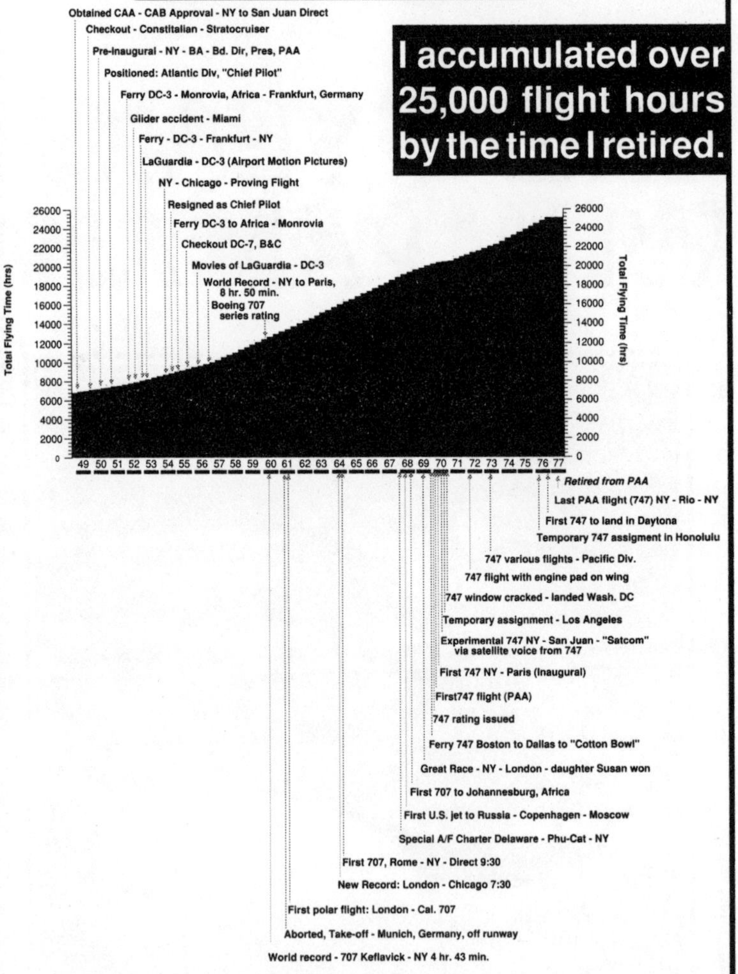

I accumulated over 25,000 flight hours by the time I retired.
Obtained CAA - CAB Approval - NY to San Juan Direct
Checkout - Constitalian - Stratocruiser
Pre-Inaugural - NY - BA - Bd. Dir, Pres, PAA
Positioned: Atlantic Div, "Chief Pilot"
Ferry DC-3 - Monrovia, Africa - Frankfurt, Germany
Glider accident - Miami
Ferry - DC-3 - Frankfurt - NY
LaGuardia - DC-3 (Airport Motion Pictures)
NY - Chicago - Proving Flight
Resigned as Chief Pilot
Ferry DC-3 to Africa - Monrovia
Checkout DC-7, B&C
Movies of LaGuardia - DC-3
World Record - NY to Paris, 8 hr. 50 min.
Boeing 707 series rating
Total Flying Time (hrs)
26000
24000
22000
20000
18000
16000
14000
12000
10000
8000
6000
4000
2000
0
49 50 51 52 53 54 55 56 57 58 59 60 61 62 63 64 65 66 67 68 69 70 71 72 73 74 75 76 77
Retired from PAA
Last PAA flight (747) NY - Rio - NY
First 747 to land in Daytona
Temporary 747 assigment in Honolulu
747 various flights - Pacific Div.
747 flight with engine pad on wing
747 window cracked - landed Wash. DC
Temporary assignment - Los Angeles
Experimental 747 NY - San Juan - "Satcom" via satellite voice from 747
First 747 NY - Paris (Inaugural)
First747 flight (PAA)
747 rating issued
Ferry 747 Boston to Dallas to "Cotton Bowl"
Great Race - NY - London - daughter Susan won
First 707 to Johannesburg, Africa
First U.S. jet to Russia - Copenhagen - Moscow
Special A/F Charter Delaware - Phu-Cat - NY
First 707, Rome - NY - Direct 9:30
New Record: London - Chicago 7:30
First polar flight: London - Cal. 707
Aborted, Take-off - Munich, Germany, off runway
World record - 707 Keflavick - NY 4 hr. 43 min.

Chapter Twenty-Eight

When reviewing aviation history, the singular contributions of Pan American cannot be overlooked or minimized. Of course, my 36 years inside the airline might be considered subjective, for part of the joy and ongoing impetus for affiliation with Pan American World Airways has been its history for being first. Throughout the world, its name and logo have become symbols of the United States on a par with Coca Cola and Kodak.

Pan American's pioneering, technical and business leadership gave the United States primacy throughout the world with its establishment of air transport service over the international trade routes considered of first importance to our commerce, postal service and national defense.

The years of planning and action have brought about the development of suitable aircraft, communication, navigation, and meteorological facilities. The airline's struggle for perfecting operating techniques and procedures, adaptation of laws and regulations relative to the requirements of international air transport, and solicitation and promotion of air traffic was complicated by the struggle for position against heavily subsidized airlines of foreign nations.

Pan Am can take you to every continent in the world Except one. Antarctica.
PAN AM
America's airline to the world.

The installation of airports, terminals, maintenance facilities, even the necessity of establishing completely self sufficient communities in remote and inaccessible locations resulted in the negotiation of operating concession contracts with foreign governments.

Under the aggressive and able guidance of Juan T. Trippe, for over 40 years, there were many Pan American "firsts." Pan American's initial route from Key West, Florida to Havana, Cuba dates back to 1927. Its operations in the Alaska region commenced in 1932. The first trans-Pacific scheduled air services were those of Pan American (the China Clipper) inaugurated in 1935.

Juan T. Trippe

The thrilling 1930's, or "Golden Years of Aviation" as they are now known, stand alone for the explosive growth and sheer luxury our Clipper series provided. The romance and adventure of those years remains a constant even to the uninitiated in aviation, and for those of us who shared the dreams, daring, and pioneering, they represent some of the finest hours of aviation adventure and development.

Operations to Bermuda began in 1937. The first regularly scheduled air service between the United States and Europe was initiated by our airline in 1939. Trans-Alantic service to Africa was begun December 6, 1941, the day before the Japanese attacked Pearl Harbor.

When World War II was declared, like millions of other Americans, Pan American enlisted for the duration. Suspending all commercial flying, the airlines flew more than 90 million miles, carrying top secret personnel and war materials. During those years Pan American established 50 airports and trained thousands of flyers, navigators and maintenance crews to aid the war effort.

Pan American was the first airline to acquire U.S. jet transports and, in 1958, the first to put them into service. Ours was the first 747 service, continuing our pattern of being the launching customer for the advances and innovations of aircraft design and production.

On March 1, 1977 I retired from my position with Pan American after nearly four exhilarating decades of learning,

Scenes from my last flight

teaching, testing, re-testing, laughing, enjoying, and "flying in fog". I am forever grateful for the many firsts in which I was able to participate as a Pan American pilot including: the pre-inaugural flight on the 377 Stratocruiser-New York to South America; the world record flight from New York to Paris (for propeller driven aircraft), time: 8 hours and 50 minutes; the first 707 flight to Russia; the first 707 flight to Johannesburg, South Africa; and the first 747 flight from New York to Paris.

Jockeying for business with the other national and international competition over purchase of new large body transports, the 1973 Arab oil embargo, over-expansion and take over of other airlines, and the airline deregulation have reduced the profitability and world wide power of Pan American. However, nothing can dim the achievements and revolutionizing influence the airline has been able to exert in over 6 decades of operations.

Substantial achievements, or our "firsts," accomplished by Pan American were, in most instances, a culmination of extensive planning, financial risk, diligent effort, and the overcoming of obstacles of either technological, political or economic significance. Most such accomplishments are based in aviation history, the full understanding and romance of which is lost in describing the ultimate event only in terms of the end result.

I feel compelled to describe the end result though, so I am providing a brief chronological description of many of those "firsts":

1927-First American airline to operate a permanent international service.
1927-First American airline to operate land planes over water on regularly scheduled flights.
1927-First American airline to schedule multi-engine aircraft permanently.
1928-First American airline to use radio.
1928-First American airline to use multiple flight crews.

1928-First American airline to develop airport and airways traffic control system.
1928-First airline to order and purchase aircraft built to its own specifications (Sikorsky 38).
1929-First airline to develop and use instrument flying techniques.
1929-First American airline to develop a complete avi—ation weather service.
1929-First airline to employ cabin attendants and serve meals aloft.
1930-First American airline to offer international air express service.
1931-First American airline to develop and operate four engined flying boats. (Sikorsky S-40).
1932-First airline to sell all expense international air tours.
1935-First airline to develop and use long range weather forecasting.
1935-First airline to install facilities for heating food aboard an aircraft.
1935-First airline to operate scheduled trans-Pacific service.
1937-First airline to operate, in continuous service, a transport aircraft with a pressurized cabin.
1939-First airline to provide trans-Atlantic passenger and mail service.
1942-First airline to complete a round the world flight.
1942-First airline to operate international service with all cargo service.
1944-First airline to propose a plan for low cost, mass transportation on a world wide basis.
1945-First airline to use high speed commercial land planes on a trans-oceanic route (DC-4).
1946-First American airline to install ground controlled approach in overseas operations.
1947-First airline to operate a scheduled commercial

round the world service.

1948-First airline to provide tourist class service outside the continental limits of the United States.

1949-First airline approved to fly New York-San Juan direct without a celestial navigator.

1948-First airline to link the United States and South Africa with regular service.

1950-First commercial airline to enter the Korean air lift.

1952-First airline to use aircraft built specifically for tourist class service on the trans-Atlantic route.

1955-First airline to order U. S. commercial jet trans ports.

1958-First airline to operate scheduled trans-Atlantic service with American built jets (Boeing 707).

1959-First airline to open a scheduled round the world jet service.

1961-First airline to offer a world wide marketing service for shippers and importers around the world.

1962-First airline to make 100,000 trans-Atlantic flights.

1963-First airline to operate the Boeing 707-321C pure jet freighters.

1964-First airline to relay in-flight messages via satellite Syncom III.

1965-First airline to operate round the world jet freighters.

1966-First airline to order the 747 Superjet.

1967-First airline to make fully automatic approach and landing in scheduled service.

Aerodynamic technical improvements fostered by Pan American include high wing loadings, high aspect ratio wings, and flush riveting. In 1934, the Sikorsky S-42 was flown at a wing loading of 28.6 pounds per square foot, later being increased to 33.7, and gradually increasing until the Constellation arrived with a wing loading of 49.7. The high aspect ratio wings increased aerodynamic efficiency. In 1936 an aspect ratio of 10.4 was used in the Sikorsky S-42A, a figure which has not been exceeded on any other air transport airplane used in regular service. Our flush riveting technique, including the fuselage, decreased drag to permit higher speed.

Pan American sponsored considerable research on aircraft hydrodynamic characteristics. A single example is the expenditure of more than $40.000, to improve the water handling characteristics of the Boeing 314. In addition, many tests were conducted for, and with, the N. A. C.A. and aircraft manufacturers concerning longitudinal, directional, and lateral stability of seaplanes.

The airline's efforts to improve aircraft structures were successful in increasing load carrying through utilization of a high ratio of useful load to gross weight. The Martin 130 had the highest ratio of useful load gross weight ever achieved in a U. S. transport plane until the development of the Martin Mars.

Other singular structural innovations include, installation of integral fuel tanks, wing flaps to permit higher wing loadings, implementation of water tight wings to provide emergency flotation, fuel dump valves to permit weight reduction for safety in emergency landings, installation of emergency exits, installation of oxygen supply for all passengers, winterization of aircraft, cowl flaps to provide improved engine cooling, installation of explosion proof electric motors, specification for flame proofing of interior fabrics, incorporation of accessibility of engines in flight, and flight training of design engineers.

Pan American made the first installation of twin row engines and production Wright Cyclone 14 engines (1500 horsepower) in air transport planes, reducing fuel consumption, and improving foil design and techniques as early as

1932.

The variable pitch propeller (providing higher efficiency for takeoff and cruising), installation of a propeller braking device (combining variable pitch and propeller brake with less drag), specification of the hydromatic full feathering propeller, and improved propeller air foil sections were significant Pan American fostered technical improvements.

Pan American sponsored the development of the first fuel flow meter and totalizer used for other than test purposes. The first of the improved design was installed in the 314 in 1939, and is now a standard instrument adopted by the airlines for all long range air transport. We were the first airline to install remote indicating instruments in commercial aircraft, the first to install a visual engine synchronizer, and we aided in the development of aircraft octants for improved navigation instrumentation.

At the forefront of operating techniques, we were the first to limit flight time of pilots to a maximum number of hours per year, develop procedure and equipment for night landings, implement docking procedure for airplanes, extensively use higher altitudes in cruising, and provide for continuous overhaul of aircraft without removing them from service for long periods.

The adventures, misadventures, goofs, puzzles, predicaments, exhilaration, enthrallment, joy, innovations, dead ends, new beginnings, and, most of all, the ability to pursue projects, reaching for the best, have been the gift of my years with Pan American. I was able to enjoy an era when the prestige and the potential capacity for adventure by airline captains was at its zenith.

In fairness to my readers, I close with one of the most profound descriptions of my profession I have heard, and one to which I give real credit. In response to a classroom assignment, an unknown fifth grader wrote:

> *"I want to be an airline pilot when I grow up because it is fun and easy to do. Pilots don't need*

much school, they just have to learn numbers so they can read instruments. I guess they should be able to read maps so they can find their way if they are lost. Pilots should be brave so they won't be scared if it's foggy and they can't see or if a wing or motor falls off they could stay calm so they'll know what to do. Pilots have to have good eyes so they can see through clouds and they can't be afraid of lightning or thunder because they are closer to them than we are. The salary pilots make is another thing I like. They make more money than they can spend. This is because most people think airplane flying is dangerous except pilots don't because they know how easy it is. There isn't much I don't like except girls like pilots and all the stewardesses want to marry them so they always have to chase them away so they won't bother them. I hope I don't get airsick because if I do I couldn't be a pilot and would have to go to work."

About the Author

Captain Kimball J. Scribner, Pan American World Airways Master Pilot and Chief Pilot, retired in 1977 at age sixty. He has 46 years of flying-over 36 with Pan American, with 35 years flying as a captain. He was designated Master Pilot of Flying Boats. As chief pilot for Pan American for seven years, he flew the first Boeing Stratocruiser to South America. On July 23, 1968, he was captain of the first U. S. transport-a Boeing 707- to fly into Moscow, Russia. On October 2, 1968, he flew the first jet transport to Johannesburg, South Africa. His actual flying time with Pan American exceeds three years (over 27,000 hours).

He served as consultant for Bendix Avionics Division, Fort Lauderdale, Florida, where he produced a visual training program on Digital Radar for the aviation industry and U.S. government.

As an author and lecturer, Captain Scribner has given lectures throughout the United States and in Europe.

Elected to the Board of Trustees of Embry Riddle Aeronautical University in 1969, Captain Scribner is now Trustee Emeritus, and Chairman of their International Advisory

Council. He served as the first Chairman of the Board of Directors of Daytona Beach Aviation, Inc., a fixed base operation owned by Embry Riddle.

EDUCATION

University of Maryland (1936-1939).

Completed Pan American pilot, navigation, and aircraft schools.

University of Virginia

Certificate, Nuclear Radiation Safety Officer, 1977.

ORGANIZATIONS

Elected Fellow Member, The Explorers Club, 1953.

Former Vice President and Director.

Former Chairman, Southeast Chapter.

Vice President, Explorers Research Corporation.

Chairman, Aviation Research Committee.

Member, National Soaring Society of America.

Member, Board of Trustees, Elmira, New York, Soaring Museum.

Board of Trustees, Embry Riddle Aeronautical University.

Trustee Emeritus, Embry Riddle Aeronautical University.

Chairman, International Advisory Council

Former Trustee, Golden Hills Academy, Ocala, Florida.

Member:

Aviation Space Writers Association. Airline Pilots Association: Quiet Birdmen, International Order of Characters. Member of Silver Wings, Sigma Chi, OX-5 Club "Hall of Fame", Cosmos Club, Wings Club, Airline Pilots Association (Retired), Pan American Airways Clipper Pioneers.

GENERAL AVIATION EXPERIENCE

1933

First parachute jump (16 years old).

Soloed (16 years old).

1938
Invented and tested first steerable parachute.

1938-1939
Appointed Chief Pilot and Flight Instructor for Congressional School of Aeronautics, Rockville, Maryland.

1940
Designated Flight Examiner, No. 228 By CAA. Taught flight training and ground school courses at George Washington University and University of Maryland.

Employed as Advanced Ground School Instructor and Flight Instructor at Embry Riddle Flying School, Miami Florida.

Taught University of Miami students advanced aerobatic flight and ground school training for commercial pilot licenses under the auspices of the Civilian Pilot Training Program.

1941-1977
Employed by Pan American World Airways.

1941
Employed by Pan American as copilot on flying boats in Miami. Qualified to fly four engine flying boat, the Sikorsky S-42. Checked out as a solo pilot to fly twin engine S-38s for local seaplane experience. Transferred to New York, Atlantic Division as Fourth Officer Ocean Pilot. Graduated as Second Officer from Pan American Celestial Navigation, on Boeing 314 Flying Clippers. Qualified and promoted to First Officer.

1942
Transferred to Miami and promoted to DC-3 captain. After 1,000 hours of command captain time, was transferred to New York, Atlantic Division, to undertake preparation to be-

come Master Pilot of Ocean Flying Boats. Licensed to fly Boeing Ocean Flying Clippers, the Boeing 314 and the Navy PB2Y3. Commissioned Lieutenant Senior Grade, United States Navy.

1944
Flew as captain on U. S. Navy PB2Y3's over north and south Atlantic routes.

1945
Transferred to Miami to fly in the Africa and Orient Division of Pan American Airways. Flew Air Force C-54's and Constellation L-49s under contract with the Air Transport Command.

1946
Appointed Master Check Pilot

1947
Appointed by CAA as Airline Transport Pilot Examiner, No. 2940.

1948
Appointed Senior Check Pilot assigned to Panagra routes on DC-6s.

Appointed Sector Chief Pilot and Senior Operations Representative with the Airline Transport Association for the Latin American Division, New York, the Latin American Division, Miami, and the Pacific Division in San Francisco.

1951
Appointed Atlantic Division Chief Pilot, responsible for all pilots and flight operations out of New York, London, and Germany.

As Chief Pilot of Pan American: Established and was elected chairman of the first International Airlines Chief Pilots's Committee for Air Transport Association, Established criteria and specifications for the flying of PAA route New York to San Juan direct. Developed system for utilizing wide screen color motion picture projection of airports to qualify pilots. Submitted and obtained Civil Air regulation change for same.

Produced various films on safety and evacuation of passengers and crew ditched at sea, and aborted takeoffs.

After seven years as Chief Pilot, returned to regular international airline flying as Master Pilot on the Boeing 707.

1977
Retired from flying on March 1, 1977 as Captain, Pan American World Airways, Boeing 747.

QUALIFIED AND LICENSED AS:
Airline Transport Pilot
Ratings and Limitations: Airplane-Single and Multi-engine Land and Sea, Boeing 377, Douglas DC-3, DC-4, DC-6, DC-7, Lockheed Constellation, Boeing 707-100,200, 300, and the 747 series. Commercial Glider and Flight Instructor. Ground Instructor of navigation, meteorology, theory of flight, aircraft and engines, parachutes, and civil air regulations. Ground Instructor Ratings: aircraft Engines, civil air regulations, navigation, meteorology, and parachutes. Parachute Rigger's License. Qualified: Celestial Navigation, Loran, Doppler and Inertial Guidance Systems.

SIGNIFICANT FLIGHTS FOR PAN AMERICAN WORLD AIRWAYS:
June 30, 1950

Pre-inaugural flight on Boeing 377 Stratocruiser, New York to South America.
September 1, 1953
Flew first Distance Measuring Equipment in DC-3 as Chief Pilot.

January 30, 1957
World Record Flight, (propeller driven aircraft) New York to Paris, 8 hours, 50 minutes.

July 7, 1968
Flew first 707 passenger flight, New York to Russia.

October 2, 1968
Flew first 707 flight, New York to Johannesburg, South Africa.

March 2, 1970
Flew first Boeing 747 flight, New York to Paris.

AEROBATIC EXPERIENCE:
1945
Purchased Leister-Kaufman sailplane, was towed to 5,000 feet and taught self to fly on descent.

1946
Flew sailplane in Miami All American Air Maneuvers. Purchased P-38 fighter, modified it to reduce its weight, installed auxiliary hydraulic accumulator to permit gear and flap extension after both propellers were feathered to effect landing. Obtained National Aeronautical Association racing pilot's license. Raced P-38 and performed sailplane aerobatics in numerous Florida air shows. Participated in regional soaring contests in Virginia and New York, followed by

participation in national contests in Elmira, New York and Texas.

1947
Awarded winner of Aerobatic Contest & Spot Landing, Southern States Regional Contests. Won U.S. National Aerobatic Championship. Performed exhibitions with sailplane.

1948
Awarded title of World Sailplane Aerobatic Champion.

1949
Awarded Middle Atlantic States Soaring Championship for aerobatic, spot landing and endurance contests.

1950
Awarded Beechcraft Speed Award in U.S. National Soaring Contest.

1959
Introduced soaring to Hawaii Civil Air Patrol for cadet training.

1967
Introduced The Explorers Club project study of clear air turbulence.

INVENTIONS
Designed, built, and produced the first steerable parachute. Invented system for collapsing parachute after a normal opening.

HONORS
World Aerobatic Champion (Sailplane), 1947
Fellow Member-The Explorers Club, 1953
Honorary Doctor of Aeronautical Science, Embry Riddle Aeronautical University, 1969

Founder of E-RAU Research and Development Center
Honorary Life Member, Sigma Chi International Fraternity, 1971
Honorary Member, Alpha Rho Omega, 1972
Champion of Higher Independent Education in Florida, 1974
Honorary Member, Omecron Delta Kappa, 1977
Elected "Pilot of the Year", Internation Order of Characters (I.O.C.), 1978
Elected to "Hall of Fame", OX-5 Aviation Pioneers, 1978

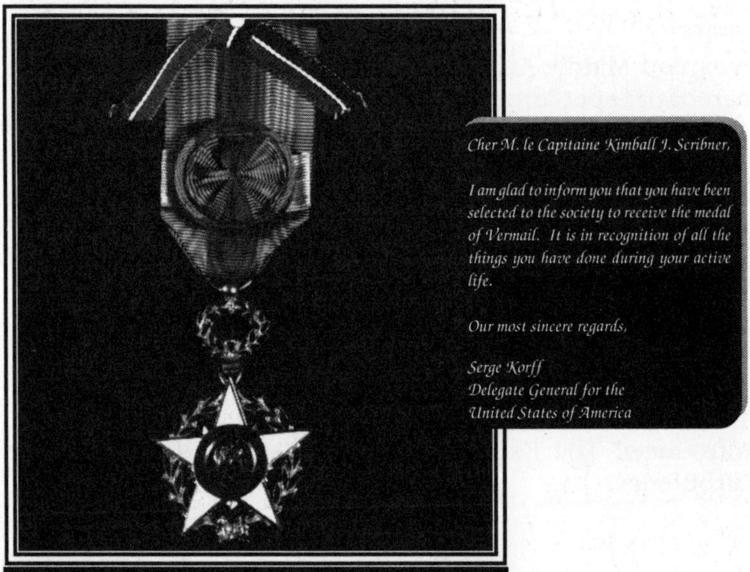
Cher M. le Capitaine Kimball J. Scribner,
I am glad to inform you that you have been selected to the society to receive the medal of Vermail. It is in recognition of all the things you have done during your active life.
Our most sincere regards,
Serge Korff
Delegate General for the
United States of America

Medaille en Vermeil", Societe d'Encouragement au Progress, Paris, France, 1982

Bishop Wright Air Industry Award, 1979
Honorary Doctor of Aeronautical Science, Salem College, West Virginia, 1984

Memorable Meetings & Moments

Vice President Hubert Humphrey

General Charles Lindbergh

Senator Jennings Randolph

Astronaut Scott Carpenter

Arthur Godfrey

Senator Barry Goldwater with my wife, Gloria

General James Doolittle

Princess Grace Kelly

Astronaut John Young

Col. Joe Kittinger (holds world records in balloon across Atlantic and highest parachute jump)

Actress Lina Romay

George R. Wallace

Richard Bach

Congressman Lyle Wolff

Lowell Thomas-President, The Explorers Club

Cartoonist Richard McNeil

Commentator Paul Harvey

Ralph Cox, at my home in Daytona

Prince Philip with my daughter, Susan

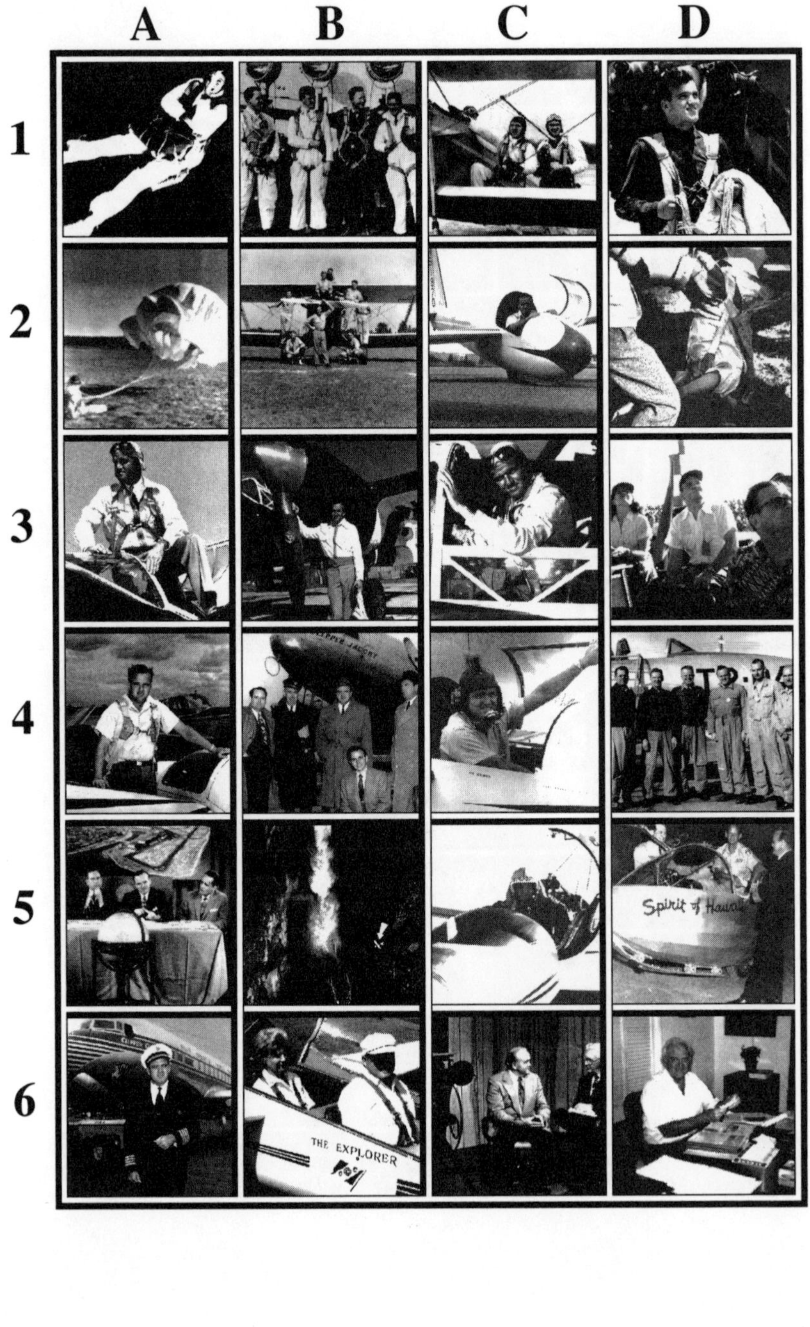
A
B
C
D
1
2
3
4
5
6
THE EXPLORER

A1-D1: *Youngest parachute jumper in USA.*
A2: *Inventor - first steerable parachute*
B2: *CPTP. training*
C2: *Sailplane flying contests*
D2: *Almost the end of a flying career*
A3-C3: *P-38 racing*
D3: *Judge - Miami aerobatic contest*
B4: *DC-3 to Africa*
C4: *Clear air turbulence study*
D4: *Air Force- senior officer jet flying course*
A5: *Qualification of pilots with motion pictures*
B5: *Angel Falls, highest falls in the world*
C5: *Rocky Mountain high altitude flights*
D5: *Sailplane for Hawaii C.A.P. - P.A.A. gift*
A6: *Member, FLA State Aviation Advisory Council*
B6: *Gloria along for a sailplane ride*
C6: *Special advisor to president of DBCC day community college; also trustee at Embry-Riddle Aeronautical University*
D6: *Author at home; expert witness - Justice Dept. of Aviation; Eastern Airlines aviation consultant*